𝔒𝔩𝔡 𝔐𝔞𝔫𝔰𝔢 𝔈𝔡𝔦𝔱𝔦𝔬𝔫

THE COMPLETE WRITINGS OF
NATHANIEL HAWTHORNE

WITH PORTRAITS, ILLUSTRATIONS, AND FACSIMILES

IN TWENTY–TWO VOLUMES

VOLUME XX

Edmund H. Garrett
St. Mary's Spire, Gloucester

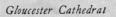

Gloucester Cathedral

THE WRITINGS OF

Nathaniel Hawthorne

HOUGHTON, MIFFLIN AND COMPANY

NOTES OF TRAVEL

BY

NATHANIEL HAWTHORNE

IN FOUR VOLUMES

VOLUME II

BOSTON AND NEW YORK

HOUGHTON, MIFFLIN AND COMPANY

The Riverside Press, Cambridge

LIST OF ILLUSTRATIONS

NOTES OF TRAVEL

II

SOUTHAMPTON, *October* 11, 1855. —
We all left London on Sunday morning,
between ten and eleven, from the Waterloo station, and arrived in Southampton about
two, without meeting with anything very remarkable on the way. We put up at Chap-
ple's Castle Hotel, which is one of the class
styled "commercial," and, though respectable,
not such a one as the nobility and gentry usually frequent. I saw little difference in the accommodation, except that young women attended us instead of men, — a pleasant change.
It was a showery day, but Julian and I walked
out to see the shore and the town and the docks,
and, if possible, the ship in which Sophia was to
sail. The most noteworthy object was the remains of an old castle, near the water-side; the
square, gray, weed-grown, weird keep of which
shows some modern chimney - pots above its
battlements, while remaining portions of the fortress are made to seem as one of the walls for
coal depots, and perhaps for small dwellings.
The English characteristically patch new things

1

into old things in this manner, materially, legally, constitutionally, and morally. Walking along the pier, we observed some pieces of ordnance, one of which was a large brass cannon of Henry VIII.'s time, about twelve feet long, and very finely made. The bay of Southampton presents a pleasant prospect, and I believe it is the great rendezvous of the yacht club. Old and young seafaring people were strolling about, and lounging at corners, just as they do on Sunday afternoons in the minor seaports of America.

From the shore we went up into the town, which is handsome, and of a cheerful aspect, with streets generally wide and well paved, — a cleanly town, not smoke-begrimed. The houses, if not modern, are, at least with few exceptions, new fronted. We saw one relic of antiquity, — a fine mediæval gateway across the principal street, much more elevated than the gates of Chester, with battlements at the top, and a spacious apartment over the great arch for the passage of carriages, and the smaller one on each side for foot-passengers. There were two statues in armor or antique costume on the hither side of the gateway, and two old paintings on the other. This, so far as I know, is the only remnant of the old wall of Southampton.

On Monday the morning was bright, alternating with a little showeriness. Una, Julian, and I went into the town to do some shopping

2

before the steamer should sail ; and a little after
twelve we drove down to the dock. The Madeira is a pleasant-looking ship enough, not very
large, but accommodating, I believe, about seventy passengers. We looked at my wife's little
stateroom, with its three berths for herself and
the two children ; and then sat down in the
saloon, and afterwards on deck, to spend the
irksome and dreary hour or two before parting.
Many of the passengers seemed to be Portu-
guese, undersized, dark, mustachioed people,
smoking cigars. John Bull was fairly represented too. . . . Una was cheerful, and Robert
seemed anxious to get off. Poor Fanny was altogether cast down, and shed tears, either from
regret at leaving her native land, or dread of sea-
sickness, or general despondency, being a person of no spring of spirits. I waited till the
captain came on board, — a middle-aged or
rather elderly man, with a sensible expression,
but, methought, with a hard, cold eye, to whom
I introduced my wife, recommending her to his
especial care, as she was unattended by any
gentleman ; and then we thought it best to cut
short the parting scene. So we bade one another farewell ; and, leaving them on the deck
of the vessel, Julian and I returned to the hotel, and, after dining at the *table d'hôte*, drove
down to the railway. This is the first great
parting that we have ever had.

It was three o'clock when we left Southampton. In order to get to Worcester, where we were to spend the night, we strode, as it were, from one line of railway to another, two or three times, and did not arrive at our journey's end till long after dark.

.   .   .   .

At Worcester we put ourselves into the hands of a cabman, who drove us to the Crown Hotel, — one of the old-fashioned hotels, with an entrance through an arched passage, by which vehicles were admitted into the inn-yard, which has also an exit, I believe, into another street. On one side of the arch was the coffee-room, where, after looking at our sleeping-chambers on the other side of the arch, we had some cold pigeon pie for supper, and for myself a pint of ale.

.   .   .   .

It should be mentioned, that in the morning, before embarking Sophia and the children on board the steamer, I saw a fragment of a rainbow among the clouds, and remembered the old adage bidding " sailors take warning." In the afternoon, as Julian and I were railing from Southampton, we saw another fragmentary rainbow, which, by the same adage, should be the " sailor's delight." The weather has rather tended to confirm the first omen, but the sea captains tell me that the steamer must have gone beyond the scope of these winds.

WORCESTER, *October* 14. — In the morning of Tuesday, after breakfast in the coffee-room, Julian and I walked about to see the remarkables of Worcester. It is not a particularly interesting city, compared with other old English cities; the general material of the houses being red brick, and almost all modernized externally, whatever may be the age of their original framework. We saw a large brick jail in castellated style, with battlements, — a very barren and dreary-looking edifice; likewise, in the more central part of the town, a Guildhall with a handsome front, ornamented with a statue of Queen Anne above the entrance, and statues of Charles I. and Charles II. on either side of the door, with the motto, "Floreat semper civitas fidelis." Worcester seems to pride itself upon its loyalty. We entered the building, and in the large interior hall saw some old armor hanging on the wall at one end, — corselets, helmets, greaves, and a pair of breeches of chain mail. An inscription told us that these suits of armor had been left by Charles II. after the battle of Worcester, and presented to the city at a much later date by a gentleman of the neighborhood. On the stone floor of the hall, under the armor, were two brass cannon, one of which had been taken from the French in a naval battle within the present century; the other was a beautiful piece, bearing, I think, the date of 1632, and manufactured in Brussels for the Count de Burgh, as a Latin inscription testified. This likewise was a relic of the battle of Worcester, where it had been lost by Charles. Many gentlemen — connected with the city government, I suppose — were passing through the hall; and, looking through its interior doors, we saw stately staircases and council-rooms panelled with oak or other dark wood. There seems to be a good deal of state in the government of these old towns.

Worcester Cathedral would have impressed me much had I seen it earlier; though its aspect is less venerable than that of Chester or Lichfield, having been faithfully renewed and repaired, and stonecutters and masons were even now at work on the exterior. At our first visit we found no entrance; but coming again at ten o'clock, when the service was to begin, we found the door open, and the chorister boys, in their white robes, standing in the nave and aisles, with elder people in the same garb, and a few black-robed ecclesiastics and an old verger. The interior of the cathedral has been covered with a light-colored paint at some recent period. There is, as I remember, very little stained glass to enrich and bedim the light; and the effect pro-

duced is a naked, daylight aspect, unlike what
I have seen in any other Gothic cathedral. The
plan of the edifice, too, is simple ; a nave and
side aisles, with great clustered pillars, from which
spring the intersecting arches ; and, somehow
or other, the venerable mystery which I have
found in Westminster Abbey and elsewhere
does not lurk in these arches and behind these
pillars. The choir, no doubt, is richer and
more beautiful ; but we did not enter it. I remember two tombs, with recumbent figures on
them, between the pillars that divide the nave
from the side aisles, and there were also mural
monuments, — one, well executed, to an officer
slain in the Peninsular war, representing him falling from his horse ; another by a young widow
to her husband, with an inscription of passionate
grief, and a record of her purpose finally to
sleep beside him. He died in 1803. I did not
see on the monument any record of the consummation of her purpose ; and so perhaps
she sleeps beside a second husband. There are
more antique memorials than these two on the
wall, and I should have been interested to examine them ; but the service was now about to
begin in the choir, and at the far-off end of the
nave the old verger waved his hand to banish
us from the cathedral. At the same time he
moved towards us, probably to say that he
would show it to us after service ; but having

little time, and being so moderately impressed with what I had already seen, I took my departure, and so disappointed the old man of his expected shilling or half-crown. The tomb of King John is somewhere in this cathedral.

We renewed our rambles through the town, and, passing the Museum of the Worcester Natural History Society, I yielded to Julian's wish to go in. There are three days in the week, I believe, on which it is open to the public; but this being one of the close days, we were admitted on payment of a shilling. It seemed a very good and well-arranged collection in most departments of Natural History, and Julian, who takes more interest in these matters than I do, was much delighted. We were left to examine the hall and galleries quite at our leisure. Besides the specimens of beasts, birds, shells, fishes, minerals, fossils, insects, and all other natural things before the flood and since, there was a stone, bearing a Roman inscription, and various antiquities, coins, and medals, and likewise portraits, some of which were old and curious.

Leaving the museum, we walked down to the stone bridge over the Severn, which is here the largest river I have seen in England, except, of course, the Mersey and the Thames. A flight of steps leads from the bridge down to a walk along the river-side, and this we followed till

8

we reached the spot where an angler was catching chubs and dace, under the walls of the bishop's palace, which here faces the river. It seems to be an old building, but with modern repairs and improvements. The angler had pretty good success while we were looking at him, drawing out two or three silvery fish, and depositing them in his basket, which was already more than half full. The Severn is not a transparent stream, and looks sluggish, but has really movement enough to carry the angler's float along pretty fast. There were two vessels of considerable size (that is, as large as small schooners) lying at the bridge. We now passed under an old stone archway, through a lane that led us from the river-side up past the cathedral, whence a gentleman and lady were just emerging, and the verger was closing the door behind them.

We returned to our hotel, and ordered luncheon, — some cold chicken, cold ham, and ale, and after paying the bill (about fifteen shillings, to which I added five shillings for attendance) we took our departure in a fly for the railway. The waiter (a young woman), chambermaid, and boots, all favored us with the most benign and deferential looks at parting, whence it was easy to see that I had given them more than they had any claim to receive. Nevertheless, this English system of fees has its good side, and I never travel without finding the advantage of it, especially on railways, where the officials are strictly forbidden to take fees, and where, in consequence, a fee secures twice as much good service as anywhere else. Be it recorded that I never knew an Englishman to refuse a shilling, — or, for that matter, a halfpenny.

From Worcester we took tickets to Wolverhampton, and thence to Birkenhead. It grew dark before we reached Chester, and began to rain ; and when we got to Birkenhead it was a pitiless, pelting storm, under which, on the deck of the steamboat, we crossed the detestable Mersey, two years' trial of which has made me detest it every day more and more. It being the night of rejoicing for the taking of Sebastopol and the visit of the Duke of Cambridge, we found it very difficult to get a cab on the Liverpool side ; but after much waiting in the rain, and afterwards in one of the refreshment-rooms on the landing stage, we took a hansom and drove off. The cloudy sky reflected the illuminations, and we saw some gas-lighted stars and other devices, as we passed, very pretty, but much marred by the wind and rain. So we finally arrived at Mrs. Blodgett's, and made a good supper of ham and cold chicken, like our luncheon, after which, wet as we were, and drizzling as the weather was, and though it was two hours beyond his bedtime, I took Julian out to see the illuminations. I wonder what his mother would have said. But the boy must now begin to see life and to feel it.

There was a crowd of people in the street; such a crowd that we could hardly make a passage through them, and so many cabs and omnibuses that it was difficult to cross the ways. Some of the illuminations were very brilliant; but there was a woful lack of variety and invention in the devices. The star of the garter, which kept flashing out from the continual extinguishment of the wind and rain, — V and A, in capital letters of light, — were repeated a hundred times; as were loyal and patriotic mottoes, — crowns formed by colored lamps. In some instances a sensible tradesman had illuminated his own sign, thereby at once advertising his loyalty and his business. Innumerable flags were suspended before the houses and across the streets, and the crowd plodded on, silent, heavy, and without any demonstration of joy, unless by the discharge of pistols close at one's ear. The rain, to be sure, was quite sufficient to damp any joyous ebullition of feeling; but the next day, when the rain had ceased, and when the streets were still thronged with people, there was the same heavy, purposeless strolling from place to place, with no more alacrity of spirit than while it rained. The English do not know how to rejoice ; and, in their present circumstances, to say the truth, have not much to rejoice for. We soon came home ; but I believe it was nearly, if not quite, eleven.

At Mrs. Blodgett's, Mr. Archer (surgeon to some prison or house of correction here in Liverpool) spoke of an attorney who many years ago committed forgery, and, being apprehended, took a dose of prussic acid. Mr. Archer came with the stomach pump, and asked the patient how much prussic acid he had taken. "Sir," he replied, attorney-like, "I decline answering that question!" He recovered, and afterwards arrived at great wealth in New South Wales.

November 14. — At dinner at Mr. Bright's, a week or two ago, Mr. Robertson Gladstone spoke of a magistrate of Liverpool, many years since, Sir John ———. Of a morning, sitting on the bench in the police court, he would take five shillings out of his pocket and say, "Here, Mr. Clerk, so much for my fine. I was drunk last night!" Mr. Gladstone witnessed this personally.

November 16. — I went to the North Hospital yesterday, to take the deposition of a dying man as to his ill treatment by the second and third mates of the ship Assyria, on the voyage from New Orleans. This hospital is a very

gloomy place, with its wide, bleak entries and
staircases, which may be very good for summer
weather, but which are most ungenial at this
bleak November season. I found the physi-
cians of the house laughing and talking very
cheerfully with Mr. Wilding, who had preceded
me. We went forthwith up two or three pairs
of stairs, to the ward where the sick man lay,
and where there were six or eight other beds, in
almost each of which was a patient, — narrow
beds, shabbily furnished. The man whom I
came to see was the only one who was not perfectly quiet; neither was he very restless. The
doctor, informing him of my presence, inti-
mated that his disease might be fatal, and that
I was come to hear what he had to say as to the
causes of his death. Afterwards, a Testament
was sought for, in order to swear him, and I
administered the oath, and made him kiss the
book. He then (in response to Mr. Wilding's
questions) told how he had been beaten and
ill treated, banged and thwacked, from the moment he came on board, to which usage he as-
cribed his death. Sometimes his senses seemed
to sink away, so that I almost thought him
dead; but by and by the questions would appear to reach him, and bring him back, and he
went on with his evidence, interspersing it, however, with dying groans, and almost death rat-
tles. In the midst of whatever he was saying,

he often recurred to a sum of four dollars and
a half, which he said he had put into the hands
of the porter of the hospital, and which he
wanted to get back. Several times he expressed his wish to return to America (of which
he was not a native), and, on the whole, I do
not think he had any real sense of his precarious
condition, notwithstanding that he assented to
the doctor's hint to that effect. He sank away
so much at one time, that they brought him
wine in a tin cup, with a spout to drink out of,
and he mustered strength to raise himself in his
bed and drink; then hemmed, with rather a
disappointed air, as if it did not stimulate and
refresh him, as drink ought to do. When he
had finished his evidence (which Mr. Wilding
took down in writing from his mouth), he
marked his cross at the foot of the paper, and
we ceased to torment him with further question.
His deposition will probably do no good, so far
as the punishment of the persons implicated is
concerned; for he appears to have come on
board in a sickly state, and never to have been
well during the passage. On a pallet, close by
his bed, lay another seaman of the same ship,
who had likewise been abused by the same men,
and bore more ostensible marks of ill usage than
this man did, about the head and face. There
is a most dreadful state of things aboard our
ships. Hell itself can be no worse than some

of them, and I do pray that some New Englander with the rage of reform in him may turn
his thoughts this way. The first step towards
better things — the best practicable step for the
present — is to legalize flogging on shipboard;
thereby doing away with the miscellaneous assaults and batteries, kickings, fisticuffings, ropes'
endings, marline spikings, which the inferior
officers continually perpetrate, as the only mode
of keeping up anything like discipline. As in
many other instances, philanthropy has over-
shot itself by the prohibition of flogging, caus-
ing the captain to avoid the responsibility of
solemn punishment, and leave his mates to make
devils of themselves, by habitual and hardly
avoidable ill treatment of the seamen.

After I left the dying sailor, his features
seemed to contract and grow sharp. Some
young medical students stood about the bed,
watching death creep upon him, and anticipat-
ing, perhaps, that in a day or two they would
have the poor fellow's body on the dissecting-
table. Dead patients, I believe, undergo this
fate, unless somebody chooses to pay their
funeral expenses; but the captain of the Assyria
(who seems to be respectable and kind hearted,
though master of a floating hell) tells me that
he means to bury the man at his own cost.
This morning there is a note from the surgeon
of the hospital, announcing his death, and like-

wise the dangerous state of his shipmate whom
I saw on the pallet beside him.

Sea captains call a dress-coat a "claw-ham-
mer."

November 22. — I went on board the ship
William Tapscott, lying in the river, yesterday,
to take depositions in reference to a homicide
committed in New York. I sat on a sofa in
the cabin, and Mr. Wilding at a table, with his
writing-materials before him, and the crew were
summoned, one by one, — rough, piratical-look-
ing fellows, contrasting strongly with the gew-
gaw cabin in which I received them. There is
no such finery on land as in the cabin of one
of these ships in the Liverpool trade, finished
off with a complete panelling of rosewood, mahogany, and bird's-eye maple, polished and var-
nished, and gilded along the cornices and the
edges of the panels. It is all a piece of elaborate cabinet-work ; and one does not altogether
see why it should be given to the gales, and the
salt-sea atmosphere, to be tossed upon the waves,
and occupied by a rude shipmaster in his dread-
naught clothes, when the fairest lady in the land
has no such boudoir. A telltale compass hung
beneath the skylight, and a clock was fastened
near it, and ticked loudly. A stewardess, with
the aspect of a woman at home, went in and

out of the cabin, about her domestic calls.
Through the cabin door (it being a house on
deck) I could see the arrangement of the ship.

The first sailor that I examined was a black-
haired, powerful fellow, in an oil-skin jacket,
with a good face enough, though he, too, might
have been taken for a pirate. In the affray in
which the homicide occurred, he had received a
cut across the forehead, and another slantwise
across his nose, which had quite cut it in two,
on a level with the face, and had thence gone
downward to his lower jaw. But neither he nor
any one else could give any testimony eluci-
dating the matter into which I had come to inquire. A seaman had been stabbed just before
the vessel left New York, and had been sent on
shore and died there. Most of these men were
in the affray, and all of them were within a few
yards of the spot where it occurred ; but those
actually present all pleaded that they were so
drunk that the whole thing was now like a
dream, with no distinct images ; and, if any had
been sober, they took care to know nothing
that could inculpate any individual. Perhaps
they spoke truth ; they certainly had a free and
honest-like way of giving their evidence, as if
their only object was to tell all the truth they
knew. But I rather think, in the forecastle,
and during the night-watches, they have whispered to one another a great deal more than

they told me, and have come to a pretty accurate conclusion as to the man who gave the stab.

While the examination proceeded, there was a drawing of corks in a side closet; and, at its conclusion, the captain asked us to stay to dinner, but we excused ourselves, and drank only a glass of wine. The captain apologized for not joining us, inasmuch as he had drunk no wine for the last seventeen years. He appears to be a particularly good and trustworthy man, and is the only shipmaster whom I have met with who says that a crew can best be governed by kindness. In the inner closet there was a cage containing two land-birds, who had come aboard him, tired almost to death, three or four hundred miles from shore; and he had fed them and been tender of them, from a sense of what was due to hospitality. He means to give them to Julian.

November 28. — I have grown wofully aristocratic in my tastes, I fear, since coming to England; at all events, I am conscious of a certain disgust at going to dine in a house with a small entrance hall and a narrow staircase, parlor with chintz curtains, and all other arrangements on a similar scale. This is pitiable. However, I really do not think I should mind these things, were it not for the bustle, the affectation,

18

the intensity, of the mistress of the house.   It
is certain that a woman in England is either decidedly a lady or decidedly not a lady.   There
seems to be no respectable medium.   Bill of
fare : broiled soles, half of a roast pig, a haricot
of mutton, stewed oysters, a tart, pears, figs,
with sherry and port wine, both good, and the
port particularly so.   I ate some pig, and could
hardly resist the lady's importunities to eat more,
though to my fancy it tasted of swill, — had a
flavor of the pigsty.   On the parlor-table were
some poor editions of popular books, Longfellow's poems and others.   The lady affects a
literary taste, and bothered me about my own
productions.

A beautiful subject for a romance, or for a sermon, would be the subsequent life of the young
man whom Jesus bade to sell all he had and
give to the poor ; and he went away sorrowful,
and is not recorded to have done what he was
bid.

.   .   .   .

December 11. — This has been a foggy morning and forenoon, snowing a little now and then,
and disagreeably cold.   The sky is of an inexpressibly dreary dun color.   It is so dark at
times that I have to hold my book close to my
eyes, and then again it lightens up a little.   On

the whole, disgustingly gloomy; and thus it has been for a long while past, although the disagreeableness seems to lie very near the earth, and just above the steeples and house-tops very probably there may be a bright, sunshiny day. At about twelve there is a faint glow of sunlight, like the gleaming reflection from a not highly polished copper kettle.

December 26. — On Christmas Eve and yesterday, there were little branches of mistletoe hanging in several parts of the house, in the kitchen, the entries, the parlor, and the smoking-room, — suspended from the gas-fittings. The maids of the house did their utmost to entrap the gentlemen boarders, old and young, under the privileged places, and there to kiss them, after which they were expected to pay a shilling. It is very queer, being customarily so respectful, that they should assume this license now, absolutely trying to pull the gentlemen into the kitchen by main force, and kissing the harder and more abundantly the more they were resisted. A little rosy-cheeked Scotch lass — at other times very modest — was the most active in this business. I doubt whether any gentleman but myself escaped. I heard old Mr. S—— parleying with the maids last evening, and pleading his age; but he seems to have met with no mercy, for there was a sound of prodigious smacking immediately afterwards.   Julian was assaulted, and fought most vigorously; but was outrageously kissed, — receiving some scratches, moreover, in the conflict.   The mistletoe has white, wax-looking berries, and dull green leaves, with a parasitical stem.

Early in the morning of Christmas Day, long before daylight, I heard music in the street, and a woman's voice, powerful and melodious, singing a Christmas hymn.   Before bedtime I presume one half of England, at a moderate calculation, was the worse for liquor.

The market-houses, at this season, show the national taste for heavy feeding, — carcasses of prize oxen, immensely fat and bulky; fat sheep, with their woolly heads and tails still on, and stars and other devices ingeniously wrought on the quarters; fat pigs, adorned with flowers, like corpses of virgins; hares, wild-fowl, geese, ducks, turkeys; and green boughs and banners suspended about the stalls, — and a great deal of dirt and griminess on the stone floor of the market-house, and on the persons of the crowd.

There are some Englishmen whom I like, — one or two for whom I might say I have an affection; but still there is not the same union between us as if they were Americans.   A cold, thin medium intervenes betwixt our most intimate approaches.   It puts me in mind of Alnaschar and his princess, with the cold steel blade of his scimitar between them. Perhaps if I were at home I might feel differently; but in a foreign land I can never forget the distinction between English and American.

January 1, 1856. — Last night, at Mrs. Blodgett's, we sat up till twelve o'clock to open the front door, and let the New Year in. After the coming guest was fairly in the house, the back door was to be opened, to let the Old Year out; but I was tired, and did not wait for the latter ceremony. When the New Year made its entrance, there was a general shaking of hands, and one of the shipmasters said that it was customary to kiss the ladies all round; but, to my great satisfaction, we did not proceed to such extremity. There was singing in the streets, and many voices of people passing, and when twelve had struck, all the bells of the town, I believe, rang out together. I went up stairs, sad and lonely, and stepping into Julian's little room, wished him a Happy New Year, as he slept, and many of them.

To a cool observer, a country does not show to best advantage during a time of war. All its self-conceit is doubly visible, and, indeed, is sedulously kept uppermost by direct appeals to it. The country must be humbugged, in order to keep its courage up.

Sentiment seems to me more abundant in middle-aged ladies in England than in the United States. I don't know how it may be with young ladies.

The shipmasters bear testimony to the singular delicacy of common sailors in their behavior in the presence of women ; and they say that this good trait is still strongly observable even in the present race of seamen, greatly deteriorated as it is. On shipboard, there is never an indecorous word or unseemly act said or done by sailors when a woman can be cognizant of it ; and their deportment in this respect differs greatly from that of landsmen of similar position in society. This is remarkable, considering that a sailor's female acquaintances are usually and exclusively of the worst kind, and that his intercourse with them has no relation whatever to morality or decency. For this very reason, I suppose, he regards a modest woman as a creature divine and to be reverenced.

January 16. — I have suffered wofully from low spirits for some time past ; and this has not often been the case since I grew to be a man, even in the least auspicious periods of my life. My desolate bachelor condition, I suppose, is the cause. Really, I have no pleasure in anything, and I feel my tread to be heavier, and my physical movement more sluggish, than in happier times.   A weight is always upon me. My appetite is not good.   I sleep ill, lying awake till late at night, to think sad thoughts and to imagine sombre things, and awaking before light with the same thoughts and fancies still in my mind.   My heart sinks always as I ascend the stairs to my office, from a dim augury of ill news from Lisbon that I may perhaps hear, — of black-sealed letters, or some such horrors.   Nothing gives me any joy.   I have learned what the bitterness of exile is, in these days ; and I never should have known it but for the absence of ——.   " Remote, unfriended, melancholy, slow," — I can perfectly appreciate that line of Goldsmith ; for it well expresses my own torpid, unenterprising, joyless state of mind and heart.   I am like an uprooted plant, wilted and drooping.   Life seems so purposeless as not to be worth the trouble of carrying it on any further.

I was at a dinner, the other evening, at Mr. B——'s, where the entertainment was almost entirely American, — New York oysters, raw, stewed, and fried ; soup of American partridges, particularly good ; also terrapin soup, rich, but not to my taste ; American pork and beans, baked in Yankee style ; a noble American turkey, weighing thirty-one pounds ; and, at the other end of the table, an American round of beef, which the Englishmen present allowed to be delicious, and worth a guinea an ounce. I forget the other American dishes, if there were any more. — O yes ! — canvas-back ducks, coming on with the sweets, in the usual English fashion. We ought to have had Catawba wine ; but this was wanting, although there was plenty of hock, champagne, sherry, madeira, port, and claret. Our host is a very jolly man, and the dinner was a merrier and noisier one than any English dinner within my experience.

February 8. — I read to-day, in the little office Bible (greasy with perjuries) St. Luke's account of the agony, the trial, the crucifixion, and the resurrection ; and how Christ appeared to the two disciples, on their way to Emmaus, and afterwards to a company of disciples. On both these latter occasions he expounded the Scriptures to them, and showed the application of the old prophecies to himself ; and it is to be supposed that he made them fully, or at least sufficiently, aware what his character was, — whether God, or man, or both, or something between, together with all other essential points of doctrine. But none of this doctrine or of these expositions is recorded, the mere facts being most simply stated, and the conclusion to which he led them, that, whether God himself, or the Son of God, or merely the Son of man, he was, at all events, the Christ foretold in the Jewish Scriptures. This last, therefore, must have been the one essential point.

February 18. — On Saturday there called on me an elderly Robinson Crusoe sort of man, Mr. H——, shipwright, I believe, of Boston, who has lately been travelling in the East. About a year ago he was here, after being shipwrecked on the Dutch coast, and I assisted him to get home. Again, I have supplied him with five pounds, and my credit for an outside garment. He is a spare man, with closely cropped gray, or rather white hair, close-cropped whiskers fringing round his chin, and a close-cropped white mustache, with his under-lip and a portion of his chin bare beneath, — sunburnt and weather worn. He has been in Syria and Jerusalem, through the Desert, and at Sebastopol; and says he means to get Ticknor to publish his travels, and the story of his whole adventurous life, on his return home. A freespoken, confiding, hardy, religious, unpolished, simple, yet world-experienced man; very talkative, and boring me with longer visits than I like. He has brought home, among other curiosities, "a lady's arm," as he calls it, two thousand years old, — a piece of a mummy, of course; also some coins, one of which, a gold coin of Vespasian, he showed me, and said he bought it of an Arab of the desert. The Bedouins possess a good many of these coins, handed down immemorially from father to son, and never sell them unless compelled by want. He had likewise a Hebrew manuscript of the Book of Ruth, on a parchment roll, which was put into his care to be given to Lord Haddo.

He was at Sebastopol during the siege, and nearly got his head knocked off by a cannon-ball. His strangest statement is one in reference to Lord Raglan. He says that an English officer told him that his Lordship shut himself up, desiring not to be disturbed, as he needed sleep. When fifteen hours had gone by, his attendants thought it time to break open the door; and Lord Raglan was found dead, with a bottle of strychnine by the bedside. The affair, so far as the circumstances indicated suicide, was hushed up, and his death represented as a natural one. The English officer seems to have been an unscrupulous fellow, jesting thus with the fresh memory of his dead commander; for it is imposible to believe a word of the story. Even if Lord Raglan had wished for death, he would hardly have taken strychnine, when there were so many chances of being honorably shot. In Wood's Narrative of the Campaign, it is stated that he died surrounded by the members of his staff, after having been for some time ill.

It appears, however, by the same statement, that no serious apprehensions had been entertained, until, one afternoon, he shut himself up, desiring not to be disturbed till evening. After two or three hours he called Lord Burghersh, — "Frank, Frank!" and was found to be almost in a state of collapse, and died that evening. Mr. H——'s story might very well have been a camp rumor.

It seems to me that the British Ministry, in its notion of a life-peerage, shows an entire misunderstanding of what makes people desire the peerage. It is not for the immediate personal distinction; but because it removes the peer and his consanguinity from the common rank of men, and makes a separate order of them, as if they should grow angelic. A life-peer is but a mortal amid the angelic throng.

February 28. — I went yesterday with Mrs. —— and another lady, and Mr. M——, to the West Derby Workhouse. . . .

[Here comes in the visit to the West Derby Workhouse, which was made the subject of a paper in Our Old Home, called Outside Glimpses of English Poverty. As the purpose in publishing these passages from the private note-books is to give to those who ask for a memoir of Mr. Hawthorne every possible incident recorded by himself which shows his character and nature, the editor thinks it proper to disclose the fact that Mr. Hawthorne was himself the gentleman of that party who took up in his arms the little child, so fearfully repulsive in its condition. And it seems better to quote his own words in reference to it, than merely to say it was he.

Under date February 28, 1856.

"After this we went to the ward where the children were kept, and, on entering this, we saw, in the first place, two or three unlovely and unwholesome little imps, who were lazily playing together. One of them (a child about six years old, but I know not whether girl or boy) immediately took the strangest fancy for me. It was a wretched, pale, half-torpid little thing, with a humor in its eyes which the Governor said was the scurvy. I never saw, till a few moments afterwards, a child that I should feel less inclined to fondle. But this little, sickly, humor-eaten fright prowled around me, taking hold of my skirts, following at my heels, and at last held up its hands, smiled in my face, and, standing directly before me, insisted on my taking it up! Not that it said a word, for I rather think it was underwitted, and could not talk; but its face expressed such perfect confidence that it was going to be taken up and made much of, that it was impossible not to do it. It was

29

as if God had promised the child this favor on my behalf, and that I must needs fulfil the contract. I held my undesirable burden a little while; and, after setting the child down, it still followed me, holding two of my fingers and playing with them, just as if it were a child of my own. It was a foundling, and out of all human kind it chose me to be its father! We went up stairs into another ward; and, on coming down again, there was this same child waiting for me, with a sickly smile round its defaced mouth, and in its dim red eyes. . . . I never should have forgiven myself if I had repelled its advances."
— S. H.

After leaving the workhouse, we drove to Norris Green; and Mrs. —— showed me round the grounds, which are very good and nicely kept. O, these English homes, what delightful places they are! I wonder how many people live and die in the workhouse, having no other home, because other people have a great deal more home than enough. . . . We had a very pleasant dinner, and Mr. M—— and I walked back, four miles and a half, to Liverpool, where we arrived just before midnight.

Why did Christ curse the fig-tree? It was not in the least to blame; and it *seems* most unreasonable to have expected it to bear figs out of season. Instead of withering it away, it would have been as great a miracle, and far more beautiful, — and, one would think, of more beneficent influence, — to have made it suddenly rich with ripe fruit.   Then, to be sure, it might have died joyfully, having answered so good a purpose.   I have been reminded of this miracle by the story of a man in Heywood, a town in Lancashire, who used such horribly profane language that a plane-tree in front of his cottage is said to have withered away from that hour.   I can draw no moral from the incident of the fig-tree, unless it be that all things perish from the instant when they cease to answer some divine purpose.

March 6. — Yesterday I lunched on board Captain Russell's ship, the Princeton.   These daily lunches on shipboard might answer very well the purposes of a dinner; being, in fact, noontide dinners, with soup, roast mutton, mutton chops, and a macaroni pudding, — brandy, port and sherry wines.   There were three elderly Englishmen at table, with white heads, — which, I think, is oftener the predicament of elderly heads here than in America.   One of these was a retired Custom House officer, and the other two were connected with shipping in some way. There is a satisfaction in seeing Englishmen eat and drink, they do it so heartily, and, on the whole, so wisely, — trusting so entirely that there is no harm in good beef and mutton, and a reasonable quantity of good liquor ; and these three hale old men, who had acted on this wholesome faith for so long, were proofs that it is well on earth to live like earthly creatures. In America, what squeamishness, what delicacy, what stomachic apprehension, would there not be among three stomachs of sixty or seventy years' experience ! I think this failure of American stomachs is partly owing to our ill usage of our digestive powers, and partly to our want of faith in them.

After lunch we all got into an omnibus, and went to the Mersey Iron Foundry, to see the biggest piece of ordnance in the world, which is almost finished. The overseer of the works received us, and escorted us courteously throughout the establishment ; which is very extensive, giving employment to a thousand men, what with night-work and day-work. The big gun is still on the axle, or turning machine, by means of which it has been bored. It is made entirely of wrought and welded iron, fifty tons of which were originally used ; and the gun, in its present state, bored out and smoothed away, weighs nearly twenty-three tons. It has, as yet, no trunnions, and does not look much like a cannon, but only a huge iron cylinder, immensely solid, and with a bore so large that a young man of nineteen shoved himself into it, the whole length, with a light, in order to see whether it is duly smooth and regular. I suppose it will have a better effect, as to the impression of size, when it is finished, polished, mounted, and fully equipped, after the fashion of ordinary cannon. It is to throw a ball of three hundred pounds' weight five miles, and woe be to whatever ship or battlement shall bear the brunt!

After inspecting the gun we went through other portions of the establishment, and saw iron in various stages of manufacture. I am not usually interested in manufacturing processes, being quite unable to understand them, at least in cotton machinery and the like; but here there were such exhibitions of mighty strength, both of men and machines, that I had a satisfaction in looking on. We saw lumps of iron, intensely white-hot, and in all but a melting state, passed through rollers of various size and pressure, and speedily converted into long bars, which came curling and waving out of the rollers like great red ribbons, or like fiery serpents wriggling out of Tophet; and finally, being straightened out, they were laid to cool in heaps. Trip-hammers are very pleasant things to look at, working so massively as they do, and yet so accurately; chewing up the hot iron, as it were, and fashioning it into shape, with a sort of mighty and gigantic gentleness in their mode of action. What great things man has contrived, and is continually performing! What a noble brute he is!

Also, I found much delight in looking at the molten iron, boiling and bubbling in the furnace, and sometimes slopping over, when stirred by the attendant. There were numberless fires on all sides, blinding us with their intense glow; and continually the pounding strokes of huge hammers, some wielded by machinery and others by human arms. I had a respect for these stalwart workmen, who seemed to be near kindred of the machines amid which they wrought, — mighty men, smiting stoutly, and looking into the fierce eyes of the furnace fearlessly, and handling the iron at a temperature which would have taken the skin off from ordinary fingers. They looked strong, indeed, but pale; for the hot atmosphere in which they live cannot but be deleterious, and I suppose their very strength wears them quickly out. But I would rather live ten years as an iron-smith than fifty as a tailor.

So much heat can be concentrated into a mass of iron, that a lump a foot square heats all the atmosphere about it, and burns the face at a considerable distance. As the trip-hammer strikes the lump, it seems still more to intensify the heat by squeezing it together, and the fluid iron oozes out like sap or juice.

" He was ready for the newest fashions ! " —
This expression was used by Mrs. Blodgett in
reference to Mr. —— on his first arrival in England, and it is a very tender way of signifying
that a person is rather poorly off as to apparel.

March 15. — Mr. ——, our new ambassador,
arrived on Thursday afternoon by the Atlantic,
and I called at the Adelphi Hotel, after dinner, to pay him my respects.   I found him and
his family at supper. . . . They seem to be
plain, affable people. . . .   The ambassador is a
venerable old gentleman, with a full head of
perfectly white hair, looking not unlike an old-
fashioned wig ; and this, together with his col-
larless white neckcloth and his brown coat, gave
him precisely such an aspect as one would expect in a respectable person of pre-revolutionary
days.   There was a formal simplicity, too, in
his manners, that might have belonged to the
same era.   He must have been a very handsome man in his youthful days, and is now
comely, very erect, moderately tall, not over-
burdened with flesh ; of benign and agreeable
address, with a pleasant smile ; but his eyes,
which are not very large, impressed me as sharp
and cold.   He did not at all stamp himself upon
me as a man of much intellectual or characteristic vigor.   I found no such matter in his conversation, nor did I feel it in the indefinable way

35

by which strength always makes itself acknow-
ledged. B——, though somehow plain and uncouth, yet vindicates himself as a large man of
the world, able, experienced, fit to handle difficult circumstances of life ; dignified, too, and
able to hold his own in any society. Mr. ——
has a kind of venerable dignity ; but yet, if a
person could so little respect himself as to in-
sult him, I should say that there was no innate
force in Mr. —— to prevent it. It is very
strange that he should have made so considerable a figure in public life, filling offices that the
strongest men would have thought worthy of
their highest ambition. There must be something shrewd and sly under his apparent simplicity ; narrow, cold, selfish, perhaps. I fancied
these things in his eyes. He has risen in life
by the lack of too powerful qualities, and by
a certain tact, which enables him to take advantage of circumstances and opportunities, and
avail himself of his unobjectionableness, just at
the proper time. I suppose he must be pronounced a humbug, yet almost or quite an inno-
cent one. Yet he is a queer representative to
be sent from brawling and boisterous America
at such a critical period. It will be funny if
England sends him back again, on hearing the
news of ——'s dismissal. Mr. —— gives me
the impression of being a very amiable man in
his own family. He has brought his son with

36

him, as Secretary of Legation, — a small young man, with a little mustache. It will be a feeble embassy.

I called again the next morning, and introduced Mrs. ——, who, I believe, accompanied the ladies about town. This simplicity in Mr. ——'s manner puzzles and teases me ; for, in spite of it, there was a sort of self-consciousness, as if he were being looked at, — as if he were having his portrait taken.

LONDON, *March* 22. — Yesterday, — no, day before yesterday, — I left Liverpool for London by rail, from the Lime Street station. The journey was a dull and monotonous one, as usual. Three passengers were in the same carriage with me at starting, but they dropped off, and from Rugby I was alone. We reached London after ten o'clock ; and I took a cab for St. James's Place, No. 32, where I found Mr. B. —— expecting me. He had secured a bedroom for me at this lodging-house, and I am to be free of his drawing-room during my stay. We breakfasted at nine, and then walked down to his counting-room, in Old Broad Street in the city. It being a dim, dingy morning, London looked very dull, the more so as it was Good Friday, and therefore the streets were comparatively thin of people and vehicles, and had on their Sunday aspect. If it were not for the hu-

man life and bustle of London, it would be a
very stupid place, with a heavy and dreary monotony of unpicturesque streets. We went up
Bolt Court, where Dr. Johnson used to live;
and this was the only interesting site we saw.
After spending some time in the counting-
room, while Mr. —— read his letters, we went
to London Bridge, and took the steamer for
Waterloo Bridge, with partly an intent to go to
Richmond, but the day was so damp and dusky
that we concluded otherwise. So we came home,
visiting, on our way, the site of Covent Garden Theatre, lately burnt down. The exterior
walls still remain perfect, and look quite solid
enough to admit of the interior being renewed,
but I believe it is determined to take them
down.

After a slight lunch and a glass of wine, we
walked out, along Piccadilly and to Hyde Park,
which already looks very green, and where there
were a good many people walking and driving,
and rosy-faced children at play. Somehow or
other the shine and charm are gone from London, since my last visit; and I did not very
much· admire, nor feel much interested in anything. We returned (and I, for my part, was
much wearied) in time for dinner at five. The
evening was spent at home in various talk, and
I find Mr. —— a very agreeable companion,
and a young man of thought and information,

with a self-respecting character, and I think him a safe person to live with.

This St. James's Place is in close vicinity to St. James's Palace, the gateway and not very splendid front of which we can see from the corner. The club-houses and the best life of the town are near at hand. Addison, before his marriage, used to live in St. James's Place, and the house where Mr. Rogers recently died is up the court, — not that this latter residence excites much interest in my mind. I remember nothing else very noteworthy in this first day's experience, except that on Sir Watkins Williams Wynn's door, not far from this house, I saw a gold knocker, which is said to be unscrewed every night lest it should be stolen. I don't know whether it be really gold; for it did not look so bright as the generality of brass ones. I received a very good letter from Julian this morning. He was to go to Mr. Bright's, at Sandhays, yesterday, and remain till Monday.

After writing the above, I walked along the Strand, Fleet Street, Ludgate Hill and Cheapside to Wood Street, — a very narrow street, insomuch that one has to press close against the wall to escape being grazed when a cart is passing. At No. 77 I found the place of business of Mr. Bennoch, who came to see me at Rock Ferry with Mr. Jerdan, not long after my arrival in England. I found him in his office ;

but he did not at first recognize me, so much stouter have I grown during my residence in England, — a new man, as he says. Mr. Bennoch is a kindly, frank, very good man, and was bounteous in his plans for making my time pass pleasantly. We talked of ——, from whom he had just received a letter, and who says he will fight for England in case of a war. I let Bennoch know that I, at least, should take the other side.

.   .   .   .

After arranging to go to Greenwich Fair, and afterwards to dine with Bennoch, I left him and went to Mr. ——'s office, and afterwards strayed forth again, and crossed London Bridge. Thence I rambled rather drearily along through several shabby and uninteresting streets on the other side of the Thames ; and the dull streets in London are really the dullest and most disheartening in the world. By and by I found my way to Southwark Bridge, and so crossed to Upper Thames Street, which was likewise very stupid, though I believe Clennam's paternal house in Little Dorrit stands thereabouts. . . . Next I got into Ludgate Hill, near St. Paul's, and being quite foot-weary, I took a Paddington omnibus, and rode up into Regent Street, whence I came home.

March 24. — Yesterday being a clear day

for England, we determined upon an expedition to Hampton Court; so walked out betimes towards the Waterloo station; but first crossed the Thames by Westminster Bridge, and went to Lambeth Palace. It stands immediately on the bank of the river, not far above the bridge. We merely walked round it, and saw only an old stone tower or two, partially renewed with brick, and a high connecting wall, within which appeared gables and other portions of the palace, all of an ancient plan and venerable aspect, though evidently much patched up and restored in the course of the many ages since its foundation. There is likewise a church, part of which looks old, connected with the palace. The streets surrounding it have many gabled houses, and a general look of antiquity, more than some other parts of London.

We then walked to the Waterloo station, on the same side of the river; and at twenty minutes past one took the rail for Hampton Court, distant some twelve or fifteen miles. On arriving at the terminus, we beheld Hampton Palace, on the other side of the Thames, — an extensive structure, with a front of red brick, long and comparatively low, with the great Hall which Wolsey built rising high above the rest. We crossed the river (which is here but a narrow stream) by a stone bridge. The entrance to the palace is about half a quarter of a mile from the railway, through arched gates, which give a long perspective into the several quadrangles. These quadrangles, one beyond another, are paved with stone, and surrounded by the brick walls of the palace, the many windows of which look in upon them. Soldiers were standing sentinels at the exterior gateways, and at the various doors of the palace; but they admitted everybody without question and without fee. Policemen, or other attendants, were in most of the rooms, but interfered with no one ; so that, in this respect, it was one of the pleasantest places to visit that I have found in England. A good many people, of all classes, were strolling through the apartments.

We first went into Wolsey's great Hall, up a most spacious staircase, the walls and ceiling of which were covered with an allegorical fresco by Verrio, wonderfully bright and well preserved ; and without caring about the design or execution, I greatly liked the brilliancy of the colors. The great Hall is a most noble and beautiful room, above a hundred feet long and sixty high and broad. Most of the windows are of stained or painted glass, with elaborate designs, whether modern or ancient I know not, but certainly brilliant in effect. The walls, from the floor to perhaps half their height, are covered with antique tapestry, which, though a good deal faded, still retains color enough to be

a very effective adornment, and to give an idea
of how rich a mode of decking a noble apartment this must have been.   The subjects represented were from Scripture, and the figures
seemed colossal.   On looking closely at this
tapestry, you could see that it was thickly in-
terwoven with threads of gold, still glistening.
The windows, except one or two that are long,
do not descend below the top of this tapestry,
and are therefore twenty or thirty feet above
the floor ; and this manner of lighting a great
room seems to add much to the impressiveness
of the enclosed space.   The roof is very magnificent, of carved oak, intricately and elaborately
arched, and still as perfect to all appearance as
when it was first made.   There are banners,
so fresh in their hues, and so untattered, that
I think they must be modern, suspended along
beneath the cornice of the hall, and exhibiting
Wolsey's arms and badges.   On the whole, this
is a perfect sight in its way.

Next to the hall there is a withdrawing-room,
more than seventy feet long, and twenty-five
feet high.   The walls of this apartment, too,
are covered with ancient tapestry, of allegorical
design, but more faded than that of the hall.
There is also a stained-glass window; and a
marble statue of Venus on a couch, very lean
and not very beautiful ; and some cartoons of
Carlo Cignani, which have left no impression

on my memory; likewise, a large model of a splendid palace of some East Indian nabob.

I am not sure, after all, that Verrio's frescoed grand staircase was not in another part of the palace; for I remember that we went from it through an immensely long suite of apartments, beginning with the Guard-chamber. All these rooms are wainscoted with oak, which looks new, being, I believe, of the date of King William's reign. Over many of the doorways, or around the panels, there are carvings in wood by Gibbons, representing wreaths of flowers, fruit, and foliage, the most perfectly beautiful that can be conceived; and the wood being of a light hue (lime-wood, I believe), it has a fine effect on the dark oak panelling. The apartments open one beyond another, in long, long, long succession, — rooms of state, and kings' and queens' bedchambers, and royal closets bigger than ordinary drawing-rooms, so that the whole suite must be half a mile, or it may be a mile, in extent. From the windows you get views of the palace grounds, broad and stately walks, and groves of trees, and lawns, and fountains, and the Thames and adjacent country beyond. The walls of all these rooms are absolutely covered with pictures, including works of all the great masters, which would require long study before a new eye could enjoy them; and, seeing so many of them at once, and hav-

44

ing such a nothing of time to look at them all,
I did not even try to see any merit in them.
Vandyke's picture of Charles I., on a white
horse beneath an arched gateway, made more
impression on me than any other, and as I re-
call it now, it seems as if I could see the king's
noble, melancholy face, and armed form, remembered not in picture, but in reality. All
Sir Peter Lely's lewd women, and Kneller's
too, were in these rooms; and the jolly old stupidity of George III. and his family, many times
repeated; and pictures by Titian, Rubens, and
other famous hands, intermixed with many by
West, which provokingly drew the eye away
from their betters. It seems to me that a picture, of all other things, should be by itself;
whereas people always congregate them in galleries. To endeavor really to see them, so arranged, is like trying to read a hundred poems
at once, — a most absurd attempt. Of all these
pictures, I hardly recollect any so well as a
ridiculous old travesty of the Resurrection and
Last Judgment, where the dead people are represented as coming to life at the sound of the
trumpet, — the flesh reëstablishing itself on the
bones, — one man picking up his skull, and
putting it on his shoulders, — and all appearing
greatly startled, only half awake, and at a loss
what to do next. Some devils are dragging
away the damned by the heels and on sledges,

and above sits the Redeemer and some angelic and sainted people, looking complacently down upon the scene!

We saw, in one of the rooms, the funeral canopy beneath which the Duke of Wellington lay in state, — very gorgeous, of black velvet embroidered with silver and adorned with escutcheons; also, the state bed of Queen Anne, broad, and of comfortable appearance, though it was a queen's, — the materials of the curtains, quilt, and furniture, red velvet, still brilliant in hue; also King William's bed and his queen Mary's, with enormously tall posts, and a good deal the worse for time and wear.

The last apartment we entered was the gallery containing Raphael's cartoons, which I shall not pretend to admire nor to understand. I can conceive, indeed, that there is a great deal of expression in them, and very probably they may, in every respect, deserve all their fame; but on this point I can give no testimony. To my perception they were a series of very much faded pictures, dimly seen (for this part of the palace was now in shadow), and representing figures neither graceful nor beautiful, nor, as far as I could discern, particularly grand. But I came to them with a wearied mind and eye; and also I had a previous distaste to them through the medium of engravings.

But what a noble palace, nobly enriched, is this

46

Hampton Court! The English Government does well to keep it up, and to admit the people freely into it, for it is impossible for even a Republican not to feel something like awe — at least a profound respect — for all this state, and for the institutions which are here represented, the sovereigns whose moral magnificence demands such a residence; and its permanence, too, enduring from age to age, and each royal generation adding new splendors to those accumulated by their predecessors. If one views the matter in another way, to be sure, we may feel indignant that such dolt-heads, rowdies, and every way mean people, as many of the English sovereigns have been, should inhabit these stately halls, contrasting its splendors with their littleness; but, on the whole, I readily consented within myself to be impressed for a moment with the feeling that royalty has its glorious side. By no possibility can we ever have such a place in America.

Leaving Hampton Court at about four o'clock, we walked through Bushy Park, — a beautiful tract of ground, well wooded with fine old trees, green with moss all up their twisted trunks, — through several villages, Twickenham among the rest, to Richmond. Before entering Twickenham, we passed a lath and plaster castellated edifice, much time-worn, and with the plaster peeling off from the laths, which I fancied might be Horace Walpole's toy-castle. Not that it really could have been; but it was like the image, wretchedly mean and shabby, which one forms of such a place, in its decay. From Hampton Court to the Star and Garter, on Richmond Hill, is about six miles. After glancing cursorily at the prospect, which is famous, and doubtless very extensive and beautiful if the English mistiness would only let it be seen, we took a good dinner in the large and handsome coffee-room of the hotel, and then wended our way to the rail station, and reached home between eight and nine o'clock. We must have walked not far from fifteen miles in the course of the day.

March 25. — Yesterday, at one o'clock, I called by appointment on Mr. Bennoch, and lunched with him and his partners and clerks. This lunch seems to be a legitimate continuation of the old London custom of the master living at the same table with his apprentices. The meal was a dinner for the latter class. The table was set in an upper room of the establishment; and the dinner was a large joint of roast mutton, to which ten people sat down, including a German silk merchant as a guest, besides myself. Mr. Bennoch was at the head of the table, and one of his partners at the foot. For the apprentices there was porter to drink, and for the partners and guests some sparkling Moselle, and we had a sufficient dinner with agreeable conversation.   Bennoch said that G. G——— used to be very fond of these lunches while in England.

After lunch, Mr. Bennoch took me round the establishment, which is quite extensive, occupying, I think, two or three adjacent houses, and requiring more.   He showed me innumerable packages of ribbons, and other silk manufactures, and all sorts of silks, from the raw thread to the finest fabrics.   He then offered to show me some of the curiosities of old London, and took me first to Barber-Surgeons' Hall, in Monkwell Street.   It was at this place that the first anatomical studies were instituted in England. At the time of its foundation, the Barbers and Surgeons were one company ; but the latter, I believe, are now the exclusive possessors of the hall.   The edifice was built by Inigo Jones, and the principal room is a fine one, with finely carved wood-work on the ceiling and walls.   There is a skylight in the roof, letting down a sufficient radiance on the long table beneath, where, no doubt, dead people have been dissected, and where, for many generations, it has been the custom of the society to hold its stated feasts. In this room hangs the most valuable picture by Holbein now in existence, representing the company of Barber-Surgeons kneeling before Henry

VIII., and receiving their charter from his hands. The picture is about six feet square. The king is dressed in scarlet, and quite fulfils one's idea of his aspect. The Barber-Surgeons, all portraits, are an assemblage of grave-looking personages, in dark costumes. The company has refused five thousand pounds for this unique picture; and the keeper of the Hall told me that Sir Robert Peel had offered a thousand pounds for liberty to take out only one of the heads, that of a person named Pen, he conditioning to have a perfect facsimile painted in. I did not see any merit in this head over the others.

Beside this great picture hung a most exquisite portrait by Vandyke; an elderly, bearded man, of noble and refined countenance, in a rich, grave dress. There are many other pictures of distinguished men of the company, in long past times, and of some of the kings and great people of England, all darkened with age, and producing a rich and sombre effect, in this stately old hall. Nothing is more curious in London than these ancient localities and customs of the City Companies, — each trade and profession having its own hall, and its own institutions. The keeper next showed us the plate which is used at the banquets.

.   .   .   .

I should like to be present at one of these feasts. I saw also an old vellum manuscript, in black-letter, which appeared to be a record of the proceedings of the company ; and at the end there were many pages ruled for further entries, but none had been made in the volume for the last three or four hundred years.

I think it was in the neighborhood of Barber-Surgeons' Hall, which stands amid an intricacy of old streets, where I should never have thought of going, that I saw a row of ancient almshouses, of Elizabethan structure. They looked woefully dilapidated. In front of one of them was an inscription, setting forth that some worthy alderman had founded this establishment for the support of six poor men, — and these six, or their successors, are still supported, but no larger number, although the value of the property left for that purpose would now suffice for a much larger number.

Then Mr. Bennoch took me to Cripplegate, and, entering the door of a house, which proved to be a sexton's residence, we passed by a side entrance into the church porch of St. Giles, of which the sexton's house seems to be an indivisible contiguity. This is a very ancient church, that escaped the great fire of London. The galleries are supported by arches, the pillars of which are cased high upwards with oak ; but all this oaken work and the oaken pews are comparatively modern, though so solid and dark that they agree well enough with the general effect of the church. Proceeding to the high altar, we found it surrounded with many very curious old monuments and memorials, some in carved oak, some in marble ; grim old worthies, mostly in the costume of Queen Elizabeth's time.   Here was the bust of Speed, the historian ; here was the monument of Fox, author of The Book of Martyrs.   High up on the wall, beside the altar, there was a black wooden coffin, and a lady sitting upright within it, with her hands clasped in prayer, it being her awakening moment at the Resurrection.   Thence we passed down the centre aisle, and about midway we stopped before a marble bust, fixed against one of the pillars. And this was the bust of Milton ! Yes, and Milton's bones lay beneath our feet ; for he was buried under the pew over the door of which I was leaning.   The bust, I believe, is the original of the one in Westminster Abbey.

Treading over the tombstones of the old citizens of London, both in the aisles and the porch, and within doors and without, we went into the churchyard, one side of which is fenced in by a portion of London Wall, very solid, and still high, though the accumulation of human dust has covered much of its base. This is the most considerable portion now remaining of the ancient wall of London.   The sexton now asked us to go into the tower of the church, that he might show us the oldest part of the structure, and we did so, and, looking down from the organ gallery, I saw a woman sitting alone in the church, waiting for the rector, whose ghostly consolation, I suppose, she needed.

This old church tower was formerly lighted by three large windows, — one of them of very great size ; but the thrifty church-wardens of a generation or two ago had built them up with brick, to the great disfigurement of the church. The sexton called my attention to the organ pipe, which is of sufficient size, I believe, to admit three men.

From Cripplegate we went to Milton Street (as it is now called), through which we walked for a very excellent reason ; for this is the veritable Grub Street, where my literary kindred of former times used to congregate. It is still a shabby looking street, with old-fashioned houses, and inhabited chiefly by people of the poorer classes, though not by authors. Next we went to Old Broad Street, and, being joined by Mr. B——, we set off for London Bridge, turning out of our direct course to see London Stone in Watling Street. This famous stone appears now to be built into the wall of St. Swithin's Church, and is so encased that you can only see and touch the top of it through a circular hole. There are one or two long cuts or indentations in the top, which are said to have been made by Jack Cade's sword when he struck it against the stone. If so, his sword was of a redoubtable temper. Judging by what I saw, London Stone was a rudely shaped and unhewn post.

At the London Bridge station, we took the rail for Greenwich, and, it being only about five miles off, we were not long in reaching the town. It was Easter Monday; and during the first three days of Easter, from time immemorial, a fair has been held at Greenwich, and this was what we had come to see.

[This fair is described in Our Old Home, in A London Suburb.]

.   .   .   .

Reaching Mr. Bennoch's house, we found it a pretty and comfortable one, and adorned with many works of art; for he seems to be a patron of art and literature, and a warm-hearted man, of active benevolence and vivid sympathies in many directions. His face shows this. I have never seen eyes of a warmer glow than his. On the walls of one room there were a good many sketches by Haydon, and several artists' proofs of fine engravings, presented by persons to whom he had been kind. In the drawing-room there was a marble bust of Mrs. ——, and one, I think, of himself, and one of the Queen, which Mr. Bennoch said was very good, and it is unlike any other I have seen. It is intended as a gift, from a number of subscribers, to Miss Nightingale. Likewise a crayon sketch of

————, looking rather morbid and unwholesome, as the poor lady really is. Also, a small picture of Mr. Bennoch in a military dress, as an officer, probably, of city-horse. By and by came in a young gentleman, son of Haydon, the painter of high art, and one or two ladies staying in the house, and anon Mrs. ————. And so we went in to dinner.

Bennoch is an admirable host, and warms his guests like a household fire by the influence of his kindly face and glowing eyes, and by such hospitable demeanor as best suits this aspect. After the cloth was removed, came in Mr. Newton Crosland, a young man who once called on me in Liverpool, — the husband of a literary lady, formerly Camilla Toulmin. The lady herself was coming to spend the evening. The husband (and I presume the wife) is a decided believer in spiritual manifestations. We talked of politics and spiritualism and literature ; and before we rose from the table, Mr. Bennoch drank the health of the ladies, and especially of Mrs. H————, in terms very kind towards her and me. I responded in her behalf as well as I could, and left it to Mr. Bowman, as a bachelor, to respond for the ladies generally, — which he did briefly, toasting Mrs. B————.

We had heard the sound of the piano in the drawing-room for some time, and now adjourning thither, I had the pleasure to be introduced to Mrs. Newton Crosland, — a rather tall, thin, pale, and lady-like person, looking, I thought, of a sensitive character. She expressed in a low tone and quiet way great delight at seeing my distinguished self! for she is a vast admirer of The Scarlet Letter, and especially of the character of Hester; indeed, I remember seeing a most favorable criticism of the book from her pen, in one of the London magazines. . . .

At eleven o'clock Mrs. Crosland entered the tiniest pony carriage, and set forth for her own residence, with a lad walking at the pony's head, and carrying a lantern. . . .

March 26. — Yesterday was not a very eventful day. After writing in my journal I went out at twelve, and visited, for the first time, the National Gallery. It is of no use for me to criticise pictures, or to try to describe them, but I have an idea that I might acquire a taste, with a little attention to the subject, for I find I already begin to prefer some pictures to others. This is encouraging. Of those that I saw yesterday, I think I liked several by Murillo best. There were a great many people in the gallery, almost entirely of the middle, with a few of the lower classes; and I should think that the effect of the exhibition must at least tend towards refinement. Nevertheless, the only emotion that I saw displayed was in broad grins on the faces of a man and two women, at sight of a small picture of Venus, with a Satyr peeping at her with an expression of gross animal delight and merriment. Without being aware of it, this man and the two women were of that same Satyr breed.

If I lived in London, I would endeavor to educate myself in this and other galleries of art; but as the case stands, it would be of no use. I saw two of Turner's landscapes; but did not see so much beauty in them as in some of Claude's. A view of the grand canal in Venice, by Canaletto, seemed to me wonderful, — absolutely perfect, — a better reality, for I could see the water of the canal moving and dimpling; and the palaces and buildings on each side were quite as good in their way.

Leaving the gallery, I walked down into the city, and passed through Smithfield, where I glanced at St. Bartholomew's Hospital. . . . Then I went into St. Paul's, and walked all round the great cathedral, looking, I believe, at every monument on the floor. There is certainly nothing very wonderful in any of them, and I do wish it would not so generally happen that English warriors go into battle almost nude; at least, we must suppose so, from their invariably receiving their death wounds in that condition. I will not believe that a sculptor or a painter is a man of genius unless he can make

the nobleness of his subject illuminate and trans-
figure any given pattern of coat and breeches.
Nevertheless, I never go into St. Paul's without
being impressed anew with the grandeur of the
edifice, and the general effect of these same
groups of statuary ranged in their niches and at
the bases of the pillars as adornments of the
cathedral.

Coming homeward, I went into the enclosure
of the Temple, and near the entrance saw "Dr.
Johnson's staircase" printed over a doorway;
so I not only looked in, but went up the first
flight of some broad, well-worn stairs, passing
my hand over a heavy, ancient, broken balustrade, on which, no doubt, Johnson's hand has
often rested. It was here that Boswell used to
visit him, in their early acquaintance. Before
my lunch, I had gone into Bolt Court, where
he died.

.   .   .   .

This morning there have been letters from
Mr. Wilding, enclosing an invitation to me to
be one of the stewards of the anniversary dinner of the Literary Fund.

No, I thank you, gentlemen!

March 27. — Yesterday I went out at about
twelve, and visited the British Museum; an
exceedingly tiresome affair. It quite crushes a

person to see so much at once, and I wandered from hall to hall with a weary and heavy heart, wishing (Heaven forgive me !) that the Elgin Marbles and the frieze of the Parthenon were all burnt into lime, and that the granite Egyptian statues were hewn and squared into building-stones, and that the mummies had all turned to dust two thousand years ago ; and, in fine, that all the material relics of so many successive ages had disappeared with the generations that produced them.   The present is burdened too much with the past. We have not time, in our earthly existence, to appreciate what is warm with life, and immediately around us ; yet we heap up these old shells, out of which human life has long emerged, casting them off forever.   I do not see how future ages are to stagger onward under all this dead weight, with the additions that will be continually made to it.

After leaving the Museum, I went to see Bennoch, and arrange with him our expedition of to-day ; and he read me a letter from Tupper, very earnestly inviting me to come and spend a night or two with him.   Then I wandered about the city, and was lost in the vicinity of Holborn ; so that for a long while I was under a spell of bewilderment, and kept returning, in the strangest way, to the same point in Lincoln's Inn Fields. . . .

Mr. Bowman and I went to the Princess's

Theatre in the evening. Charles Kean performed in Louis XI. very well indeed, — a thoughtful and highly skilled actor, — much improved since I saw him, many years ago, in America.

April 1. — After my last date on Thursday, I visited the National Gallery. At three o'clock, having packed a travelling-bag, I went to Bennoch's office, and lunched with him ; and at about five we took the rail from the Waterloo station for Aldershott Camp. At Tamborough we were cordially received by Lieutenant Shaw, of the North Cork Rifles, and were escorted by him, in a fly, to his quarters. The camp is a large city, composed of numberless wooden barracks, arranged in regular streets, on a wide, bleak heath, with an extensive and dreary prospect on all sides. Lieutenant Shaw assigned me one room in his hut, and Bennock another, and made us as comfortable as kind hospitality could ; but the huts are very small, and the rooms have no size at all ; neither are they airtight, and the sharp wind whistles in at the crevices ; and, on the whole, of all discomfortable places, I am inclined to reckon Aldershott Camp the most so. I suppose the government has placed the camp on that windy heath, and built such wretched huts, for the very purpose of rendering life as little desirable as may be to the soldiers, so that they should throw it away the more willingly.

At seven o'clock we dined at the regimental mess, with the officers of the North Cork. The mess-room is by far the most endurable place to be found in camp. The hut is large, and the mess-room is capable of receiving between thirty and forty guests, besides the officers of the regiment, when a great dinner-party is given. As I saw it, the whole space was divided into a dining-room and two anterooms by red curtains drawn across; and the second anteroom seems to be a general rendezvous for the officers, where they meet at all times, and talk, or look over the newspapers and the army register, which constitute the chief of their reading. The Colonel and Lieutenant-Colonel of the regiment received Bennoch and me with great cordiality, as did all the other officers, and we sat down to a splendid dinner.

All the officers of the regiment are Irishmen, and all of them, I believe, men of fortune; and they do what they can towards alleviating their hardships in camp by eating and drinking of the best that can be obtained of all good things. The table service and plate were as fine as those in any nobleman's establishment; the dishes numerous and admirably got up; and the wines delectable and genuine, — as they had need to be; for there is a great consumption of them.

I liked these Irish officers exceedingly, — not that it would be possible to live long among them without finding existence a bore; for they have no thought, no intellectual movement, no ideas, that I was aware of, beyond horses, dogs, drill, garrisons, field days, whist, wine, cigars, and all that kind of thing; yet they were really gentlemen, living on the best terms with one another, — courteous, kind, most hospitable, with a rich Irish humor, softened down by social refinements, — not too refined either, but a most happy sort of behavior, as natural as that of children, and with a safe freedom that made me feel entirely at my ease. I think well of the Irish gentlemen, for their sakes; and I believe I might fairly attribute to Lieutenant-Colonel Stowell (next whom I sat) a higher and finer cultivation than the above description indicates. Indeed, many of them may have been capable of much more intellectual intercourse than that of the mess-table; but I suppose it would not have been in keeping with their camp life, nor suggested by it. Several of the elder officers were men who had been long in the army; and the Colonel — a bluff, hearty old soldier, with a profile like an eagle's head and beak — was a veteran of the Peninsula, and had a medal on his breast with clasps for three famous battles besides that of Waterloo.

The regimental band played during dinner,

and the Lieutenant-Colonel apologized to me for its not playing Hail Columbia, the tune not coming within their musical accomplishments. It was no great matter, however; for I should not have distinguished it from any other tune; but, to do me what honor was possible, in the way of national airs, the band was ordered to play a series of negro melodies, and I was entirely satisfied. It is really funny that the " wood-notes wild " of those poor black slaves should have been played in a foreign land as an honorable compliment to one of their white countrymen.

After dinner we played whist, and then had some broiled bones for supper, and finally went home to our respective huts not much earlier than four o'clock. But I don't wonder these gentlemen sit up as long as they can keep their eyes open; for never was there anything so utterly comfortless as their camp-beds. They are really worse than the bed of honor, — no wider, no softer, no warmer, and affording not nearly so sound sleep. Indeed, I got hardly any sleep at all, and almost as soon as I did close my eyes, the bugles sounded, and the drums beat reveillé, and from that moment the camp was all astir; so I pretty soon uprose, and went to the mess-room for my breakfast, feeling wonderfully fresh and well, considering what my night had been.

Long before this, however, this whole regiment, and all the other regiments, marched off
to take part in a general review, and Bennoch
and I followed, as soon as we had eaten a few
mutton chops.   It was a bright, sunshiny day ;
but with a strong east wind, as piercing and
pitiless as ever blew ; and this wide, undulating
plain of Aldershott seemed just the place where
the east wind was at home.   Still, it acted, on
the whole, like an invigorating cordial ; and
whereas in pleasanter circumstances I should
have lain down, and gone to sleep, I now felt
as if I could do without sleep for a month.

In due time we found out the place of the
North Cork Regiment in the general battle
array, and were greeted as old comrades by the
Colonel and other officers.   Soon the soldiers
(who, when we first reached them, were strolling
about, or standing at ease) were called into order ; and anon we saw a group of mounted officers riding along the lines, and among them a
gentleman in a civilian's round hat, and plain
frock and trousers, riding on a white horse.
This group of riders turned the front of the
regiment, and then passed along the rear, coming close to where we stood ; and as the plainly
dressed gentleman rode by, he bent towards
me, and I tried to raise my hat, but did not
succeed very well, because the fierce wind had
compelled me to jam it tightly upon my head.

The Duke of Cambridge (for this was he) is a comely-looking, gentlemanly man, of bluff English face, with a great deal of brown beard about it.   Though a pretty tall man, he appears, on horseback, broad and round in proportion to his height.   I looked at him with a certain sort of interest, and a feeling of kindness ; for one does feel kindly to whatever human being is any wise marked out from the rest, unless it be by his disagreeable qualities.

The troops, from twelve to fifteen thousand, now fell into marching order, and went to attack a wood, where we were to suppose the enemy to be stationed.   The sham fight seemed to me rather clumsily managed, and without any striking incident or result.   The officers had prophesied, the night before, that General K——, commanding in the camp, would make a muddle of it ; and probably he did.   After the review, the Duke of Cambridge with his attendant officers took their station, and all the regiments marched in front of him, saluting as they passed. As each colonel rode by, and as the banner of each regiment was lowered, the Duke lifted his hat.

.   .   .   .

The most splendid effect of this parade was the gleam of the sun upon the long line of bayonets, — the sheen of all that steel appearing like a wavering fringe of light upon the dark masses of troops below.   It was very fine.   But I was glad when all was done, and I could go back to the mess-room, whither I carried an excellent appetite for luncheon.   After this we walked about the camp, — looked at some model tents, inspected the arrangements and modes of living in the huts of the privates ; and thus gained more and more adequate ideas of the vile uncomfortableness of a military life. Finally, I went to the anteroom and turned over the regimental literature, — a peerage and bar-onetage, — an army and militia register, a num-ber of the Sporting Magazine, and one of the United Service, while Bennoch took another walk.   Before dinner we both tried to catch a little nap by way of compensation for last night's deficiencies ; but, for my part, the attempt was fruitless.

The dinner was as splendid and as agreeable as that of the evening before ; and I believe it was nearly two o'clock when Bennoch and I bade farewell to our kind entertainers.   For my part I fraternized with these military gentlemen in a way that augurs the very best things for the future peace of the two countries.   They all expressed the warmest sympathies towards America, and it was easy to judge from their conversation that there is no real friendliness on the part of the military towards the French.

The old antipathy is just as strong as ever,—
stronger than ever, perhaps, on account of the
comparatively more brilliant success of the
French in this Russian war. So, with most
Christian sentiments of peace and brotherly
love, we returned to our hut, and lay down,
each in his narrow bed.

Early in the morning the drums and bugles
began the usual bedevilment; and shortly after
six I dressed, and we had breakfast at the mess-
room, shook hands with Lieutenant Shaw (our
more especial host), and drove off to the railway station at Ash.

I know not whether I have mentioned that
the villages neighboring to the camp have suffered terribly as regards morality from the vicinity of the soldiers. Quiet old English towns,
that till within a little time ago had kept their
antique simplicity and innocence, have now no
such thing as female virtue in them, so far as
the lower classes are concerned. This is express-
ing the matter too strongly, no doubt; but
there is too much truth in it, nevertheless; and
one of the officers remarked that even ladies
of respectability had grown much more free in
manners and conversation than at first. I have
heard observations similar to this from a Nova
Scotian, in reference to the moral influence of
soldiers when stationed in the provinces.

. . . .

Wooton stands in a hollow, near the summit of one of the long swells that here undulate over the face of the country. There is a good deal of wood behind it, as should be the case with the residence of the author of the Sylva; but I believe few, if any, of these trees are known to have been planted by John Evelyn, or even to have been coeval with his time. The house is of brick, partly ancient, and consists of a front and two projecting wings, with a porch and entrance in the centre. It has a desolate, meagre aspect, and needs something to give it life and stir and jollity. The present proprietor is of the old Evelyn family, and is now one of the two members of Parliament for Surrey; but he is a very shy and retiring man, unmarried, sees little company, and seems either not to know how to make himself comfortable or not to care about it. A servant told us that Mr. —— had just gone out, but Tupper, who is apparently on intimate terms with him, thought it best that we should go into the house, while he went in search of the master. So the servant ushered us through a hall, — where were many family pictures by Lely, and, for aught I know, by Vandyke, and by Kneller, and other famous painters, — up a grand staircase, and into the library, the inner room of which contained the ponderous volumes which John Evelyn used to read. Nevertheless, it was a room of most barren aspect, without a carpet on the floor, with pine bookcases, with a common whitewashed ceiling, with no luxurious study-chairs, and without a fire. There was an open folio on the table, and a sheet of manuscript that appeared to have been recently written. I took down a book from the shelves (a volume of annals, connected with English history), and Tupper afterwards told us that this one single volume, for its rarity, was worth either two or three hundred pounds. Against one of the windows of this library there grows a magnolia-tree, with a very large stem, and at least fifty years old.

Mrs. Tupper and I waited a good while, and Bennoch and Tupper came back, without having found Mr. ——. Tupper wished very much to show the prayer-book used by King Charles at his execution, and some curious old manuscript volumes; but the servant said that his master always kept these treasures locked up, and trusted the key to nobody. We therefore had to take our leave without seeing them; and I have not often entered a house that one feels to be more forlorn than Wooton, — although we did have a glimpse of a dining-room, with a table laid for three or four guests, and looking quite brilliant with plate and glass and snowy napery. There was a fire, too, in this one room. Mr. —— is making extensive alterations in the house, or has recently done so, and this is perhaps one reason of its ungenial mea-greness and lack of finish.

Before our departure from Wooton, Tupper had asked me to leave my card for Mr. ———; but I had no mind to overstep any limit of formal courtesy in dealing with an Englishman, and therefore declined. Tupper, however, on his own responsibility, wrote his name, Bennoch's, and mine on a piece of paper, and told the servant to show them to Mr. ———. We soon had experience of the good effect of this; for we had scarcely got back before somebody drove up to Tupper's door, and one of the girls, looking out, exclaimed that there was Mr. ——— himself, and another gentleman. He had set out, the instant he heard of our call, to bring the three precious volumes for me to see. This surely was most kind; a kindness which I should never have dreamed of expecting from a shy, retiring man like Mr. ———.

So he and his friend were ushered into the dining-room, and introduced. Mr. ——— is a young-looking man, dark, with a mustache, rather small, and though he has the manners of a man who has seen the world, it evidently requires an effort in him to speak to anybody; and I could see his whole person slightly writhing itself, as it were, while he addressed me. This is strange in a man of his public position, member for the county, necessarily mixed up with life in many forms, the possessor of sixteen thousand pounds a year, and the representative of an ancient name. Nevertheless, I liked him, and felt as if I could become intimately acquainted with him, if circumstances were favorable; but, at a brief interview like this, it was hopeless to break through two great reserves; so I talked more with his companion — a pleasant young man, fresh from college, I should imagine — than with Mr. —— himself.

The three books were really of very great interest. One was an octavo volume of manuscript in John Evelyn's own hand, the beginning of his published Diary, written as distinctly as print, in a small, clear character. It can be read just as easily as any printed book. Another was a Church of England prayer-book, which King Charles used on the scaffold, and which was stained with his sacred blood, and underneath are two or three lines in John Evelyn's hand, certifying this to be the very book. It is an octavo, or small folio, and seems to have been very little used, scarcely opened, except in one spot; its leaves elsewhere retaining their original freshness and elasticity. It opens most readily at the commencement of the common service; and there, on the left-hand page, is a discoloration, of a yellowish or brownish hue, about two thirds of an inch large, which, two hundred years ago and a little more, was doubtless red. For on that page had fallen a drop of King Charles's blood.

The other volume was large, and contained a great many original letters, written by the king during his troubles. I had not time to examine them with any minuteness, and remember only one document, which Mr. —— pointed out, and which had a strange pathos and pitifulness in it. It was a sort of due-bill, promising to pay a small sum for beer, which had been supplied to his Majesty, so soon as God should enable him, or the distracted circumstances of his kingdom make it possible, — or some touching and helpless expression of that kind. Prince Hal seemed to consider it an unworthy matter, that a great prince should think of " that poor creature, small beer," at all ; but that a great prince should not be able to pay for it is far worse.

Mr. —— expressed his regret that I was not staying longer in this part of the country, as he would gladly have seen me at Wooton, and he succeeded in saying something about my books ; and I hope I partly succeeded in showing him that I was very sensible of his kindness in letting me see those relics. I cannot say whether or no I expressed it sufficiently. It is better with such a man, or, indeed, with any man, to say too little than too much ; and, in fact, it would have been indecorous in me to take too

much of his kindness to my own share, Bennoch being likewise in question.

We had a cup of coffee, and then took our
leave ; Tupper accompanying us part way down
the village street, and bidding us an affectionate
farewell.

.   .   .   .

Bennoch and I recommenced our travels, and,
changing from one railway to another, reached
Tunbridge Wells at nine or ten in the evening.
. . . The next day was spent at Tunbridge
Wells, which is famous for a chalybeate spring,
and is a watering-place of note, most healthily
situated on a high, breezy hill, with many pleasant walks in the neighborhood. . . . From
Tunbridge Wells we transported ourselves to
Battle, — the village in which is Battle Abbey.
It is a large village, with many antique houses
and some new ones ; and in its principal street,
on one side, with a wide, green space before it,
you see the gray, embattled, outer wall, and
great, square, battlemented entrance tower (with
a turret at each corner), of the ancient Abbey.
It is the perfect reality of a Gothic battlement
and gateway, just as solid and massive as when
it was first built, though hoary and venerable
with the many intervening centuries. There
are only two days in the week on which visitors
are allowed entrance, and this was not one of

them.   Nevertheless, Bennoch was determined
to get in, and he wished me to send Lady Webster my card with his own; but this I utterly
refused, for the honor of America and for my
own honor; because I will not do anything to
increase the reputation we already have as a very
forward people.   Bennoch, however, called at a
bookshop on the other side of the street, near
the gateway of the castle; and making friends,
as he has a marvellous tact in doing, with the
bookseller, the latter offered to take in his card
to the housekeeper, and see if Lady Webster
would not relax her rule in our favor.   Meanwhile, we went into the old church of Battle,
which was built in Norman times, though sub-
sequently to the Abbey.   As we entered the
church door, the bell rang for joy at the news
of peace, which had just been announced by
the London papers.

The church has been whitewashed in modern
times, and does not look so venerable as it
ought, with its arches and pillared aisles.   In
the chancel stands a marble tomb, heavy, rich,
and elaborate, on the top of which lie the
broken-nosed statues of Sir Anthony Browne
and his lady, who were the Lord and Lady of
Battle Abbey in Henry VIII.'s time.   The
knight is in armor, and the lady in stately garb,
and (save for their broken noses) they are in
excellent preservation: The pavement of the

chancel and aisles is all laid with tombstones, and on two or three of these there were engraved brasses, representing knights in armor, and churchmen, with inscriptions in Latin. Some of them are very old. On the walls, too, there are various monuments, principally of dignitaries connected with the Abbey. Two hatchments, in honor of persons recently dead, were likewise suspended in the chancel. The best pew of the church is, of course, that of the Webster family. It is curtained round, carpeted, furnished with chairs and footstools, and more resembles a parlor than a pew; especially as there is a fireplace in one of the pointed archways, which I suppose has been bricked up in order to form it. On the opposite side of the aisle is the pew of some other magnate, containing a stove. The rest of the parishioners have to keep themselves warm with the fervor of their own piety. I have forgotten what else was interesting, except that we were shown a stone coffin, recently dug up, in which was hollowed a place for the head of the corpse.

Returning to the bookshop, we found that Lady Webster had sent her compliments, and would be very happy to have us see the Abbey. How thoroughly kind these English people can be when they like, and how often they like to be so!

We lost no time in ringing the bell at the

arched entrance, under the great tower, and were admitted by an old woman who lives, I believe, in the thickness of the wall. She told us her room used to be the prison of the Abbey, and under the great arch she pointed to a projecting beam, where she said criminals used to be hanged. At two of the intersecting points of the arches, which form the roof of the gateway, were carved faces of stone, said to represent King Harold and William the Conqueror. The exterior wall, of which this tower is the gateway, extends far along the village street, and encloses a very large space, within which stands the mansion, quite secluded from unauthorized visitors, or even from the sight of those without, unless it be at very distant eyeshot.

We rang at the principal door of the edifice (it is under a deep arch, in the Norman style, but of modern date), and a footman let us in, and then delivered us over to a respectable old lady in black. She was a Frenchwoman by birth, but had been very long in the service of the family, and spoke English almost without an accent; her French blood being indicated only by her thin and withered aspect, and a greater gentility of manner than would have been seen in an Englishwoman of similar station. She ushered us first into a grand and noble hall, the arched and carved oaken roof of which ascended into the gable. It was nearly

sixty feet long, and its height equal to its length,
— as stately a hall, I should imagine, as is
anywhere to be found in a private mansion.
It was lighted, at one end, by a great window,
beneath which, occupying the whole breadth of
the hall, hung a vast picture of the Battle of
Hastings; and, whether a good picture or no,
it was a rich adornment of the hall. The walls
were wainscoted high upward with oak: they
were almost covered with noble pictures of ancestry, and of kings and great men, and beautiful women; there were trophies of armor hung
aloft; and two armed figures, one in brass mail,
the other in bright steel, stood on a raised dais,
underneath the great picture. At the end of
the hall, opposite the picture, a third of the way
up towards the roof, was a gallery. All these
things that I have enumerated were in perfect
condition, without rust, untouched by decay or
injury of any kind; but yet they seemed to belong to a past age, and were mellowed, softened
in their splendor, a little dimmed with time, —
toned down into a venerable magnificence. Of
all domestic things that I have seen in England, it satisfied me most.

Then the Frenchwoman showed us into various rooms and offices, most of which were contrived out of the old abbey cloisters, and the
vaulted cells and apartments in which the monks
used to live. If any house be haunted, I should

suppose this might be. If any church property bring a curse with it, as people say, I do not see how the owners of Battle Abbey can escape it, taking possession of and dwelling in these holy precincts, as they have done, and laying their kitchen hearth with the stones of overthrown altars. The Abbey was first granted, I believe, to Sir Anthony Browne, whom I saw asleep with his lady in the church. It was his first wife. I wish it had been his second; for she was Surrey's Geraldine. The posterity of Sir Anthony kept the place till 1719, and then sold it to the Websters, a family of Baronets, who are still the owners and occupants. The present proprietor is Sir Augustus Webster, whose mother is the lady that so kindly let us into the Abbey.

Mr. Bennoch gave the nice old French lady half a crown, and we next went round among the ruined portions of the Abbey, under the gardener's guidance. We saw two ivied towers, insulated from all other ruins; and an old refectory, open to the sky, and a vaulted crypt, supported by pillars; and we saw, too, the foundation and scanty remains of a chapel, which had been long buried out of sight of man, and only dug up within present memory, — about forty years ago. There had always been a tradition that this was the spot where Harold had planted his standard, and where his body was found after the battle; and the discovery of the ruined chapel confirmed the tradition.

I might have seen a great deal more, had there been time; and I have forgotten much of what I did see; but it is an exceedingly interesting place. There is an avenue of old yew-trees, which meet above like a cloistered arch; and this is called the Monks' Walk. I rather think they were ivy, though growing unsupported.

As we were retiring, the gardener suddenly stopped, as if he were alarmed, and motioned to us to do the same, saying, "I believe it is my lady!" And so it was, — a tall and stately lady in black, trimming shrubs in the garden. She bowed to us very graciously, — we raised our hats, and thus we met and parted without more ado. As we went through the arch of the entrance tower, Bennoch gave the old female warder a shilling, and the gardener followed us to get half a crown.

We took a fly and driver from the principal hotel of Battle, and drove off for Hastings, about seven miles distant. Hastings is now a famous watering and sea-bathing place, and seems to be well sheltered from the winds, though open to the sea, which here stretches off towards France. We climbed a high and steep hill, terraced round its base with streets of modern lodging-houses, and crowned on its summit with the ruins of a castle, the foundation of which was anterior to the Conquest. This castle has no wall towards the sea, the precipice being too high and sheer to admit of attack on that side. I have quite exhausted my descriptive faculty for the present, so shall say nothing of this old castle, which indeed (the remains being somewhat scanty and scraggling) is chiefly picturesque and interesting from its bold position on such a headlong hill.

Clambering down on another side from that of our ascent, we entered the town of Hastings, which seems entirely modern, and made up of lodging-houses, shops, hotels, parades, and all such makings up of watering-places generally. We took a delightful warm bath, washing off all weariness and naughtiness, and coming out new men. Then we walked to St. Leonard's, — a part of Hastings, I believe, but a mile or two from the castle, and there called at the lodgings of two friends of Bennoch.

These were Mr. Martin, the author of Bon Gaultier's ballads, and his wife, the celebrated actress, Helen Faucit. Mr. Martin is a barrister, a gentleman whose face and manners suited me at once; a simple, refined, sincere, not too demonstrative person. His wife, too, I liked; a tall, dark, fine, and lady-like woman, with the simplest manners, that give no trouble at all, and so must be perfect. With these two persons I felt myself, almost in a moment, on friendly terms, and in true accord, and so I talked, I think, more than I have at any time since coming to London.

We took a pleasant lunch at their house; and then they walked with us to the railway station, and there they took leave of Bennoch affectionately, and of me hardly less so; for in truth, we had grown to be almost friends in this very little while. And as we rattled away, I said to Bennoch earnestly, "What good people they are!"—and Bennoch smiled, as if he had known perfectly well that I should think and say so. And thus we rushed onward to London; and I reached St. James's Place between nine and ten o'clock, after a very interesting tour, the record of which I wish I could have kept as we went along, writing each day's history before another day's adventures began.

LONDON, *April* 4, 1856. — On Tuesday I went to No. 14, Ludgate Hill, to dine with Bennoch at the Milton Club; a club recently founded for dissenters, non-conformists, and people whose ideas, religious or political, are not precisely in train with the establishment in church and state. I was shown into a large reading-room, well provided with periodicals and newspapers, and found two or three persons there; but Bennoch had not yet arrived. In a few moments, a tall gentleman with white hair came in, — a fine and intelligent-looking man, whom I guessed to be one of those who were to meet me. He walked about, glancing at the periodicals; and soon entered Mr. Tupper, and, without seeing me, exchanged warm greetings with the white-haired gentleman. "I suppose," began Mr. Tupper, "you have come to meet" — Now, conscious that my name was going to be spoken, and not knowing but the excellent Mr. Tupper might say something which he would not quite like me to overhear, I advanced at once, with outstretched hand, and saluted him. He expressed great joy at the recognition, and immediately introduced me to Mr. Hall.

The dining-room was pretty large and lofty, and there were sixteen guests at table, most of them authors, or people connected with the press; so that the party represented a great deal of the working intellect of London at this present day and moment, — the men whose plays, whose songs, whose articles, are just now in vogue. Mr. Tom Taylor was one of the very few whose writings I had known anything about. He is a tall, slender, dark young man, not English-looking, and wearing colored spectacles, so that I should readily have taken him for an American literary man. I did not have much opportunity of talking with him, nor with anybody else, except Dr. ———, who seemed a shrewd, sensible man, with a certain slight acerbity of thought. Mr. Herbert Ingram, recently elected member of Parliament, was likewise present, and sat on Bennoch's left.

It was a very good dinner, with an abundance of wine, which Bennoch sent round faster than was for the next day's comfort of his guests. It is singular that I should thus far have quite forgotten W—— H——, whose books I know better than those of any other person there. He is a white-headed, stout, firm-looking, and rather wrinkle-faced old gentleman, whose temper, I should imagine, was not the very sweetest in the world. There is an abruptness, a kind of sub-acidity, if not bitterness, in his address; he seemed not to be, in short, so genial as I should have anticipated from his books.

As soon as the cloth was removed, Bennoch, without rising from his chair, made a speech in honor of his eminent and distinguished guest, which illustrious person happened to be sitting in the self-same chair that I myself occupied. I have no recollection of what he said, nor of what I said in reply, but I remember that both of us were cheered and applauded much more than the occasion deserved. Then followed about fifty other speeches; for every single individual at table was called up (as Tupper said,

83

" toasted and roasted "), and, for my part, I was done entirely brown (to continue T——'s figure). Everybody said something kind, not a word or idea of which can I find in my memory. Certainly, if I never get any more praise in my life, I have had enough of it for once. I made another little bit of a speech, too, in response to something that was said in reference to the present difficulties between England and America, and ended, as a proof that I deemed war impossible, with drinking success to the British army, and calling on Lieutenant Shaw, of the Aldershott Camp, to reply. I am afraid I must have said something very wrong, for the applause was vociferous, and I could hear the gentlemen whispering about the table, " Good ! " " Good ! " " Yes, he is a fine fellow," — and other such ill-earned praises ; and I took shame to myself and held my tongue (publicly) the rest of the evening. But in such cases something must be allowed to the excitement of the moment, and to the effect of kindness and good-will, so broadly and warmly displayed ; and even a sincere man must not be held to speak as if he were under oath.

We separated, in a blessed state of contentment with one another, at about eleven ; and (lest I should starve before morning) I went with Mr. D—— to take supper at his house in Park Lane. Mr. D—— is a pale young gen-

tleman, of American aspect, being a West Indian by birth.   He is one of the principal
writers of editorials for the Times.   We were
accompanied in the carriage by another gentleman, Mr. M——, who is connected with the
management of the same paper.   He wrote the
letters from Scutari, which drew so much attention to the state of the hospitals.   Mr. D——
is the husband of the former Miss —— the actress, and when we reached his house, we found
that she had just come home from the theatre,
and was taking off her stage-dress.   Anon she
came down to the drawing-room, — a seemingly
good, simple, and intelligent lady, not at all
pretty, and, I should think, older than her husband.   She was very kind to me, and told me
that she had read one of my books — The
House of the Seven Gables — thirteen years
ago, which I thought remarkable, because I did
not write it till eight or nine years afterwards.

The principal talk during supper (which consisted of Welsh-rabbit and biscuits, with champagne and soda-water) was about the Times,
and the two contributors expressed vast admiration of Mr. ——, who has the chief editorial
management of the paper.   It is odd to find
how little we outsiders know of men who really
exercise a vast influence on affairs, for this Mr.
—— is certainly of far more importance in the
world than a minister of state.   He writes no-

thing himself; but the character of the Times seems to depend upon his intuitive, unerring judgment; and if ever he is absent from his post, even for a day or two, they say that the paper immediately shows it. In reply to my questions, they appeared to acknowledge that he was a man of expediency, but of a very high expediency, and that he gave the public the very best principles which it was capable of receiving. Perhaps it may be so; the Times's articles are certainly not written in so high a moral vein as might be wished; but what they lack in height they gain in breadth. Every sensible man in England finds his own best common sense there; and, in effect, I think its influence is wholesome.

Apropos of public speaking, Dr. —— said that Sir Lytton Bulwer asked him (I think the anecdote was personal to himself) whether he felt his heart beat when he was going to speak. "Yes." "Does your voice frighten you?" "Yes." "Do all your ideas forsake you?" "Yes." Do you wish the floor to open and swallow you?" "Yes." "Why, then, you'll make an orator!" Dr. —— told Canning, too, how once, before rising to speak in the House of Commons, he bade his friend feel his pulse, which was throbbing terrifically. "I know I shall make one of my best speeches," said Canning, "because I'm in such an awful

86

funk!" President Pierce, who has a great deal
of oratorical power, is subject to a similar horror
and reluctance.

April 5. — On Thursday, at eight o'clock, I
went to the Reform Club to dine with Dr. ——.
The waiter admitted me into a great basement
hall with a tessellated or mosaic or somehow
figured floor of stone, and lighted from a dome
of lofty height. In a few minutes Dr. ——
appeared, and showed me about the edifice,
which is very noble and of a substantial magnificence that was most satisfactory to behold,
— no woodwork imitating better materials, but
pillars and balustrades of marble, and everything that it purports to be. The reading-room
is very large, and luxuriously comfortable, and
contains an admirable library : there are rooms
and conveniences for every possible purpose ;
and whatever material for enjoyment a bachelor
may need, or ought to have, he can surely find
it here, and on such reasonable terms that a
small income will do as much for him as a far
greater one on any other system.

In a colonnade, on the first floor, surrounding the great basement hall, there are portraits
of distinguished reformers, and blank niches for
others yet to come. Joseph Hume, I believe,
is destined to fill one of these blanks ; but I remarked that the larger part of the portraits, al-

ready hung up, are of men of high rank, — the Duke of Sussex, for instance ; Lord Durham, Lord Grey ; and, indeed, I remember no commoner. In one room, I saw on the wall the facsimile, so common in the United States, of our Declaration of Independence.

Descending again to the basement hall, an elderly gentleman came in, and was warmly welcomed by Dr. ——. He was a very short man, but with breadth enough, and a back excessively bent, — bowed almost to deformity ; very gray hair, and a face and expression of remarkable briskness and intelligence. His profile came out pretty boldly, and his eyes had the prominence that indicates, I believe, volubility of speech, nor did he fail to talk from the instant of his appearance ; and in the tone of his voice, and in his glance, and in the whole man, there was something racy, — a flavor of the humorist. His step was that of an aged man, and he put his stick down very decidedly at every footfall ; though, as he afterwards told me that he was only fifty-two, he need not yet have been infirm. But perhaps he has had the gout ; his feet, however, are by no means swollen, but unusually small. Dr. —— introduced him as Mr. Douglas Jerrold, and we went into the coffee-room to dine.

The coffee-room occupies one whole side of the edifice, and is provided with a great many

tables, calculated for three or four persons to
dine at ; and we sat down at one of these, and
Dr. —— ordered some mulligatawny soup, and
a bottle of white French wine.   The waiters in
the coffee-room are very numerous, and most
of them dressed in the livery of the Club, comprising plush breeches and white-silk stockings ;
for these English Reformers do not seem to
include Republican simplicity of manners in
their system.   Neither, perhaps, is it anywise
essential.

After the soup we had turbot, and by and
by a bottle of Chateau Margaux, very delectable ; and then some lambs' feet, delicately
done, and some cutlets of I know not what
peculiar type ; and finally a ptarmigan, which is
of the same race of birds as the grouse, but
feeds high up towards the summits of the Scotch
mountains.   Then some cheese, and a bottle
of Chambertin.   It was a very pleasant dinner,
and my companions were both very agreeable
men ; both taking a shrewd, satirical, yet not
ill-natured view of life and people ; and as for
Mr. Douglas Jerrold, he often reminded me of
E—— C——, in the richer veins of the latter,
both by his face and expression, and by a tinc-
ture of something at once wise and humorously
absurd in what he said.   But I think he has a
kinder, more genial, wholesomer nature than
E——, and under a very thin crust of outward

acerbity I grew sensible of a very warm heart, and even of much simplicity of character, in this man, born in London, and accustomed always to London life.

I wish I had any faculty whatever of remembering what people say ; but, though I appreciate anything good at the moment, it never stays in my memory ; nor do I think, in fact, that anything definite, rounded, pointed, separable, and transferable from the general lump of conversation was said by anybody. I recollect that they laughed at Mr. ——, and at his shedding a tear into a Scottish river, on occasion of some literary festival. . . . They spoke approvingly of Bulwer, as valuing his literary position, and holding himself one of the brotherhood of authors ; and not so approvingly of Charles Dickens, who, born a plebeian, aspires to aristocratic society. But I said that it was easy to condescend, and that Bulwer knew he could not put off his rank, and that he would have all the advantages of it in spite of his authorship. We talked about the position of men of letters in England, and they said that the aristocracy hated and despised and feared them ; and I asked why it was that literary men, having really so much power in their hands, were content to live unrecognized in the State.

Douglas Jerrold talked of Thackeray and his success in America, and said that he himself purposed going and had been invited thither to lecture. I asked him whether it was pleasant to a writer of plays to see them performed; and he said it was intolerable, the presentation of the author's idea being so imperfect; and Dr. —— observed that it was excruciating to hear one of his own songs sung. Jerrold spoke of the Duke of Devonshire with great warmth, as a true, honest, simple, most kind-hearted man, from whom he himself had received great courtesies and kindnesses (not, as I understood, in the way of patronage or essential favors); and I (Heaven forgive me!) queried within myself whether this English reforming author would have been quite so sensible of the Duke's excellence if his Grace had not been a duke. But indeed a nobleman, who is at the same time a true and whole-hearted man, feeling his brotherhood with men, does really deserve some credit for it.

In the course of the evening Jerrold spoke with high appreciation of Emerson; and of Longfellow, whose Hiawatha he considered a wonderful performance; and of Lowell, whose Fable for Critics he especially admired. I mentioned Thoreau, and proposed to send his works to Dr. ——, who, being connected with the Illustrated News, and otherwise a writer, might be inclined to draw attention to them. Douglas Jerrold asked why he should not have them too.   I hesitated a little, but as he pressed me, and would have an answer, I said that I did not feel quite so sure of his kindly judgment on Thoreau's books ; and it so chanced that I used the word " acrid" for lack of a better, in endeavoring to express my idea of Jerrold's way of looking at men and books. It was not quite what I meant; but, in fact, he often *is* acrid, and has written pages and volumes of acridity, though, no doubt, with an honest purpose, and from a manly disgust at the cant and humbug of the world. Jerrold said no more, and I went on talking with Dr. ——— ; but, in a minute or two, I became aware that something had gone wrong, and, looking at Douglas Jerrold, there was an expression of pain and emotion on his face. By this time a second bottle of Burgundy had been opened (Clos Vougeot, the best the Club could produce, and far richer than the Chambertin), and that warm and potent wine may have had something to do with the depth and vivacity of Mr. Jerrold's feelings. But he was indeed greatly hurt by that little word " acrid." " He knew," he said, " that the world considered him a sour, bitter, ill-natured man ; but that such a man as I should have the same opinion was almost more than he could bear." As he spoke, he threw out his arms, sank back in his seat, and I was really a little apprehensive of his actual dissolution

into tears.   Hereupon I spoke, as was good
need, and though, as usual, I have forgotten
everything I said, I am quite sure it was to the
purpose, and went to this good fellow's heart,
as it came warmly from my own.   I do remember saying that I felt him to be as genial as the
glass of Burgundy which I held in my hand;
and I think that touched the very right spot;
for he smiled and said he was afraid the Burgundy was better than he, but yet he was com-
forted.   Dr. ——— said that he likewise had a
reputation for bitterness; and I assured him,
if I might venture to join myself to the brotherhood of two such men, that I was considered a
very ill-natured person by many people in my
own country.   Douglas Jerrold said he was
glad of it.

We were now in sweetest harmony, and Jerrold spoke more than it would become me to
repeat in praise of my own books, which he
said he admired, and he found the man more
admirable than his books!   I hope so, certainly.

We now went to the Haymarket Theatre,
where Douglas Jerrold is on the free list; and
after seeing a ballet by some Spanish dancers,
we separated, and betook ourselves to our several homes.   I like Douglas Jerrold very much.

April 8. — On Saturday evening at ten

o'clock, I went to a supper - party at Mr.
D———'s, and there met five or six people, —
Mr. Faed, a young and distinguished artist;
Dr. Eliotson, a dark, sombre, taciturn, power-
ful-looking man, with coal-black hair, and a
beard as black, fringing round his face; Mr.
Charles Reade, author of Christie Johnstone
and other novels, and many plays, — a tall man,
more than thirty, fair-haired, and of agreeable
talk and demeanor.

.   .   .   .

On April 6th, I went to the Waterloo station,
and there meeting Bennoch and Dr. ———, took
the rail for Woking, where we found Mr. Hall's
carriage waiting to convey us to Addlestone,
about five miles off. On arriving we found that
Mr. and Mrs. Hall had not yet returned from
church. Their place is an exceedingly pretty
one, and arranged in very good taste. The
house is not large; but is filled, in every room,
with fine engravings, statuettes, ingenious pretti-
nesses or beautifulnesses in the way of flower-
stands, cabinets, and things that seem to have
bloomed naturally out of the characters of its
occupants. There is a conservatory connected
with the drawing-room, and enriched with lovely
plants, one of which has a certain interest as
being the plant on which Coleridge's eyes were
fixed when he died. This conservatory is like-

wise beautified with several very fine casts of
statues by modern sculptors, among which was
the Greek Slave of Powers, which my English
friends criticised as being too thin and meagre;
but I defended it as in accordance with American ideas of feminine beauty. From the conservatory we passed into the garden, but did
not minutely examine it, knowing that Mr.
Hall would wish to lead us through it in person. So, in the mean time, we took a walk in
the neighborhood, over stiles and along by-
paths, for two or three miles, till we reached
the old village of Chertsey. In one of its streets
stands an ancient house, gabled, and with the
second story projecting over the first, and bearing an inscription to the purport that the poet
Cowley had once resided, and, I think, died
there. Thence we passed on till we reached a
bridge over the Thames, which at this point,
about twenty-five miles from London, is a narrow river, but looks clean and pure, and uncon-
scious what abominations the city sewers will
pour into it anon. We were caught in two or
three showers in the course of our walk; but
got back to Firfield without being very much
wetted.

Our host and hostess had by this time returned from church, and Mrs. Hall came
frankly and heartily to the door to greet us,
scolding us (kindly) for having got wet. . . .

I liked her simple, easy, gentle, quiet manners,
and I liked her husband too.

.   .   .   .

He has a wide and quick sympathy, and expresses it freely. . . . The world is the better
for him.

The shower being now over, we went out
upon the beautiful lawn before his house, where
there were a good many trees of various kinds,
many of which have been set out by persons of
great or small distinction, and are labelled with
their names.   Thomas Moore's name was appended to one ; Maria Edgeworth's to another ;
likewise Fredrika Bremer's, Jenny Lind's ; also
Grace Greenwood's, and I know not whose besides.   This is really a pleasant method of enriching one's grounds with memorials of friends,
nor is there any harm in making a shrubbery
of celebrities.   Three holes were already dug,
and three new trees lay ready to be planted,
and for me there was a sumach to plant, — a
tree I never liked ; but Mr. Hall said that they
had tried to dig up a hawthorn, but found it
clung too fast to the soil.   So, since better
might not be, and telling Mr. Hall that I supposed I should have a right to hang myself on
this tree whenever I chose, I seized a spade,
and speedily shovelled in a great deal of dirt ;
and there stands my sumach, an object of interest to posterity !   Bennoch also and Dr. ——

set out their trees, and, indeed, it was in some sense a joint affair, for the rest of the party held up each tree, while its godfather shovelled in the earth; but, after all, the gardener had more to do with it than we. After this important business was over, Mr. Hall led us about his grounds, which are very nicely planned and ordered; and all this he has bought, and built, and laid out, from the profits of his own and his wife's literary exertions.

We dined early, and had a very pleasant dinner, and, after the cloth was removed, Mr. Hall was graciously pleased to drink my health, following it with a long tribute to my genius. I answered briefly; and one half of my short speech was in all probability very foolish. . . .

After the ladies (there were three, one being a girl of seventeen, with rich auburn hair, the adopted daughter of the Halls) had retired, Dr. ———, having been toasted himself, proposed Mrs. Hall's health.

.   .   .   .

I did not have a great deal of conversation with Mrs. Hall; but enough to make me think her a genuine and good woman, unspoilt by a literary career, and retaining more sentiment than even most girls keep beyond seventeen. She told me that it had been the dream of her life to see Longfellow and myself! . . . Her dream is half accomplished now, and, as they

97

say Longfellow is coming over this summer, the
remainder may soon be rounded out. On taking leave, our kind hosts presented me with
some beautiful flowers, and with three volumes
of a work, by themselves, on Ireland ; and Dr.
—— was favored also with some flowers, and
a plant in a pot, and Bennoch too had his
hands full, . . . and we went on our way rejoicing.

[Here follows an account of the Lord May-
or's dinner, taken mostly for Our Old Home ;
but I think I will copy this more exact description of the lady mentioned in Civic Banquets.
— S. H.]

. . . My eyes were mostly drawn to a young
lady, who sat nearly opposite me, across the
table. She was, I suppose, dark, and yet not
dark, but rather seemed to be of pure white
marble, yet not white ; but the purest and finest complexion, without a shade of color in it,
yet anything but sallow or sickly. Her hair
was a wonderful deep raven-black — black as
night, black as death ; not raven-black, for that
has a shiny gloss, and hers had not, but it was
hair never to be painted nor described, — wonderful hair, Jewish hair. Her nose had a beautiful outline, though I could see that it was Jewish too ; and that, and all her features, were
so fine that sculpture seemed a despicable art
beside her, and certainly my pen is good for no-

thing. If any likeness could be given, however,
it must be by sculpture, not painting. She was
slender and youthful, and yet had a stately and
cold, though soft and womanly grace; and, looking at her, I saw what were the wives of the
old patriarchs in their maiden or early-married
days, — what Judith was, for, womanly as she
looked, I doubt not she could have slain a man
in a just cause, — what Bathsheba was, only she
seemed to have no sin in her, — perhaps what
Eve was, though one could hardly think her
weak enough to eat the apple. . . . Whether
owing to distinctness of race, my sense that she
was a Jewess, or whatever else, I felt a sort of
repugnance, simultaneously with my perception
that she was an admirable creature.

At ten o'clock the next day [after the Lord
Mayor's dinner] I went to lunch with Bennoch,
and afterwards accompanied him to one of the
government offices in Downing Street. He
went thither, not on official business, but on
a matter connected with a monument to Miss
Mitford, in which Mr. Harness, a clergyman
and some sort of a government clerk, is interested. I gathered from this conversation that
there is no great enthusiasm about the monumental affair among the British public. It surprised me to hear allusions indicating that Miss
Mitford was not the invariably amiable person

that her writings would suggest; but the whole
drift of what they said tended, nevertheless, towards the idea that she was an excellent and
generous person, loved most by those who
knew her best.

From Downing Street we crossed over and
entered Westminster Hall, and passed through
it, and up the flight of steps at its farthest end,
and along the avenue of statues, into the vestibule of the House of Commons. It was now
somewhat past five, and we stood at the inner
entrance of the House, to see the members pass
in, Bennoch pointing out to me the distinguished ones. I was not much impressed with
the appearance of the members generally ; they
seemed to me rather shabbier than English gentlemen usually, and I saw or fancied in many
of them a certain self-importance, as they passed
into the interior, betokening them to be very
full of their dignity. Some of them looked
more American — more like American politi-
cians — than most Englishmen do. There was
now and then a gray-headed country gentleman,
the very type of stupidity ; and two or three
city members came up and spoke to Bennoch,
and showed themselves quite as dull, in their
aldermanic way, as the country squires. . . .
Bennoch pointed out Lord John Russell, a
small, very short, elderly gentleman, in a brown
coat, and so large a hat — not large of brim,

but large like a peck - measure — that I saw
really no face beneath it. By and by came a
rather tall, slender person, in a black frock-coat,
buttoned up, and black pantaloons, taking long
steps, but I thought rather feebly or listlessly.
His shoulders were round, or else he had a
habitual stoop in them. He had a prominent
nose, a thin face, and a sallow, very sallow complexion ; . . . and had I seen him in America,
I should have taken him for a hard-worked editor of a newspaper, weary and worn with night-
labor and want of exercise, — aged before his
time. It was Disraeli, and I never saw any
other Englishman look in the least like him ;
though, in America, his appearance would not
attract notice as being unusual. I do not remember any other noteworthy person whom
we saw enter ; in fact, the House had already
been some time in session, and most of the
members were in their places.

We were to dine at the Refectory of the
House with the new member for Boston ; and
meanwhile Bennoch obtained admittance for us
into the Speaker's gallery, where we had a view
of the members, and could hear what was going
on. A Mr. Muntz was speaking on the Income Tax, and he was followed by Sir George
Cornewall Lewis and others ; but it was all very
uninteresting, without the slightest animation
or attempt at oratory, — which, indeed, would

have been quite out of place. We saw Lord Palmerston; but at too great a distance to distinguish anything but a gray head. The House had daylight in it when we entered, and for some time afterwards; but, by and by, the roof, which I had taken to be a solid and opaque ceiling, suddenly brightened, and showed itself to be transparent; a vast expanse of tinted and figured glass, through which came down a great, mild radiance on the members below. The character of the debate, however, did not grow more luminous or vivacious; so we went down into the vestibule, and there waited for Mr. ——, who soon came and led us into the Refectory. It was very much like the coffee-room of a club. The strict rule forbids the entrance of any but members of Parliament; but it seems to be winked at, although there is another room, opening beyond this, where the law of seclusion is strictly enforced.

The dinner was good, not remarkably so, but good enough,—a soup, some turbot or salmon, cutlets, and I know not what else, and claret, sherry, and port; for, as Mr. —— said, "he did not wish to be stingy." Mr. —— is a self-made man, and a strong instance of the difference between the Englishman and the American, when self-made, and without early education. He is no more a gentleman now than when he began life,—not a whit more refined, either outwardly or inwardly; while the American would have been, after the same experience, not distinguishable outwardly, and perhaps as refined within, as nine tenths of the gentlemen born, in the House of Commons. And besides, an American comes naturally to any distinctions to which success in life may bring him; he takes them as if they were his proper inheritance, and in no wise to be wondered at. Mr. ——, on the other hand, took evidently a childish delight in his position, and felt a childish wonder in having arrived at it; nor did it seem real to him, after all. . . .

We again saw Disraeli, who has risen from the people by modes perhaps somewhat like those of Mr. ——. He came and stood near our table, looking at the bill of fare, and then sat down on the opposite side of the room with another gentleman, and ate his dinner. The story of his marriage does him much credit; and indeed I am inclined to like Disraeli, as a man who has made his own place good among a hostile aristocracy, and leads instead of following them.

From the House of Commons we went to Albert Smith's exhibition, or lecture, of the ascent of Mont Blanc, to which Bennoch had orders. It was very amusing, and in some degree instructive. We remained in the saloon at the conclusion of the lecture; and when the audience had dispersed, Mr. Albert Smith made his appearance. . . .

Nothing of moment happened the next day, at least, not till two o'clock, when I went with Mr. Bowman to Birch's eating-house (it is not Birch's now, but this was the name of the original founder, who became an alderman, and has long been dead) for a basin of turtle-soup.   It was very rich, very good, better than we had at the Lord Mayor's, and the best I ever ate.

In the evening, Mr. J. B. Davis, formerly our Secretary of Legation, called to take us to dine at Mr. ——— ———'s in Camden Town. Mr. ——— calls his residence Vermont House; but it hardly has a claim to any separate title, being one of the centre houses of a block.   I forget whether I mentioned his calling on me. He is a Vermonter, a graduate of Yale College, who has been here several years, and has established a sort of book brokerage, buying libraries for those who want them, and rare works and editions for American collectors.   His business naturally brings him into relations with literary people; and he is himself a kindly and pleasant man.   On our arrival we found Mr. D——— and one of his sisters already there, and soon came a Mr. Peabody, who, if I mistake not, is one of the Salem Peabodys, and has some connection with the present eminent London Mr. Peabody.   At any rate, he is a very sensible,

well-instructed, and widely and long-travelled
man.   Mr. Tom Taylor was also expected ; but,
owing to some accident or mistake, he did not
come for above an hour, all which time our
host waited. . . . But Mr. Tom Taylor, a wit,
a satirist, and a famous diner out, is too formidable and too valuable a personage to be
treated cavalierly.

In the interim Mr. —— showed us some
rare old books, which he has in his private collection, a black-letter edition of Chaucer, and
other specimens of the early English printers ;
and I was impressed, as I have often been, with
the idea that we have made few, if any, improvements in the art of printing, though we
have greatly facilitated the modes of it.   He
showed us Dryden's translation of Virgil, with
Dr. Johnson's autograph in it ; and a large collection of Bibles, of all dates, — church Bibles,
family Bibles of the common translation, and
older ones.   He says he has written or is writing a history of the Bible (as a printed work, I
presume).   Many of these Bibles had, no doubt,
been in actual and daily use from generation to
generation ; but they were now all splendidly
bound, and were likewise very clean and smooth,
— in fact, every leaf had been cleansed by a
delicate process, a part of which consisted in
soaking the whole book in a tub of water, during several days.   Mr. —— is likewise rich in

manuscripts, having a Spanish document with the signature of the son of Columbus; a whole little volume in Franklin's handwriting, being the first specimen of it; and the original manuscripts of many of the songs of Burns. Among these I saw Auld Lang Syne, and Bruce's Address to his Army. We amused ourselves with these matters as long as we could; but at last, as there was to be a party in the evening, dinner could no longer be put off; so we took our seats at table, and immediately afterwards Mr. Taylor made his appearance with his wife and another lady.

Mr. Taylor is reckoned a brilliant conversationist; but I suppose he requires somebody to draw him out and assist him; for I could hear nothing that I thought very remarkable on this occasion. He is not a kind of man whom I can talk with, or greatly help to talk; so, though I sat next to him, nothing came of it. He told me some stories of his life in the Temple, — little funny incidents, that he afterwards wrought into his dramas; in short, a sensible, active-minded, clearly perceptive man, with a humorous way of showing up men and matters. . . . I wish I could know exactly what the English style good conversation. Probably it is something like plum pudding, — as heavy, but seldom so rich.

After dinner Mr. Tom Taylor and Mr.

D——, with their respective ladies, took their leave; but when we returned to the drawing-room, we found it thronged with a good many people. Mr. S. C. Hall was there with his wife, whom I was glad to see again, for this was the third time of meeting her, and, in this whirl of new acquaintances, I felt quite as if she were an old friend. Mr. William Howitt was also there, and introduced me to his wife, — a very natural, kind, and pleasant lady; and she presented me to one or two daughters. Mr. Marston, the dramatist, was also introduced to me; and Mr. Helps, a thin, scholarly, cold sort of a man. Dr. Mackay and his wife were there, too; and a certain Mr. Jones, a sculptor, — a jolly, large, elderly person, with a twinkle in his eye. Also a Mr. Godwin, who impressed me as quite a superior person, gentlemanly, culti-vated, a man of sensibility; but it is quite im-possible to take a clear imprint from any one character, where so many are stamped upon one's notice at once. This Mr. Godwin, as we were discussing Thackeray, said that he is most beautifully tender and devoted to his wife, when-ever she can be sensible of his attentions. He says that Thackeray, in his real self, is a sweet, sad man. I grew weary of so many people, especially of the ladies, who were rather super-fluous in their oblations, quite stifling me, in-deed, with the incense that they burnt under my

nose.   So far as I could judge, they had all
been invited there to see me.   It is ungracious,
even hoggish, not to be gratified with the interest they expressed in me ; but then it is really
a bore, and one does not know what to do or
say.   I felt like the hippopotamus, or — to use
a more modest illustration — like some strange
insect imprisoned under a tumbler, with a dozen
eyes watching whatever I did.   By and by Mr.
Jones, the sculptor, relieved me by standing
up against the mantelpiece, and telling an Irish
story, not to two or three auditors, but to the
whole drawing-room, all attentive as to a set
exhibition.   It was very funny.

The next day after this I went with Mr. Bowman to call on our minister, and found that he,
and four of the ladies of his family, with his son,
had gone to the Queen's Drawing-room.   We
lunched at the Wellington ; and spent an hour
or more in looking out of the window of that
establishment at the carriages, with their pom-
pous coachmen and footmen, driving to and
from the Palace of St. James, and at the Horse-
Guards, with their bright cuirasses, stationed
along the street. . . . Then I took the rail for
Liverpool. . . . While I was still at breakfast at
the Waterloo, Julian came in, ruddy cheeked,
smiling, very glad to see me, and looking, I
thought, a good deal taller than when I left him.
And so ended my London excursion, which has

certainly been rich in incident and character, though my account of it be but meagre.

May 10. — Last Friday, May 2d, I took the rail, with Mr. Bowman, from the Lime Street station, for Glasgow. There was nothing of much interest along the road, except that, when we got beyond Penrith, we saw snow on the tops of some of the hills. Twilight came on as we were entering Scotland ; and I have only a recollection of bleak and bare hills and villages dimly seen, until, nearing Glasgow, we saw the red blaze of furnace-lights at frequent iron-founderies. We put up at the Queen's Hotel, where we arrived about ten o'clock ; a better hotel than I have anywhere found in England, — new, well arranged, and with brisk attendance.

In the morning I rambled largely about Glasgow, and found it to be chiefly a modern-built city, with streets mostly wide and regular, and handsome houses and public edifices of a dark gray stone. In front of our hotel, in an enclosed green space, stands a tall column surmounted by a statue of Sir Walter Scott, — a good statue, I should think, as conveying the air and personal aspect of the man. There is a bronze equestrian statue of the Queen in one of the streets, and one or two more equestrian or other statues of eminent persons. I passed through the Trongate and the Gallow-Gate, and visited the Salt-Market, and saw the steeple of the Tolbooth, all of which Scott has made interesting; and I went through the gate of the University, and penetrated into its enclosed courts, round which the College edifices are built. They are not Gothic, but of the age, I suppose, of James I., — with odd-looking, conical-roofed towers, and here and there the bust of a benefactor in niches round the courts, and heavy stone staircases ascending from the pavement, outside the buildings, all of dark gray granite, cold, hard, and venerable. The University stands in High Street, in a dense part of the town, and a very old and shabby part, too. I think the poorer classes of Glasgow excel even those in Liverpool in the bad eminence of filth, uncombed and unwashed children, drunkenness, disorderly deportment, evil smell, and all that makes city poverty disgusting. In my opinion, however, they are a better-looking people than the English (and this is true of all classes), more intelligent of aspect, with more regular features. I looked for the high cheek bones, which have been attributed, as a characteristic feature, to the Scotch, but could not find them. What most distinguishes them from the English is the regularity of the nose, which is straight, or sometimes a little curved inward; whereas the English nose has no law whatever, but disports itself in all manner of irregularity.

I very soon learned to recognize the Scotch face, and when not too Scotch, it is a handsome one.

.   .   .   .

In another part of the High Street, up a pretty steep slope, and on one side of a public green, near an edifice which I think is a medical college, stands St. Mungo's Cathedral. It is hardly of cathedral dimensions, though a large and fine old church. The price of a ticket of admittance is twopence; so small that it might be as well to make the entrance free. The interior is in excellent repair, with the nave and side aisles, and clustered pillars, and intersecting arches, that belong to all these old churches; and a few monuments along the walls. I was going away without seeing any more than this; but the verger, a friendly old gentleman, with a hearty Scotch way of speaking, told me that the crypts were what chiefly interested strangers; and so he guided me down into the foundation story of the church, where there is an intricacy and entanglement of immensely massive and heavy arches, supporting the structure above. The view through these arches, among the great shafts of the columns, was very striking. In the central part is a monument; a recumbent figure, if I remember rightly, but it is not known whom it commemorates. There is also a monument to a Scotch prelate, which

seems to have been purposely defaced, probably
in Covenant times.   These intricate arches were
the locality of one of the scenes in Rob Roy,
when Rob gives Frank Osbaldistone some message or warning, and then escapes from him into
the obscurity behind.   In one corner is St.
Mungo's well, secured with a wooden cover;
but I should not care to drink water that comes
from among so many old graves.

After viewing the cathedral, I got back to the
hotel just in time to go from thence to the
steamer wharf, and take passage up the Clyde.
There was nothing very interesting in this little
voyage. We passed many small iron steamers,
and some large ones ; and green fields along the
river-shores, villas, villages, and all such suburban objects ; neither am I quite sure of the
name of the place we landed at, though I think
it was Bowling.   Here we took the railway for
Balloch ; and the only place or thing I remember during this transit was a huge bluff or crag,
rising abruptly from a river-side, and looking,
in connection with its vicinity to the Highlands,
just such a site as would be taken for the foundation of a castle.   On inquiry it turned out
that this abrupt and double-headed hill (for it
has two summits, with a cleft between) is the
site of Dumbarton Castle, for ages one of the
strongest fortresses in Scotland, and still kept
up as a garrisoned place.   At the distance and

point of view at which we passed it, the castle made no show.

Arriving at Balloch, we found it a small village, with no marked features, and a hotel, where we got some lunch, and then we took a stroll over the bridge across the Leven, while waiting for the steamer to take us up Loch Lomond. It was a beautiful afternoon, warm and sunny; and after walking about a mile, we had a fine view of Loch Lomond, and of the mountains around and beyond it, — Ben Lomond among the rest. It is vain, at a week's distance, to try to remember the shapes of mountains; so I shall attempt no description of them, and content myself with saying that they did not quite come up to my anticipations. In due time we returned to our hotel, and found in the coffee-room a tall, white-haired, venerable gentleman, and a pleasant-looking young lady, his daughter. They had been eating lunch, and the young lady helped her father on with his outside garment, and his comforter, and gave him his stick, just as any other daughter might do, — all of which I mention because he was a nobleman; and, moreover, had engaged all the post-horses at the inn, so that we could not continue our travels by land, along the side of Loch Lomond, as we had first intended. At four o'clock the railway train arrived again, with a very moderate number of passengers, who (and

we among them) immediately embarked on
board a neat little steamer which was waiting
for us.

The day was bright and cloudless ; but there
was a strong, cold breeze blowing down the
lake, so that it was impossible, without vast discomfort, to stand in the bow of the steamer and
look at the scenery. I looked at it, indeed,
along the sides, as we passed, and on our track
behind ; and no doubt it was very fine ; but
from all the experience I have had, I do not
think scenery can be well seen from the water.
At any rate, the shores of Loch Lomond have
faded completely out of my memory ; nor can
I conceive that they really were very striking.
At a year's interval, I can recollect the cluster
of hills around the head of Lake Windermere ;
at twenty years' interval, I remember the shores
of Lake Champlain ; but of the shores of this
Scottish lake I remember nothing except some
oddly shaped rocks, called " The Cobbler and
his Daughter," on a mountain-top, just before
we landed. But, indeed, we had very imperfect
glimpses of the hills along the latter part of the
course, because the wind had grown so very
cold that we took shelter below, and merely
peeped at Loch Lomond's sublimities from the
cabin windows.

The whole voyage up Loch Lomond is, I
think, about thirty-two miles ; but we landed

at a place called Tarbet, much short of the ulti-
mate point.   There is here a large hotel; but
we passed it, and walked onward a mile or two
to Arroquhar, a secluded glen among the hills,
where is a new hotel, built in the old manor-
house style, and occupying the site of what was
once a castle of the chief of the MacFarlanes.
Over the portal is a stone taken from the former house, bearing the date 1697.   There is a
little lake near the house, and the hills shut in
the whole visible scene so closely that there appears no outlet nor communication with the
external world; but in reality this little lake is
connected with Loch Long, and Loch Long is
an arm of the sea; so that there is water communication between Arroquhar and Glasgow.   We
found this a very beautiful place; and being quite
sheltered from all winds that blew, we strolled
about late into the prolonged twilight, and admired the outlines of the surrounding hills, and
fancied resemblances to various objects in the
shapes of the crags against the evening sky.
The sun had not set till nearly, if not quite,
eight o'clock; and before the daylight had quite
gone, the northern lights streamed out, and I do
not think that there was much darkness over the
glen of Arroquhar that night.   At all events,
before the darkness came, we withdrew into the
coffee-room.

We had excellent beds and sleeping-rooms

in this new hotel, and I remember nothing more till morning, when we were astir betimes, and had some chops for breakfast. Then our host, Mr. Macgregor, who is also the host of our hotel at Glasgow, and has many of the characteristics of an American landlord, claiming to be a gentleman and the equal of his guests, took us in a drosky, and drove us to the shore of Loch Lomond, at a point about four miles from Arroquhar. The lake is here a mile and a half wide, and it was our object to cross to Inversnaid, on the opposite shore; so first we waved a handkerchief, and then kindled some straw on the beach, in order to attract the notice of the ferryman at Inversnaid. It was half an hour before our signals and shoutings resulted in the putting off of a boat, with two oarsmen, who made the transit pretty speedily; and thus we got across Loch Lomond. At Inversnaid there is a small hotel, and over the rock on which it stands a little waterfall tumbles into the lake, — a very little one, though I believe it is reckoned among the other picturesque features of the scene.

We were now in Rob Roy's country, and at the distance of a mile or so, along the shore of the lake, is Rob Roy's cave, where he and his followers are supposed to have made their abode in troublous times. While lunch was getting ready, we again took the boat, and went thither.

Landing beneath a precipitous, though not very lofty crag, we clambered up a rude pathway, and came to the mouth of the cave, which is nothing but a fissure or fissures among some great rocks that have tumbled confusedly together. There is hardly anywhere space enough for half a dozen persons to crowd themselves together, nor room to stand upright. On the whole, it is no cave at all, but only a crevice; and, in the deepest and darkest part, you can look up and see the sky. It may have sheltered Rob Roy for a night, and might partially shelter any Christian during a shower.

Returning to the hotel, we started in a drosky (I do not know whether this is the right name of the vehicle, or whether it has a right name, but it is a carriage in which four persons sit back to back, two before and two behind) for Aberfoyle. The mountain-side ascends very steeply from the inn door, and, not to damp the horse's courage in the outset, we went up on foot. The guide-book says that the prospect from the summit of the ascent is very fine; but I really believe we forgot to turn round and look at it. All through our drive, however, we had mountain views in plenty, — especially of great Ben Lomond, with his snow-covered head, round which, since our entrance into the Highlands, we had been making a circuit. Nothing can possibly be drearier than the mountains at this season; bare, barren, and bleak, with black patches of withered heath variegating the dead brown of the herbage on their sides; and as regards trees the hills are perfectly naked. There were no frightful precipices, no boldly picturesque features, along our road; but high, weary slopes, showing miles and miles of heavy solitude, with here and there a highland hut, built of stone and thatched; and, in one place, an old gray, ruinous fortress, a station of the English troops after the Rebellion of 1745; and once or twice a village of huts, the inhabitants of which, old and young, ran to their doors to stare at us. For several miles after we left Inversnaid, the mountain stream which makes the waterfall brawled along the roadside. All the hills are sheep pastures, and I never saw such wild, rough, ragged-looking creatures as the sheep, with their black faces and tattered wool. The little lambs were very numerous, poor things, coming so early in the season into this inclement region; and it was laughable to see how invariably, when startled by our approach, they scampered to their mothers, and immediately began to suck. It would seem as if they sought a draught from the maternal udder, wherewith to fortify and encourage their poor little hearts; but I suppose their instinct merely drove them close to their dams, and, being there, they took advantage of their oppor-

tunity. These sheep must lead a hard life
during the winter; for they are never fed nor
sheltered.

The day was sunless, and very uncomfort-
ably cold; and we were not sorry to walk whenever the steepness of the road gave us cause. I
do not remember what o'clock it was, but not
far into the afternoon, when we reached the
Baillie Nicol-Jarvie Inn at Aberfoyle; a scene
which is much more interesting in the pages of
Rob Roy than we found it in reality. Here
we got into a sort of cart, and set out, over
another hill-path, as dreary as or drearier than
the last, for the Trosachs. On our way, we
saw Ben Venue, and a good many other famous
Bens, and two or three lochs — and when we
reached the Trosachs, we should probably have
been very much enraptured if our eyes had not
already been weary with other mountain shapes.
But, in truth, I doubt if anybody ever does
really see a mountain, who goes for the set and
sole purpose of seeing it. Nature will not let
herself be seen in such cases. You must patiently bide her time; and by and by, at some
unforeseen moment, she will quietly and suddenly unveil herself, and for a brief space allow
you to look right into the heart of her mystery.
But if you call out to her peremptorily, Nature!
unveil yourself this very moment! she only
draws her veil the closer: and you may look

with all your eyes, and imagine that you see all
that she can show, and yet see nothing. Thus,
I saw a wild and confused assemblage of heights,
crags, precipices, which they call the Trosachs,
but I saw them calmly and coldly, and was glad
when the drosky was ready to take us on to
Callender. The hotel at the Trosachs, by the
bye, is a very splendid one, in the form of an
old feudal castle, with towers and turrets. All
among these wild hills there is set preparation
for enraptured visitants; and it seems strange
that the savage features do not subside of their
own accord, and that there should still be cold
winds and snow on the top of Ben Lomond,
and rocks and heather, and ragged sheep, now
that there are so many avenues by which the
commonplace world is sluiced in among the
Highlands. I think that this fashion of the picturesque will pass away.

We drove along the shore of Lake Venna-
char, and onward to Callender, which I believe
is either the first point in the Lowlands or the
last in the Highlands. It is a large village on
the river Teith. We stopped here to dine, and
were some time in getting any warmth into our
benumbed bodies; for, as I said before, it was
a very cold day. Looking from the window of
the hotel, I saw a young man in Highland dress,
with bare thighs, marching through the village
street towards the Lowlands, with a martial and

elastic step, as if he were going forth to conquer and occupy the world. I suppose he was a soldier who had been absent on leave, returning to the garrison at Stirling. I pitied his poor thighs, though he certainly did not look uncomfortable.

After dinner, as dusk was coming on and we had still a long drive before us (eighteen miles, I believe), we took a close carriage and two horses, and set off for Stirling. The twilight was too obscure to show many things along the road, and by the time we drove into Stirling we could but dimly see the houses in the long street in which stood our hotel. There was a good fire in the coffee-room, which looked like a drawing-room in a large old-fashioned mansion, and was hung around with engravings of the portraits of the county members, and a master of fox-hounds, and other pictures. We made ourselves comfortable with some tea, and retired early.

In the morning we were stirring betimes, and found Stirling to be a pretty large town, of rather ancient aspect, with many gray stone houses, the gables of which are notched on either side, like a flight of stairs. The town stands on the slope of a hill, at the summit of which, crowning a long ascent, up which the paved street reaches all the way to its gate, is Stirling Castle. Of course we went thither, and

found free entrance, although the castle is garrisoned by five or six hundred men, among
whom are bare-legged Highlanders (I must say
that this costume is very fine and becoming,
though their thighs did look blue and frostbit-
ten) and also some soldiers of other Scotch regiments, with tartan trousers. Almost immediately on passing the gate, we found an old artil-
leryman, who undertook to show us round the
castle. Only a small portion of it seems to be
of great antiquity. The principal edifice within
the castle wall is a palace, that was either built
or renewed by James VI.; and it is ornamented
with strange old statues, one of which is his own.
The old Scottish Parliament House is also here.
The most ancient part of the castle is the tower,
where one of the Earls of Douglas was stabbed
by a king, and afterwards thrown out of the
window. In reading this story, one imagines a
lofty turret, and the dead man tumbling headlong from a great height; but in reality, the
window is not more than fifteen or twenty feet
from the garden into which he fell. This part
of the castle was burned last autumn; but is
now under repair, and the wall of the tower is
still stanch and strong. We went up into the
chamber where the murder took place, and
looked through the historic window.

Then we mounted the castle wall, where it
broods over a precipice of many hundred feet

perpendicular, looking down upon a level plain below, and forth upon a landscape, every foot of which is richly studded with historic events. There is a small peep-hole in the wall, which Queen Mary is said to have been in the habit of looking through. It is a most splendid view, — in the distance the blue Highlands, with a variety of mountain outlines that I could have studied unweariably ; and in another direction, beginning almost at the foot of the Castle Hill, were the Links of Forth, where, over a plain of miles in extent, the river meandered and circled about, and returned upon itself again and again and again, as if knotted into a silver chain which it was difficult to imagine to be all one stream. The history of Scotland might be read from this castle wall, as on a book of mighty page ; for here, within the compass of a few miles, we see the field where Wallace won the battle of Stirling, and likewise the battlefield of Bannockburn, and that of Falkirk, and Sheriffmuir, and I know not how many besides.

Around the Castle Hill there is a walk, with seats for old and infirm persons, at points sheltered from the wind. We followed it downward, and I think we passed over the site where the games used to be held, and where, this morning, some of the soldiers of the garrison were going through their exercises. I ought to have mentioned, that, passing through the inner gateway of the castle, we saw the round tower, and glanced into the dungeon, where the Roderick Dhu of Scott's poem was left to die. It is one of the two round towers, between which the portcullis rose and fell.

At eleven o'clock we took the rail for Edinburgh, and I remember nothing more, except that the cultivation and verdure of the country were very agreeable, after our experience of Highland barrenness and desolation, until we found the train passing close at the base of the rugged crag of Edinburgh Castle. We established ourselves at Queen's Hotel, in Prince's Street, and then went out to view the city. The monument to Sir Walter Scott — a rather fantastic and not very impressive affair, I thought — stands almost directly in front of a hotel. We went along Prince's Street, and thence, by what turns I know not, to the Palace of Holyrood, which stands on a low and sheltered site, and is a venerable edifice. Arthur's Seat rises behind it, — a high hill, with a plain between. As we drew near the Palace, Mr. Bowman, who has been here before, pointed out the windows of Queen Mary's apartments, in a circular tower on the left of the gateway. On entering the enclosed quadrangle, we bought tickets for sixpence each, admitting us to all parts of the Palace that are shown to visitors; and first we went into a noble hall or gallery, — a long and

stately room, hung with pictures of ancient
Scottish kings ; and though the pictures were
none of them authentic, they, at least, answer
an excellent purpose in the way of upholstery.
It was here that the young Pretender gave
the ball which makes one of the scenes in Wa-
verley.

Thence we passed into the old historic rooms
of the Palace, — Darnley's and Queen Mary's
apartments, which everybody has seen and described. They are very dreary and shabby-look-
ing rooms, with bare floors, and here and there
a piece of tapestry, faded into a neutral tint ;
and carved and ornamented ceilings, looking
shabbier than plain whitewash. We saw Queen
Mary's old bedstead, low, with four tall posts,
— and her looking - glass, which she brought
with her from France, and which has often reflected the beauty that set everybody mad, —
and some needle-work and other womanly matters of hers ; and we went into the little closet
where she was having such a cosy supper-party
with two or three friends, when the conspirators
broke in, and stabbed Rizzio before her face.
We saw, too, the blood-stain at the threshold
of the door in the next room, opening upon the
stairs. The body of Rizzio was flung down here,
and the attendant told us that it lay in that spot
all night. The blood-stain covers a large space,
— much larger than I supposed, — and it gives

the impression that there must have been a great
pool and sop of blood on all the spot covered
by Rizzio's body, — staining the floor deeply
enough never to be washed out. It is now of
a dark brown hue ; and I do not see why it may
not be the genuine, veritable stain. The floor,
thereabouts, appears not to have been scrubbed
much ; for I touched it with my finger, and
found it slightly rough ; but it is strange that
the many footsteps should not have smoothed
it, in three hundred years.

One of the articles shown us in Queen Mary's
apartments was the breastplate supposed to have
been worn by Lord Ruthven at the murder, a
heavy plate of iron, and doubtless a very uncomfortable waistcoat.

From the Palace we passed into the contiguous ruin of Holyrood Abbey ; which is roofless,
although the front and some broken columns
along the nave, and fragments of architecture
here and there, afford hints of a magnificent
Gothic church in by-gone times. It deserved
to be magnificent ; for here have been stately
ceremonials, marriages of kings, coronations,
investitures, before the high altar, which has
now been overthrown or crumbled away ; and
the floor — so far as there is any floor — consists of tombstones of the old Scottish nobility. There are likewise monuments, bearing
the names of illustrious Scotch families ; and

inscriptions, in the Scotch dialect, on the walls.

In one of the front towers, — the only remaining one, indeed, — we saw the marble tomb of a nobleman, Lord Belhaven, who is represented reclining on the top, — with a bruised nose, of course. Except in Westminster Abbey, I do not remember ever to have seen an old monumental statue with the nose entire. In all political or religious outbreaks, the mob's first impulse is to hit the illustrious dead on their noses.

At the other end of the Abbey, near the high altar, is the vault where the old Scottish kings used to be buried ; but, looking in through the window, I saw only a vacant space, — no skull, no bone, nor the least fragment of a coffin. In fact, I believe the royal dead were turned out of their last home, on occasion of the Revolutionary movements at the accession of William III.

Quitting the Abbey and the Palace, we turned into the Canongate, and passed thence into High Street, which, I think, is a continuation of the Canongate ; and being now in the old town of Edinburgh, we saw those immensely tall houses, seven stories high, where the people live in tiers, all the way from earth to middle air. They were not so quaint and strange looking as I expected ; but there were some houses

of very antique individuality, and among them
that of John Knox, which looks still in good
repair. One thing did not in the least fall short
of my expectations, — the evil odor, for which
Edinburgh has an immemorial renown, — nor
the dirt of the inhabitants, old and young. The
town, to say the truth, when you are in the
midst of it, has a very sordid, grimy, shabby,
unswept, unwashen aspect, grievously at vari-
ance with all poetic and romantic associations.

From the High Street we turned aside into
the Grass-Market, the scene of the Porteous
Mob; and we found in the pavement a cross
on the site where the execution of Porteous is
supposed to have taken place.

Returning then to the High Street, we followed it up to the Castle, which is nearer the
town, and of more easy access from it, than I
had supposed. There is a large court or parade
before the castle gate, with a parapet on the
abrupt side of the hill, looking towards Arthur's
Seat and Salisbury Crags, and overhanging a
portion of the old town. As we leaned over
this parapet, my nose was conscious of the bad
odor of Edinburgh, although the streets whence
it must have come were hundreds of feet below.
I have had some experience of this ugly smell
in the poor streets of Liverpool; but I think
I never perceived it before crossing the Atlantic. It is the odor of an old system of life;

the scent of the pine forests is still too recent with us for it to be known in America.

The Castle of Edinburgh is free (as appears to be the case with all garrisoned places in Great Britain) to the entrance of any peaceable person. So we went in, and found a large space enclosed within the walls, and dwellings for officers, and accommodation for soldiers, who were being drilled or loitering about; and as the hill still ascends within the external wall of the castle, we climbed to the summit, and there found an old soldier, whom we engaged to be our guide. He showed us Mons Meg, a great old cannon, broken at the breech, but still aimed threateningly from the highest ramparts; and then he admitted us into an old chapel, said to have been built by a Queen of Scotland, the sister of Harold, King of England, and occupying the very highest part of the hill. It is the smallest place of worship I ever saw, but of venerable architecture, and of very solid construction. The old soldier had not much more to show us; but he pointed out the window whence one of the kings of Scotland is said, when a baby, to have been lowered down, the whole height of the castle, to the bottom of the precipice on which it stands, — a distance of seven hundred feet.

After the soldier had shown us to the extent of his jurisdiction, we went into a suite of rooms, in one of which I saw a portrait of Queen Mary, which gave me, for the first time, an idea that she was really a very beautiful woman.   In this picture she is wonderfully so, — a tender womanly grace, which was none the less tender and graceful for being equally imbued with queenly dignity and spirit.   It was too lovely a head to be cut off.   I should be glad to know the authenticity of this picture.

I do not know that we did anything else worthy of note, before leaving Edinburgh. There is matter enough, in and about the town, to interest the visitor for a very long time ; but when the visit is calculated on such brevity as ours was, we get weary of the place before even these few hours come to an end.   Thus, for my part, I was not sorry when, in the course of the afternoon, we took the rail for Melrose, where we duly arrived, and put up at the George Inn.

Melrose is a village of rather antique aspect, situated on the slope and at the bottom of the Eildon Hills, which, from this point of view, appear like one hill with a double summit. The village, as I said, has an old look, though many of the houses have at least been refronted at some recent date ; but others are as ancient, I suppose, as the days when the Abbey was in its splendor, — a rustic and peasant-like antiquity, however, low-roofed and straw-thatched. There is an aged cross of stone in the centre of the town.

Our first object, of course, was to see the Abbey, which stands just on the outskirts of the village, and is attainable only by applying at a neighboring house, the inhabitant of which probably supports himself, and most comfortably too, as a showman of the ruin. He unlocked the wooden gate, and admitted us into what is left of the Abbey, comprising only the ruins of the church, although the refectory, the dormitories, and the other parts of the establishment, formerly covered the space now occupied by a dozen village houses. Melrose Abbey is a very satisfactory ruin, all carpeted along its nave and transepts with green grass ; and there are some well-grown trees within the walls. We saw the window, now empty, through which the tints of the painted glass fell on the tombstone of Michael Scott, and the tombstone itself, broken in three pieces, but with a cross engraven along its whole length. It must have been the monument of an old monk or abbot, rather than a wizard. There, too, is still the " marble stone" on which the monk and warrior sat them down, and which is supposed to mark the resting-place of Alexander of Scotland. There are remains, both without and within the Abbey, of

most curious and wonderfully minute old sculpture, — foliage, in places where it is almost impossible to see them, and where the sculptor
could not have supposed that they would be
seen, but which yet are finished faithfully, to
the very veins of each leaf, in stone; and there
is a continual variety of this accurate toil. On
the exterior of the edifice there is equal minuteness of finish, and a great many niches for
statues; all of which, I believe, are now gone,
although there are carved faces at some points
and angles. The graveyard around the Abbey
is still the only one which the village has, and is
crowded with gravestones, among which I read
the inscription of one erected by Sir Walter
Scott to the memory of Thomas Purdy, one of
his servants. Some sable birds — either rooks
or jackdaws — were flitting about the ruins, inside and out.

Mr. Bowman and I talked about revisiting
Melrose by moonlight; but, luckily, there was
to be no moon that evening. I do not myself
think that daylight and sunshine make a ruin
less effective than twilight or moonshine. In
reference to Scott's description, I think he de-
plorably diminishes the impressiveness of the
scene by saying that the alternate buttresses,
seen by moonlight, look as if made of ebon and
ivory. It suggests a small and very pretty piece
of cabinet-work; not these gray, rough walls,

which Time has gnawed upon for a thousand years without eating them away.

Leaving the Abbey, we took a path or a road which led us to the river Tweed, perhaps a quarter of a mile off; and we crossed it by a foot-bridge, — a pretty wide stream, a dimpling breadth of transparent water flowing between low banks, with a margin of pebbles. We then returned to our inn and had tea, and passed a quiet evening by the fireside. This is a good, unpretentious inn; and its visitors' book indicates that it affords general satisfaction to those who come here.

In the morning we breakfasted on broiled salmon, taken, no doubt, in the neighboring Tweed. There was a very coarse-looking man at table with us, who informed us that he owned the best horse anywhere round the Eildon Hills, and could make the best cast for a salmon, and catch a bigger fish than anybody, — with other self-laudation of the same kind. The waiter afterwards told us that he was the son of an Admiral in the neighborhood; and soon, his horse being brought to the door, we saw him mount and ride away. He sat on horseback with ease and grace, though I rather suspect, early as it was, that he was already in his cups. The Scotch seem to me to get drunk at very unseasonable hours. I have seen more drunken people here than during all my residence in

England, and, generally, early in the day. Their liquor, so far as I have observed, makes them good-natured and sociable, imparting a perhaps needed geniality to their cold natures.

After breakfast we took a drosky, or whatever these fore-and-aft-seated vehicles are called, and set out for Dryburgh Abbey, three miles distant. It was a cold though rather bright morning, with a most shrewd and bitter wind, which blew directly in my face as I sat beside the driver. An English wind is bad enough, but methinks a Scotch one is rather worse; at any rate, I was half frozen, and wished Dryburgh Abbey in Tophet, where it would have been warmer work to go and see it. Some of the border hills were striking, especially the Cowden Knowe, which ascends into a prominent and lofty peak. Such villages as we passed did not greatly differ from English villages. By and by we came to the banks of the Tweed, at a point where there is a ferry. A carriage was on the river bank, the driver waiting beside it; for the people who came in it had already been ferried across to see the Abbey.

The ferryman here is a young girl; and, stepping into the boat, she shoved off, and so skilfully took advantage of the eddies of the stream, which is here deep and rapid, that we were soon on the other side. She was by no means an uncomely maiden, with pleasant Scotch features, and a quiet intelligence of aspect, gleaming into a smile when spoken to ; much tanned with all kinds of weather, and, though slender, yet so agile and muscular that it was no shame for a man to let himself be rowed by her.

From the ferry we had a walk of half a mile, more or less, to a cottage, where we found another young girl, whose business it is to show the Abbey. She was of another mould than the ferry-maiden, — a queer, shy, plaintive sort of a body, — and answered all our questions in a low, wailing tone. Passing through an apple orchard, we were not long in reaching the Abbey, the ruins of which are much more extensive and more picturesque than those of Melrose, being overrun with bushes and shrubbery, and twined about with ivy, and all such vegetation as belongs, naturally, to old walls. There are the remains of the refectory, and other domestic parts of the Abbey, as well as the church, and all in delightful state of decay, — not so far gone but that we had bits of its former grandeur in the columns and broken arches, and in some portions of the edifice that still retain a roof.

In the chapter-house we saw a marble statue of Newton, woefully maltreated by damps and weather; and though it had no sort of business there, it fitted into the ruins picturesquely enough. There is another statue, equally unauthorized; both having been placed here by a former Earl of Buchan, who seems to have been a little astray in his wits.

On one side of the church, within an arched recess, are the monuments of Sir Walter Scott and his family, — three ponderous tombstones of Aberdeen granite, polished, but already dimmed and dulled by the weather. The whole floor of the recess is covered by these monuments, that of Sir Walter being the middle one, with Lady (or, as the inscription calls her, Dame) Scott beyond him, next to the church wall, and some one of his sons or daughters on the hither side. The effect of his being buried here is to make the whole of Dryburgh Abbey his monument. There is another arched recess, twin to the Scott burial-place and contiguous to it, in which are buried a Pringle family; it being their ancient place of sepulture. The spectator almost inevitably feels as if they were intruders, although their rights here are of far older date than those of Scott.

Dryburgh Abbey must be a most beautiful spot of a summer afternoon; and it was beautiful even on this not very genial morning, especially when the sun blinked out upon the ivy, and upon the shrubberied paths that wound about the ruins. I think I recollect the birds chirruping in this neighborhood of it. After viewing it sufficiently, — sufficiently for this one time, — we went back to the ferry, and, being set across by the same Undine, we drove back to Melrose. No longer riding against the wind, I found it not nearly so cold as before. I now noticed that the Eildon Hills, seen from this direction, rise from one base into three distinct summits ranged in a line. According to The Lay of the Last Minstrel, they were cleft into this shape by the magic of Michael Scott. Reaching Melrose . . . without alighting, we set off for Abbotsford, three miles off. The neighborhood of Melrose, leading to Abbotsford, has many handsome residences of modern build and very recent date, — suburban villas each with its little lawn and garden ground, such as we see in the vicinity of Liverpool. I noticed, too, one castellated house, of no great size, but old, and looking as if its tower were built, not for show, but for actual defence in the old border warfare.

We were not long in reaching Abbotsford. The house, which is more compact, and of considerably less extent than I anticipated, stands in full view from the road, and at only a short distance from it, lower down towards the river. Its aspect disappointed me; but so does everything. It is but a villa, after all; no castle, nor even a large manor-house, and very unsatisfactory when you consider it in that light. Indeed, it impressed me, not as a real house, intended for the home of human beings, — a house to die in or to be born in, — but as a plaything, — something in the same category as Horace Walpole's Strawberry Hill. The present owner seems to have found it insufficient for the actual purposes of life; for he is adding a wing, which promises to be as extensive as the original structure.

We rang at the front door (the family being now absent), and were speedily admitted by a middle-aged or somewhat elderly man, — the butler, I suppose, or some upper servant, — who at once acceded to our request to be permitted to see the house. We stepped from the porch immediately into the entrance-hall; and having the great Hall of Battle Abbey in my memory, and the idea of a baronial hall in my mind, I was quite taken aback at the smallness and narrowness and lowness of this; which, however, is a very fine one, on its own little scale. In truth, it is not much more than a vestibule. The ceiling is carved; and every inch of the walls is covered with claymores, targets, and other weapons and armor, or old-time curiosities, tastefully arranged, many of which, no doubt, have a history attached to them, — or had in Sir Walter's own mind. Our attendant was a very intelligent person, and pointed out much that was interesting; but in such a multitudinous variety it was almost impossible to fix the eye upon any one thing. Probably the apartment looked smaller than it really was, on account of being so wainscoted and festooned with curiosities. I remember nothing particularly, unless it be the coal-grate in the fireplace, which was one formerly used by Archbishop Sharpe, the prelate whom Balfour of Burley murdered. Either in this room or the next one, there was a glass case containing the suit of clothes last worn by Scott, — a short green coat, somewhat worn, with silvered buttons, a pair of gray tartan trousers, and a white hat. It was in the hall that we saw these things; for there too, I recollect, were a good many walking-sticks that had been used by Scott, and the hatchet with which he was in the habit of lopping branches from his trees, as he walked among them.

From the hall we passed into the study, — a small room, lined with the books which Sir Walter, no doubt, was most frequently accustomed to refer to; and our guide pointed out some volumes of the Moniteur, which he used while writing the history of Napoleon. Probably these were the dryest and dullest volumes in his whole library. About mid-height of the walls of the study there is a gallery, with a short flight of steps for the convenience of getting at the upper books. A study-table occupied the centre of the room, and at one end of the table stands an easy-chair, covered with morocco, and

with ample space to fling one's self back. The
servant told me that I might sit down in this
chair, for that Sir Walter sat there while writing
his romances, "and perhaps," quoth the man,
smiling, "you may catch some inspiration."
What a bitter word this would have been if he
had known me to be a romance-writer! "No,
I never shall be inspired to write romances!"
I answered, as if such an idea had never occurred to me. I sat down, however. This study
quite satisfied me, being planned on principles
of common-sense, and made to work in, and
without any fantastic adaptation of old forms to
modern uses.

Next to the study is the library, an apartment of respectable size, and containing as many
books as it can hold, all protected by wire-
work. I did not observe what or whose works
were here; but the attendant showed us one
whole compartment full of volumes having reference to ghosts, witchcraft, and the supernatu-
ral generally. It is remarkable that Scott should
have felt interested in such subjects, being such
a worldly and earthly man as he was; but then,
indeed, almost all forms of popular superstition
do clothe the ethereal with earthly attributes,
and so make it grossly perceptible.

The library, like the study, suited me well —
merely the fashion of the apartment, I mean —
and I doubt not it contains as many curious

volumes as are anywhere to be met with within
a similar space.   The drawing-room adjoins it;
and here we saw a beautiful ebony cabinet,
which was presented to Sir Walter by George
IV.; and some pictures of much interest, — one
of Scott himself at thirty-five, rather portly,
with a heavy face, but shrewd eyes, which seem
to observe you closely.   There is a full-length
of his eldest son, an officer of dragoons, leaning
on his charger; and a portrait of Lady Scott,
— a brunette, with black hair and eyes, very
pretty, warm, vivacious, and un-English in her
aspect.   I am not quite sure whether I saw all
these pictures in the drawing-room, or some of
them in the dining-room; but the one that
struck me most — and very much indeed —
was the head of Mary Queen of Scots: literally the head cut off, and lying on a dish.   It
is said to have been painted by an Italian or
French artist, two days after her death.   The
hair curls or flows all about it; the face is of a
death-like hue, but has an expression of quiet,
after much pain and trouble, — very beautiful,
very sweet and sad; and it affected me strongly
with the horror and strangeness of such a head
being severed from its body.   Methinks I should
not like to have it always in the room with me.
I thought of the lovely picture of Mary that
I had seen at Edinburgh Castle, and reflected
what a symbol it would be, — how expressive

of a human being having her destiny in her own hands, — if that beautiful young queen were painted as carrying this dish, containing her own woeful head, and perhaps casting a curious and pitiful glance down upon it, as if it were not her own.

Also, in the drawing-room, there was a plaster cast of Sir Walter's face, taken after death; the only one in existence, as our guide assured us. It is not often that one sees a homelier set of features than this; no elevation, no dignity, whether bestowed by nature or thrown over them by age or death; sunken cheeks, the bridge of the nose depressed, and the end turned up; the mouth puckered, and no chin whatever, or hardly any. The expression was not calm and happy; but rather as if he were in a perturbed slumber, perhaps nothing short of nightmare. I wonder that the family allow this cast to be shown, — the last record that there is of Scott's personal reality, and conveying such a wretched and unworthy idea of it.

Adjoining the drawing-room is the dining-room, in one corner of which, between two windows, Scott died. It was now a quarter of a century since his death; but it seemed to me that we spoke with a sort of hush in our voices, as if he were still dying here, or had but just departed. I remember nothing else in this room. The next one is the armory, which is

the smallest of all that we had passed through;
but its walls gleam with the steel blades of
swords, and the barrels of pistols, matchlocks,
firelocks, and all manner of deadly weapons,
whether European or Oriental; for there are
many trophies here of East Indian warfare.   I
saw Rob Roy's gun, rifled and of very large
bore; and a beautiful pistol, formerly Claverhouse's; and the sword of Montrose, given him
by King Charles, the silver hilt of which I
grasped.   There was also a superb claymore,
in an elaborately wrought silver sheath, made
for Sir Walter Scott, and presented to him by
the Highland Society, for his services in mar-
shalling the clans when George IV. came to
Scotland.   There were a thousand other things,
which I knew must be most curious, yet did
not ask nor care about them, because so many
curiosities drive one crazy, and fret one's heart
to death.   On the whole, there is no simple
and great impression left by Abbotsford; and
I felt angry and dissatisfied with myself for not
feeling something which I did not and could not
feel.   But it is just like going to a museum,
if you look into particulars; and one learns
from it, too, that Scott could not have been
really a wise man, nor an earnest one, nor one
that grasped the truth of life; he did but play,
and the play grew very sad toward its close.
In a certain way, however, I understand his

romances the better for having seen his house; and his house the better for having read his romances. They throw light on one another.

We had now gone through all the show-rooms; and the next door admitted us again into the entrance hall, where we recorded our names in the visitors' book. It contains more names of Americans, I should judge, from casting my eyes back over last year's record, than of all other people in the world, including Great Britain.

Bidding farewell to Abbotsford, I cannot but confess a sentiment of remorse for having visited the dwelling-place — as just before I visited the grave — of the mighty minstrel and romancer with so cold a heart and in so critical a mood, — *his* dwelling-place and *his* grave whom I had so admired and loved, and who had done so much for my happiness when I was young. But I, and the world generally, now look at him from a different point of view; and, besides, these visits to the actual haunts of famous people, though long dead, have the effect of making us sensible, in some degree, of their human imperfections, as if we actually saw them alive. I felt this effect, to a certain extent, even with respect to Shakespeare, when I visited Stratford-on-Avon. As for Scott, I still cherish him in a warm place, and I do not know that I have any pleasanter anticipation, as regards

books, than that of reading all his novels over
again after we get back to the Wayside.

[This Mr. Hawthorne did, aloud to his
family, the year following his return to America.
— S. H.]

It was now one or two o'clock, and time for
us to take the rail across the borders.   Many
a mile behind us, as we rushed onward, we could
see the threefold Eildon Hill, and probably
every pant of the engine carried us over some
spot of ground which Scott has made fertile
with poetry.   For Scotland — cold, cloudy,
barren little bit of earth that it is — owes all the
interest that the world feels in it to him.   Few
men have done so much for their country as he.
However, having no guide-book, we were none
the wiser for what we saw out of the window
of the rail carriage ; but now and then a castle
appeared, on a commanding height, visible for
miles round, and seemingly in good repair, —
now, in some low and sheltered spot, the gray
walls of an abbey ; now, on a little eminence, the
ruin of a border fortress, and near it the modern residence of the laird, with its trim lawn and
shrubbery.

We were not long in coming to Berwick, a
town which seems to belong both to England
and Scotland, or perhaps is a kingdom by itself,
for it stands on both sides of the boundary river,
the Tweed, where it empties into the German

Ocean. From the railway bridge we had a good
view over the town, which looks ancient, with
red roofs on all the gabled houses ; and it being
a sunny afternoon, though bleak and chill, the
sea view was very fine. The Tweed is here
broad, and looks deep, flowing far beneath the
bridge, between high banks. This is all that I
can say of Berwick (pronounced Berrick), for
though we spent above an hour at the station
waiting for the train, we were so long in getting
our dinner that we had not time for anything
else. I remember, however, some gray walls,
that looked like the last remains of an old castle,
near the railway station.

We next took the train for Newcastle, the
way to which, for a considerable distance, lies
within sight of the sea ; and in close vicinity to
the shore we saw Holy Isle, on which are the
ruins of an abbey. Norham Castle must be
somewhere in this neighborhood, on the English shore of the Tweed. It was pretty late in
the afternoon — almost nightfall — when we
reached Newcastle, over the roofs of which, as
over those of Berwick, we had a view from the
railway, and like Berwick, it was a congregation
of mostly red roofs ; but, unlike Berwick (the
atmosphere over which was clear and transparent), there came a gush of smoke from every
chimney, which made it the dimmest and smok-
iest place I ever saw. This is partly owing to

the iron founderies and furnaces ; but each domestic chimney, too, was smoking on its own
account, — coal being so plentiful there, no
doubt, that the fire is always kept freshly heaped
with it, reason or none.   Out of this smoke-
cloud rose tall steeples ; and it was discernible
that the town stretched widely over an uneven
surface, on the banks of the Tyne, which is
navigable up hither ten miles from the sea for
pretty large vessels.

We established ourselves at the Station Hotel,
and then walked out to see something of the
town ; but I remember only a few streets of
duskiness and dinginess, with a glimpse of the
turrets of a castle to which we could not find
our way.   So, as it was getting twilightish and
very cold, we went back to the hotel, which is a
very good one, better than any one I have seen
in the South of England, and almost or quite as
good as those of Scotland.   The coffee-room is
a spacious and handsome apartment, adorned
with a full-length portrait of Wellington, and
other pictures, and in the whole establishment
there was a well-ordered alacrity and liberal provision for the comfort of guests that one seldom
sees in English inns.   There are a good many
American guests in Newcastle, and through all
the North.

An old Newcastle gentleman and his friend
came into the smoking-room, and drank three

glasses of hot whiskey toddy apiece, and were still going on to drink more when we left them. These respectable persons probably went away drunk that night, yet thought none the worse of themselves or of one another for it. It is like returning to times twenty years gone by for a New Englander to witness such simplicity of manners.

The next morning, May 8th, I rose and breakfasted early, and took the rail soon after eight o'clock, leaving Mr. Bowman behind; for he had business in Newcastle, and would not follow till some hours afterwards. There is no use in trying to make a narrative of anything that one sees along an English railway. All I remember of this tract of country is that one of the stations at which we stopped for an instant is called "Washington," and this is, no doubt, the old family place, where the De Wessyngtons, afterwards the Washingtons, were first settled in England. Before reaching York, first one old lady and then another (Quaker) lady got into the carriage along with me; and they seemed to be going to York, on occasion of some fair or celebration. This was all the company I had, and their advent the only incident. It was about eleven o'clock when I beheld York Cathedral rising huge above the old city, which stands on the river Ouse, separated by it from the railway station, but communicating by a ferry (or

two) and a bridge.   I wandered forth, and found my way over the latter into the ancient and irregular streets of York, crooked, narrow, or of unequal width, puzzling, and many of them bearing the name of the particular gate in the old walls of the city to which they lead.   There were no such fine, ancient, stately houses as some of those in Shrewsbury were, nor such an aspect of antiquity as in Chester ; but still York is a quaint old place, and what looks most modern is probably only something old, hiding itself behind a new front, as elsewhere in England.

I found my way by a sort of instinct, as directly as possible, to York Minster.   It stands in the midst of a small open space, — or a space that looks small in comparison with the vast bulk of the cathedral.   I was not so much impressed by its exterior as I have usually been by Gothic buildings, because it is rectangular in its general outline and in its towers, and seems to lack the complexity and mysterious plan which perplexes and wonder-strikes me in most cathedrals.   Doubtless, however, if I had known better how to admire it, I should have found it wholly admirable.   At all events, it has a satisfactory hugeness.   Seeking my way in, I at first intruded upon the Registry of Deeds, which occupies a building patched up against the mighty side of the cathedral, and hardly dis-

cernible, so small the one and so large the other.
I finally hit upon the right door, and I felt no
disappointment in my first glance around at the
immensity of enclosed space : I see now in my
mind's eye a dim length of nave, a breadth in
the transepts like a great plain, and such an airy
height beneath the central tower that a worship-
per could certainly get a good way towards
heaven without rising above it.   I only wish
that the screen, or whatever they call it, between
the choir and nave, could be thrown down, so
as to give us leave to take in the whole vast-
itude at once.   I never could understand why,
after building a great church, they choose to
sunder it in halves by this mid-partition.   But
let me be thankful for what I got, and especially for the height and massiveness of the clustered pillars that support the arches on which
rests the central tower.   I remember at Furness
Abbey I saw two tall pillars supporting a broken
arch, and thought it the most majestic fragment
of architecture that could possibly be.   But
these pillars have a nobler height, and these
arches a greater sweep.   What nonsense to try
to write about a cathedral !

There is a great, cold bareness and bleakness
about the interior ; for there are very few monuments, and those seem chiefly to be of ecclesiastical people.   I saw no armed knights, asleep
on the tops of their tombs; but there was

a curious representation of a skeleton, at full length, under the table-slab of one of the monuments. The walls are of a grayish hue, not so agreeable as the rich dark tint of the inside of Westminster Abbey; but a great many of the windows are still filled with ancient painted glass, the very small squares and pieces of which are composed into splendid designs of saints and angels, and scenes from Scripture.

There were a few watery blinks of sunshine out of doors, and whenever these came through the old painted windows, some of the more vivid colors were faintly thrown upon the pavement of the cathedral, — very faintly, it is true; for, in the first place, the sunshine was not brilliant; and painted glass, too, fades in the course of the ages, perhaps, like all man's other works. There were two or three windows of modern manufacture, and far more magnificent, as to brightness of color and material beauty, than the ancient ones; but yet they looked vulgar, glaring, and impertinent in comparison, because such revivals or imitations of a long-disused art cannot have the good faith and earnestness of the originals. Indeed, in the very coloring, I felt the same difference as between heart's blood and a scarlet dye. It is a pity, however, that the old windows cannot be washed, both inside and out, for now they have the dust of centuries upon them.

The screen or curtain between the nave and choir has eleven carved figures, at full length, which appeared to represent kings, some of them wearing crowns and bearing sceptres or swords. They were in wood, and wrought by some Gothic hand. These carvings, and the painted windows, and the few monuments, are all the details that the mind can catch hold of in the immensity of this cathedral; and I must say that it was a dreary place on that cold, cloudy day. I doubt whether a cathedral is a sort of edifice suited to the English climate. The first buildings of the kind were probably erected by people who had bright and constant sunshine, and who desired a shadowy awfulness — like that of a forest, with its arched wood-paths — into which to retire in their religious moments.

In America, on a hot summer's day, how delightful its cool and solemn depths would be! The painted windows, too, were evidently contrived, in the first instance, by persons who saw how effective they would prove when a vivid sun shone through them. But in England, the interior of a cathedral, nine days out of ten, is a vast sullenness, and as chill as death and the tomb. At any rate, it was so to-day, and so thought one of the old vergers, who kept walking as briskly as he could along the width of the transepts. There were several of these old men when I first came in, but they went off, all but this one, before I departed. None of them said a word to me, nor I to them; and admission to the Minster seems to be entirely free.

After emerging from this great gloom, I wandered to and fro about York, and contrived to go astray within no very wide space. If its history be authentic, it is an exceedingly old city, having been founded about a thousand years before the Christian era. There used to be a palace of the Roman emperors here, and the Emperor Severus died here, as did some of his successors; and Constantine the Great was born here. I know not what, if any, relics of those earlier times there may be; but York is still partly surrounded with a wall, and has several gates, which the city authorities take pains to keep in repair. I grew weary in my endeavor to find my way back to the railway, and inquired it of one of the good people of York, — a respectable, courteous, gentlemanly person, — and he told me to walk along the walls. Then he went on a considerable distance, but seemed to repent of not doing more for me; so he waited till I came up, and, walking along by my side, pointed out the castle, now the jail, and the place of execution, and directed me to the principal gateway of the city, and instructed me how to reach the ferry. The path along the wall leads, in one place, through a room over the arch of a gateway, — a low, thick-walled, stone apartment, where doubtless the gate-keeper used to lodge, and to parley with those who desired entrance.

I found my way to the ferry over the Ouse, according to this kind Yorkist's instructions. The ferryman told me that the fee for crossing was a halfpenny, which seemed so ridiculously small that I offered him more; but this un-paralleled Englishman declined taking anything beyond his rightful halfpenny. This seems so wonderful to me that I can hardly trust my own memory.

Reaching the station, I got some dinner, and at four o'clock, just as I was starting, came Mr. Bowman, my very agreeable and sensible travel-ling companion. Our journeying together was ended here; for he was to keep on to London, and I to return to Liverpool. So we parted, and I took the rail westward across England, through a very beautiful, and in some degree picturesque, tract of country, diversified with hills, through the valleys and vistas of which goes the railroad, with dells diverging from it on either hand, and streams and arched bridges, and old villages, and a hundred pleasant Eng-lish sights. After passing Rochdale, however, the dreary monotony of Lancashire succeeded this variety. Between nine and ten o'clock I reached the Tithebarn station in Liverpool.

Ever since until now, May 17th, I have employed my leisure moments in scribbling off the
journal of my tour; but it has greatly lost by
not having been written daily, as the scenes and
occurrences were fresh.   The most picturesque
points can be seized in no other way, and the
hues of the affair fade as quickly as those of a
dying dolphin; or as, according to Audubon,
the plumage of a dead bird.

One thing that struck me as much as anything else in the Highlands I had forgotten to
put down.   In our walk at Balloch, along the
road within view of Loch Lomond and the
neighboring hills, it was a brilliant sunshiny
afternoon, and I never saw any atmosphere so
beautiful as that among the mountains.   It was
a clear, transparent, ethereal blue, as distinct as
a vapor, and yet by no means vaporous, but a
pure, crystalline medium.   I have witnessed nothing like this among the Berkshire hills nor
elsewhere.

York is full of old churches, some of them
very antique in appearance, the stones weather-
worn, their edges rounded by time, blackened,
and with all the tokens of sturdy and age-long
decay; and in some of them I noticed windows
quite full of old painted glass, a dreary kind of
minute patchwork, all of one dark and dusty
hue, when seen from the outside.   Yet had I
seen them from the interior of the church, there

doubtless would have been rich and varied apparitions of saints with their glories round their heads, and bright-winged angels, and perhaps even the Almighty Father himself, so far as conceivable and representable by human powers. It requires light from heaven to make them visible. If the church were merely illuminated from the inside, — that is, by what light a man can get from his own understanding, — the pictures would be invisible, or wear at best but a miserable aspect.

LIVERPOOL, *May* 24. — Day before yesterday I had a call at the Consulate from one of the Potentates of the Earth, — a woolly-haired negro, rather thin and spare, between forty and fifty years of age, plainly dressed; at the first glimpse of whom, I could readily have mistaken him for some ship's steward, seeking to enter a complaint of his captain. However, this was President Roberts, of Liberia, introduced by a note from Mrs. O'Sullivan, whom he has recently met in Madeira. I was rather favorably impressed with him; for his deportment was very simple, and without any of the flourish and embroidery which a negro might be likely to assume on finding himself elevated from slavery to power. He is rather shy, — reserved, at least, and undemonstrative, yet not harshly so, — in fine, with manners that offer no prominent points for notice or criticism; although I felt, or thought I felt, that his color was continually before his mind, and that he walks cautiously among men, as conscious that every new introduction is a new experiment. He is not in the slightest degree an interesting man (so far as I discovered in a very brief interview), apart from his position and history; his face is not striking, nor so agreeable as if it were jet black; but there may be miles and miles of depth in him which I know nothing of. Our conversation was of the most unimportant character; for he had called merely to deliver the note, and sat only a few minutes, during which he merely responded to my observations, and originated no remarks. Intelligence, discretion, tact, — these are probably his traits; not force of character and independence.

The same day I took the rail from the Lime Street Station for Manchester, to meet Bennoch, who had asked me thither to dine with him. I had never visited Manchester before, though now so long resident within twenty miles of it; neither is it particularly worth visiting, unless for the sake of its factories, which I did not go to see. It is a dingy and heavy town, with very much the aspect of Liverpool, being, like the latter, built almost entirely within the present century. I stopped at the Albion Hotel, and,

as Bennoch was out, I walked forth to view the
city, and made only such observations as are recorded above.   Opposite the hotel stands the
Infirmary, — a very large edifice, which, when
erected, was on the outskirts, or perhaps in the
rural suburbs, of the town, but it is now almost
in its centre.   In the enclosed space before it
stands the statue of Peel, and sits a statue of
Dr. Dalton, the celebrated chemist, who was a
native of Manchester.

Returning to the hotel, I sat down in the
room where we were to dine, and in due time
Bennoch made his appearance, with the same
glow and friendly warmth in his face that I had
left burning there when we parted in London.
If this man has not a heart, then no man ever
had.   I like him inexpressibly for his heart and
for his intellect, and for his flesh and blood;
and if he has faults, I do not know them, nor
care to know them, nor value him the less if I
did know them.   He went to his room to dress;
and in the mean time a middle-aged, dark man,
of pleasant aspect, with black hair, black eyebrows, and bright, dark eyes came in, limping a
little, but not much.   He seemed not quite a
man of the world, a little shy in manner, yet he
addressed me kindly and sociably. I guessed him
to be Mr. Charles Swain, the poet, whom Mr.
Bennoch had invited to dinner.   Soon came
another guest, whom Mr. Swain introduced to

me as Mr. ——, editor of the Manchester Examiner. Then came Bennoch, who made us all regularly acquainted, or took for granted that we were so; and lastly appeared a Mr. W——, a merchant in Manchester, and a very intelligent man; and the party was then complete. Mr. Swain, the poet, is not a man of fluent conversation; he said, indeed, very little, but gave me the impression of amiability and simplicity of character, with much feeling.

. . . .

Mr. W—— is a very sensible man. He has spent two or three years in America, and seems to have formed juster conclusions about us than most of his countrymen do. He is the only Englishman, I think, whom I have met, who fairly acknowledges that the English do cherish doubt, jealousy, suspicion, — in short, an unfriendly feeling, — towards the Americans. It is wonderful how every American, whatever class of the English he mingles with, is conscious of this feeling, and how no Englishman, except this sole Mr. W——, will confess it. He expressed some very good ideas, too, about the English and American press, and the reasons why the Times may fairly be taken as the exponent of British feeling towards us, while the New York Herald, immense as its circulation is, can be considered, in no similar degree or kind, the American exponent.

We sat late at table, and after the other guests had retired, Bennoch and I had some very friendly talk, and he proposed that on my wife's return we should take up our residence in his house at Blackheath, while Mrs. Bennoch and himself were absent for two months on a trip to Germany. If his wife and mine ratify the idea, we will do so.

The next morning we went out to see the Exchange, and whatever was noticeable about the town. Time being brief, I did not visit the cathedral, which, I believe, is a thousand years old. There are many handsome shops in Manchester; and we went into one establishment, devoted to pictures, engravings, and decorative art generally, which is most perfect and extensive. The firm, if I remember, is that of the Messrs. Agnew, and, though originating here, they have now a house in London. Here I saw some interesting objects, purchased by them at the recent sale of the Rogers collection; among other things, a slight pencil and water-color sketch by Raphael. An unfinished affair, done in a moment, as this must have been, seems to bring us closer to the hand that did it than the most elaborately painted picture can. Were I to see the Transfiguration, Raphael would still be at the distance of centuries. Seeing this little sketch, I had him very near me. I know not why, — perhaps it might be fancied that he had only laid down the pencil for an instant, and would take it up again in a moment more. I likewise saw a copy of a handsome, illustrated edition of Childe Harold, presented by old John Murray to Mr. Rogers, with an inscription on the fly-leaf, purporting that it was a token of gratitude from the publisher, because, when everybody else thought him imprudent in giving four hundred guineas for the poem, Mr. Rogers told him it would turn out the best bargain he ever made.

There was a new picture by Millais, the distinguished Pre-Raphaelite artist, representing a melancholy parting between two lovers. The lady's face had a great deal of sad and ominous expression; but an old brick wall, overrun with foliage, was so exquisitely and elaborately wrought that it was hardly possible to look at the personages of the picture. Every separate leaf of the climbing and clustering shrubbery was painfully made out; and the wall was reality itself, with the weather-stains and the moss, and the crumbling lime between the bricks. It is not well to be so perfect in the inanimate, unless the artist can likewise make man and woman as lifelike, and to as great a depth, too, as the Creator does.

Bennoch left town for some place in Yorkshire, and I for Liverpool. I asked him to come and dine with me at the Adelphi, meaning to ask two or three people to meet him ; but he had other engagements, and could not spare a day at present, though he promises to come before long.

Dining at Mr. Rathbone's one evening last week (May 21st), it was mentioned that Borrow, author of The Bible in Spain, is supposed to be of gypsy descent by the mother's side. Hereupon Mr. Martineau mentioned that he had been a schoolfellow of Borrow, and though he had never heard of his gypsy blood, he thought it probable, from Borrow's traits of character. He said that Borrow had once run away from school, and carried with him a party of other boys, meaning to lead a wandering life.

If an Englishman were individually acquainted with all our twenty-five millions of Americans, and liked every one of them, and believed that each man of those millions was a Christian, honest, upright, and kind, he would doubt, despise, and hate them in the aggregate, however he might love and honor the individuals.

Captain —— and his wife Oakum : they spent an evening at Mrs. B——'s. The Captain is a Marblehead man by birth, not far from sixty years old ; very talkative and anecdotic in regard to his adventures ; funny, good humored, and full of various nautical experience. Oakum (it is a nickname which he gives his wife) is an inconceivably tall woman, — taller than he, — six feet, at least, and with a well-proportioned largeness in all respects, but looks kind and good, gentle, smiling, — and almost any other woman might sit like a baby on her lap. She does not look at all awful and belligerent, like the massive English women one often sees. You at once feel her to be a benevolent giantess, and apprehend no harm from her. She is a lady, and perfectly well mannered, but with a sort of naturalness and simplicity that becomes her ; for any the slightest affectation would be so magnified in her vast personality that it would be absolutely the height of the ridiculous. This wedded pair have no children, and Oakum has so long accompanied her husband on his voyages that I suppose by this time she could command a ship as well as he. They sat till pretty late, diffusing cheerfulness all about them, and then, " Come, Oakum," cried the Captain, " we must hoist sail ! " and up rose Oakum to the ceiling, and moved tower-like to the door, looking down with a benignant smile on the poor little pygmy women about her. " Six feet," did I say? Why, she must be seven, eight, nine ; and, whatever be her size, she is as good as she is big.

June 11. — Monday night (9th), just as I was retiring, I received a telegraphic message announcing my wife's arrival at Southampton. So, the next day, I arranged the consular business for an absence of ten days, and set forth with Julian, and reached Birmingham, between eight and nine, evening. We put up at the Queen's Hotel, a very large establishment, contiguous to the railway. Next morning we left Birmingham, and made our first stage to Leamington, where we had to wait nearly an hour, which we spent in wandering through some of the streets that had been familiar to us last year. Leamington is certainly a beautiful town, new, bright, clean, and as unlike as possible to the business towns of England. However, the sun was burning hot, and I could almost have fancied myself in America. From Leamington we took tickets for Oxford, where we were obliged to make another stop of two hours; and these we employed to what advantage we could, driving up into town, and straying hither and thither, till Julian's weariness weighed upon me, and I adjourned with him to a hotel. Oxford is an ugly old town, of crooked and irregular streets, gabled houses, mostly plastered of a buff or yellow hue; some new fronts; and as for the buildings of the University, they seem to be scattered at random, without any reference to one another. I passed through an old gateway of

Christ Church, and looked.at its enclosed square, and that is, in truth, pretty much all I then saw of the University of Oxford. From Christ Church we rambled along a street that led us to a bridge across the Isis; and we saw many row-boats lying in the river, — the lightest craft imaginable, unless it were an Indian canoe. The Isis is but a narrow stream, and with a sluggish current. I believe the students of Oxford are famous for their skill in rowing.

To me as well as to Julian the hot streets were terribly oppressive; so we went into the Roebuck Hotel, where we found a cool and pleasant coffee-room. The entrance to this hotel is through an arch, opening from High Street, and giving admission into a paved court, the buildings all around being part of the establishment, — old edifices with pointed gables and old-fashioned projecting windows, but all in fine repair, and wearing a most quiet, retired, and comfortable aspect. The court was set all round with flowers, growing in pots or large pedestalled vases; on one side was the coffee-room, and all the other public apartments, and the other side seemed to be taken up by the sleeping-chambers and parlors of the guests. This arrangement of an inn, I presume, is very ancient, and it resembles what I have seen in the hospitals, free schools, and other charitable establishments in the old English towns; and indeed, all large

165

houses were arranged on somewhat the same
principle.

By and by two or three young men came in,
in wide-awake hats, and loose, blouse-like, sum-
merish garments; and from their talk I found
them to be students of the University, although
their topics of conversation were almost entirely
horses and boats. One of them sat down to
cold beef and a tankard of ale; the other two
drank a tankard of ale together, and went away
without paying for it, — rather to the waiter's
discontent. Students are very much alike, all
the world over, and, I suppose, in all time;
but I doubt whether many of my fellows at
college would have gone off without paying for
their beer.

We reached Southampton between seven and
eight o'clock. I cannot write to-day.

June 15. — The first day after we reached
Southampton was sunny and pleasant; but we
made little use of the fine weather, except that
Sophia and I walked once along the High Street,
and Julian and I took a little ramble about town
in the afternoon. The next day there was a
high and disagreeable wind, and I did not once
stir out of the house. The third day, too, I
kept entirely within doors, it being a storm of
wind and rain. The Castle Hotel stands within
fifty yards of the water-side; so that this gusty

day showed itself to the utmost advantage, —
the vessels pitching and tossing at their moor-
ings, the waves breaking white out of a tumultuous gray surface, the opposite shore glooming
mistily at the distance of a mile or two ; and on
the hither side boatmen and seafaring people
scudding about the pier in waterproof clothes ;
and in the street, before the hotel door, a cabman or two, standing drearily beside his horse.
But we were sunny within doors.

Yesterday it was breezy, sunny, shadowy,
showery ; and we ordered a cab to take us to
Clifton Villa, to call on Mrs. ——, a friend of
B——'s, who called on us the day after our arrival. Just as we were ready to start, Mrs. ——
again called, and accompanied us back to her
house. It is in Shirley, about two miles from
Southampton pier, and is a pleasant suburban
villa, with a pretty ornamented lawn and shrubbery about it. Mrs. —— is an instructress of
young ladies ; and at B——'s suggestion, she is
willing to receive us for two or three weeks,
during the vacation, until we are ready to go to
London. She seems to be a pleasant and sensible woman, and to-morrow we shall decide
whether to go there. There was nothing very
remarkable in this drive ; and, indeed, my stay
hereabouts thus far has been very barren of sights
and incidents externally interesting, though the
inner life has been rich.

Southampton is a very pretty town, and has not the dinginess to which I have been accustomed in many English towns. The High Street reminds me very much of American streets in its general effect; the houses being mostly stuccoed white or light, and cheerful in aspect, though doubtless they are centuries old at heart. The old gateway, which I presume I have mentioned in describing my former visit to Southampton, stands across High Street, about in the centre of the town, and is almost the only token of antiquity that presents itself to the eye.

SALISBURY, *June* 17. — Yesterday morning, June 16th, Sophia, Mrs. ——, and I took the rail for Salisbury, where we duly arrived without any accident or anything noticeable, except the usual verdure and richness of an English summer landscape. From the railway station we walked up into Salisbury, with the tall spire (four hundred feet high) of the cathedral before our eyes. Salisbury is an antique city, but with streets more regular than I have seen in most old towns, and the houses have a more picturesque aspect than those of Oxford, for instance, where almost all are mean-looking alike, — though I could hardly judge of Oxford on that hot, weary day. Through one or more of the streets there runs a swift, clear little stream, which, being close to the pavement, and bordered with stone, may be called, I suppose, a kennel, though possessing the transparent purity of a rustic rivulet. It is a brook in city garb. We passed under the pointed arch of a gateway, which stands in one of the principal streets, and soon came in front of the cathedral.

I do not remember any cathedral with so fine a site as this, rising up out of the centre of a beautiful green, extensive enough to show its full proportions, relieved and insulated from all other patchwork and impertinence of rusty edifices. It is of gray stone, and looks as perfect as when just finished, and with the perfection, too, that could not have come in less than six centuries of venerableness, with a view to which these edifices seem to have been built. A new cathedral would lack the last touch to its beauty and grandeur. It needs to be mellowed and ripened, like some pictures; although I suppose this awfulness of antiquity was supplied, in the minds of the generation that built cathedrals, by the sanctity which they attributed to them. Salisbury Cathedral is far more beautiful than that of York, the exterior of which was really disagreeable to my eye; but this mighty spire and these multitudinous gray pinnacles and towers ascend towards heaven with a kind of natural beauty, not as if man had contrived them. They might be fancied to have grown up, just

as the spires of a tuft of grass do, at the same
time that they have a law of propriety and regularity among themselves. The tall spire is
of such admirable proportion that it does not
seem gigantic — and indeed the effect of the
whole edifice is of beauty rather than weight and
massiveness. Perhaps the bright, balmy sunshine in which we saw it contributed to give it
a tender glory, and to soften a little its majesty.

When we went in, we heard the organ, the
forenoon service being near conclusion. If I
had never seen the interior of York Cathedral,
I should have been quite satisfied, no doubt,
with the spaciousness of this nave and these
side aisles, and the height of their arches, and
the girth of these pillars ; but with that recollection in my mind, they fell a little short of
grandeur. The interior is seen to disadvantage,
and in a way the builder never meant it to be
seen ; because there is little or no painted glass,
nor any such mystery as it makes, but only a
colorless common daylight, revealing everything
without remorse. There is a general light hue,
moreover, like that of whitewash, over the whole
of the roof, and walls of the interior, pillars,
monuments and all ; whereas originally every
pillar was polished, and the ceiling was ornamented in brilliant colors, and the light came,
many-hued, through the windows, on all this

elaborate beauty, in lieu of which there is nothing now but space.

Between the pillars that separate the nave from the side aisles, there are ancient tombs, most of which have recumbent statues on them. One of these is Longsword, Earl of Salisbury, son of Fair Rosamond, in chain mail; and there are many other warriors and bishops, and one cross-legged Crusader, and on one tombstone a recumbent skeleton, which I have likewise seen in two or three other cathedrals. The pavement of the aisles and nave is laid in great part with flat tombstones, the inscriptions on which are half obliterated, and on the walls, especially in the transepts, there are tablets, among which I saw one to the poet Bowles, who was a canon of this cathedral. The ecclesiastical dignitaries bury themselves and monument themselves to the exclusion of almost everybody else, in these latter times; though still, as of old, the warrior has his place. A young officer, slain in the Indian wars, was memorialized by a tablet, and may be remembered by it, six hundred years hence, as we now remember the old Knights and Crusaders. It deserves to be mentioned that I saw one or two noses still unbroken among these recumbent figures. Most of the antique statues, on close examination, proved to be almost entirely covered with names and initials, scratched over the once polished surface. The cathedral and its relics must have been far less carefully watched, at some former period, than now.

Between the nave and the choir, as usual, there is a screen that half destroys the majesty of the building, by abridging the spectator of the long vista which he might otherwise have of the whole interior at a glance. We peeped through the barrier, and saw some elaborate monuments in the chancel beyond, — but the doors of the screen are kept locked, so that the vergers may raise a revenue by showing strangers through the richest part of the cathedral. By and by one of these vergers came through the screen, with a gentleman and lady whom he was taking round, and we joined ourselves to the party. He showed us into the cloisters, which had long been neglected and ruinous, until the time of Bishop Dennison, the last prelate, who has been but a few years dead. This Bishop has repaired and restored the cloisters in faithful adherence to the original plan; and they now form a most delightful walk about a pleasant and verdant enclosure, in the centre of which sleeps good Bishop Dennison, with a wife on either side of him, all three beneath broad, flat stones. Most cloisters are darksome and grim; but these have a broad, paved walk beneath the vista of arches, and are light, airy, and cheerful; and from one corner you can get the best possible view of the whole height and beautiful proportion of the cathedral spire. One side of this cloistered walk seems to be the length of the nave of the cathedral. There is a square of four such sides; and of places for meditation, grave, yet not too sombre, it seemed to me one of the best. While we stayed there, a jackdaw was walking to and fro across the grassy enclosure, and haunting around the good Bishop's grave. He was clad in black, and looked like a feathered ecclesiastic; but I know not whether it were Bishop Dennison's ghost, or that of some old monk.

On one side of the cloisters, and contiguous to the main body of the cathedral, stands the chapter-house. Bishop Dennison had it much at heart to repair this part of the holy edifice; and, if I mistake not, did begin the work; for it had been long ruinous, and in Cromwell's time his dragoons stationed their horses there. Little progress, however, had been made in the repairs when the Bishop died; and it was decided to restore the building in his honor, and by way of monument to him. The repairs are now nearly completed; and the interior of this chapter-house gave me the first idea, anywise adequate, of the splendor of these Gothic church edifices. The roof is sustained by one great central pillar of polished marble, — small pillars clustered about a great central column, which

rises to the ceiling, and there gushes out with
various beauty, that overflows all the walls; as
if the fluid idea had sprung out of that fountain, and grown solid in what we see. The
pavement is elaborately ornamented; the ceiling is to be brilliantly gilded and painted, as
it was of yore, and the tracery and sculptures
around the walls are to be faithfully renewed
from what remains of the original patterns.

After viewing the chapter-house, the verger —
an elderly man of grave, benign manner, clad in
black and talking of the cathedral and the monuments as if he loved them — led us again into
the nave of the cathedral, and thence within
the screen of the choir. The screen is as poor
as possible, — mere barren wood-work, without
the least attempt at beauty. In the chancel there
are some meagre patches of old glass, and some
of modern date, not very well worth looking
at. We saw several interesting monuments in
this part of the cathedral, — one belonging to
the ducal family of Somerset, and erected in
the reign of James I.; it is of marble, and extremely splendid and elaborate, with kneeling
figures and all manner of magnificence, — more
than I have seen in any monument except that
of Mary of Scotland in Westminster Abbey.
The more ancient tombs are also very numerous, and among them that of the Bishop who
founded the cathedral. Within the screen, against

the wall, is erected a monument, by Chantrey, to the Earl of Malmesbury; a full-length statue of the Earl in a half-recumbent position, holding an open volume, and looking upward, — a noble work, — a calm, wise, thoughtful, firm, and not unbenignant face. Beholding its expression, it really was impossible not to have faith in the high character of the individual thus represented ; and I have seldom felt this effect from any monumental bust or statue, though I presume it is always aimed at.

I am weary of trying to describe cathedrals. It is utterly useless ; there is no possibility of giving the general effect, or any shadow of it, and it is miserable to put down a few items of tombstones, and a bit of glass from a painted window, as if the gloom and glory of the edifice were thus to be reproduced. Cathedrals are almost the only things (if even those) that have quite filled out my ideal here in this old world ; and cathedrals often make me miserable from my inadequacy to take them wholly in ; and, above all, I despise myself when I sit down to describe them.

We now walked around the Close, which is surrounded by some of the quaintest and comfortablest ecclesiastical residences that can be imagined. These are the dwelling-houses of the Dean and the canons, and whatever other high officers compose the Bishop's staff; and there was one large brick mansion, old, but not so ancient as the rest, which we took to be the Bishop's palace. I never beheld anything — I must say again — so cosy, so indicative of domestic comfort for whole centuries together, — houses so fit to live in or to die in, and where it would be so pleasant to lead a young wife beneath the antique portal, and dwell with her till husband and wife were patriarchal, — as these delectable old houses. They belong naturally to the cathedral, and have a necessary relation to it, and its sanctity is somehow thrown over them all, so that they do not quite belong to this world, though they look full to overflowing of whatever earthly things are good for man. These are places, however, in which mankind makes no progress ; the rushing tumult of human life here subsides into a deep, quiet pool, with perhaps a gentle circular eddy, but no onward movement. The same identical thought, I suppose, goes round in a slow whirl from one generation to another, as I have seen a withered leaf do in the vortex of a brook. In the front of the cathedral there is a most stately and beautiful tree, which flings its verdure upward to a very lofty height ; but far above it rises the tall spire, dwarfing the great tree by comparison.

When the cathedral had sufficiently oppressed us with its beauty, we returned to sublunary matters, and went wandering about Salisbury in

search of a luncheon, which we finally took in a
confectioner's shop.   Then we inquired hither
and thither, at various livery-stables, for a conveyance to Stonehenge, and at last took a fly
from the Lamb Hotel.   The drive was over a
turnpike for the first seven miles, over a bare,
ridgy country, showing little to interest us.   We
passed a party of seven or eight men, in a coarse
uniform dress, resembling that worn by con-
victs, and apparently under the guardianship of
a stout, authoritative, yet rather kindly-looking
man with a cane.   Our driver said that they
were lunatics from a neighboring asylum, out
for a walk.

Seven miles from Salisbury we turned aside
from the turnpike, and drove two miles across
Salisbury Plain, which is an apparently bound-
less extent of unenclosed land — treeless and
houseless.   It is not exactly a plain, but a green
sea of long and gentle swells and subsidences, affording views of miles upon miles to a very far horizon.   We passed large flocks of sheep, with the
shepherds watching them ; but the dogs seemed
to take most of the care of the flocks upon their
own shoulders, and would scamper to turn the
sheep when they inclined to stray whither they
should not, — and then arose a thousand-fold
bleating, not unpleasant to the ear, for it did
not apparently indicate any fear or discomfort
on the part of the flock.   The sheep and lambs

are all black-faced, and have a very funny expression. As we drove over the plain (my seat was beside the driver), I saw at a distance a cluster of large gray stones, mostly standing upright, and some of them slightly inclined towards each other, — very irregular, and so far off forming no very picturesque or noteworthy spectacle. Of course I knew at once that this was Stonehenge, and also knew that the reality was going to dwindle woefully within my ideal, as almost everything else does. When we reached the spot, we found a picnic-party just finishing their dinner, on one of the overthrown stones of the druidical temple; and within the sacred circle an artist was painting a wretched daub of the scene, and an old shepherd — the very Shepherd of Salisbury Plain — sat erect in the centre of the ruin.

There never was a ruder thing than Stonehenge made by mortal hands. It is so very rude that it seems as if Nature and man had worked upon it with one consent, and so it is all the stranger and more impressive from its rudeness. The spectator wonders to see art and contrivance, and a regular and even somewhat intricate plan, beneath all the uncouth simplicity of this arrangement of rough stones; and certainly, whatever was the intellectual and scientific advancement of the people who built Stonehenge, no succeeding architects will ever have a right to triumph over them; for no-body's work in after times is likely to endure till it becomes a mystery as to who built it, and how, and for what purpose.   Apart from the moral considerations suggested by it, Stone-henge is not very well worth seeing.   Mate-rially, it is one of the poorest of spectacles, and when complete, it must have been even less picturesque than now, — a few huge, rough stones, very imperfectly squared, standing on end, and each group of two supporting a third large stone on their tops; other stones of the same pattern overthrown and tumbled one upon another; and the whole comprised within a circuit of about a hundred feet diameter; the short, sheep-cropped grass of Salisbury Plain growing among all these uncouth boulders.   I am not sure that a misty, lowering day would not have better suited Stonehenge, as the dreary midpoint of the great, desolate, trackless plain; not literally trackless, however, for the London and Exeter Road passes within fifty yards of the ruins, and another road intersects it.

After we had been there about an hour, there came a horseman within the Druid's circle, — evidently a clerical personage by his white neckcloth, though his loose gray riding pantaloons were not quite in keeping.   He looked at us rather earnestly, and at last ad-dressed Mrs. ——, and announced himself as

Mr. Hinchman, — a clergyman whom she had been trying to find in Salisbury, in order to avail herself of him as a cicerone ; and he had now ridden hither to meet us.   He told us that the artist whom we found here could give us more information than anybody about Stonehenge ; for it seems he has spent a great many years here, painting and selling his poor sketches to visitors and also selling a book which his father wrote about the remains.   This man showed, indeed, a pretty accurate acquaintance with these old stones, and pointed out what is thought to be the altar-stone, and told us of some relation between this stone and two other stones, and the rising of the sun at midsummer, which might indicate that Stonehenge was a temple of solar worship.   He pointed out, too, to how little depth the stones were planted in the earth, insomuch that I have no doubt the American frosts would overthrow Stonehenge in a single winter ; and it is wonderful that it should have stood so long, even in England. I have forgotten what else he said ; but I bought one of his books, and find it a very unsatisfactory performance, being chiefly taken up with an attempt to prove these remains to be an antediluvian work, constructed, I think the author says, under the superintendence of Father Adam himself !   Before our departure we were requested to write our names in the album which the artist keeps for the purpose ; and he pointed out Ex-President Fillmore's autograph, and those of one or two other Americans who have been here within a short time. It is a very curious life that this artist leads, in this great solitude, and haunting Stonehenge like the ghost of a Druid ; but he is a brisk little man, and very communicative on his one sub-ject.   •

Mr. Hinchman rode with us over the plain, and pointed out Salisbury spire, visible close to Stonehenge.   Under his guidance we returned by a different road from that which brought us thither, — and a much more delightful one.   I think I never saw such continued sylvan beauty as this road showed us, passing through a good deal of woodland scenery, — fine old trees, standing each within its own space, and thus having full liberty to outspread itself, and wax strong and broad for ages, instead of being crowded, and thus stifled and emaciated, as human beings are here, and forest-trees are in America.   Hedges, too, and the rich, rich ver-dure of England ; and villages full of pictur-esque old houses, thatched and ivied, or perhaps overrun with roses, — and a stately mansion in the Elizabethan style ; and a quiet stream, glid-ing onward without a ripple from its own mo-tion, but rippled by a large fish darting across it ; and over all this scene a gentle, friendly sunshine, not ardent enough to crisp a single leaf or blade of grass. Nor must the village church be forgotten, with its square, battlemented tower, dating back to the epoch of the Normans. We called at a house where one of Mrs. ——'s pupils was residing with her aunt, — a thatched house of two stories high, built in what was originally a sand-pit, but which, in the course of a good many years, has been transformed into the most delightful and homelike little nook almost that can be found in England. A thatched cottage suggests a very rude dwelling indeed; but this had a pleasant parlor and drawing-room, and chambers with lattice windows opening close beneath the thatched roof; and the thatch itself gives an air to the place as if it were a bird's-nest, or some such simple and natural habitation. The occupants are an elderly clergyman, retired from professional duty, and his sister; and having nothing else to do, and sufficient means, they employ themselves in beautifying this sweet little retreat, — planting new shrubbery, laying out new walks around it, and helping Nature to add continually another charm; and Nature is certainly a more genial playfellow in England than in my own country. She is always ready to lend her aid to any beautifying purpose.

Leaving these good people, who were very hospitable, giving tea and offering wine, we reached Salisbury in time to take the train for Southampton.

June 18. — Yesterday we left the Castle Hotel, after paying a bill of £20 for a little more than a week's board.   In America we could not very well have lived so simply, but we might have lived luxuriously for half the money. This Castle Hotel was once an old Roman castle, the landlord says, and the circular sweep of the tower is still seen towards the street, although, being painted white, and built up with modern additions, it would not be taken for an ancient structure.   There is a dungeon beneath it, in which the landlord keeps his wine.

Julian and I, quitting the hotel, walked towards Shirley, along the water-side, leaving the rest of the family to follow in a fly.   There are many traces, along the shore, of the fortifications by which Southampton was formerly defended towards the water, and very probably their foundations may be as ancient as Roman times. Our hotel was no doubt connected with this chain of defences, which seems to have consisted of a succession of round towers, with a wall extending from one to another.   We saw two or three of these towers still standing, and likely to stand, though ivy-grown and ruinous at the summit, and intermixed and even amalgamated with pot-houses and mean dwellings ; and often, through an antique arch, there was a narrow doorway, giving access to the house of some sailor or laborer or artisan, and his wife gossiping at it with her neighbor, or his children playing about it.

After getting beyond the precincts of Southampton our walk was not very interesting, except to Julian, who kept running down to the verge of the water, looking for shells and sea insects.

June 29. — Yesterday, 28th, I left Liverpool from the Lime Street station; an exceedingly hot day for England, insomuch that the rail carriages were really uncomfortable. I have now passed over the London and Northwestern Railway so often that the northern part of it is very wearisome, especially as it has few features of interest even to a new observer. At Stafford — no, at Wolverhampton — we diverged to a track which I have passed over only once before. We stopped an hour and a quarter at Wolverhampton, and I walked up into the town, which is large and old, — old, at least, in its plan, or lack of plan, — the streets being irregular, and straggling over an uneven surface. Like many of the English towns, it reminds me of Boston, though dingier. The sun was so hot that I actually sought the shady sides of the streets; and this, of itself, is one long step

towards establishing a resemblance between an
English town and an American one.

English railway carriages seem to me more
tiresome than any other; and I suppose it is
owing to the greater motion, arising from their
more elastic springs. A slow train, too, like
that which I was now in, is more tiresome than
a quick one, at least to the spirits, whatever it
may be to the body. We loitered along through
afternoon and evening, stopping at every little
station, and nowhere getting to the top of our
speed; till at last, in the late dusk, we reached
Gloucester, and I put up at the Wellington
Hotel, which is but a little way from the station. I took tea and a slice or two of ham in
the coffee-room, and had a little talk with two
people there; one of whom, on learning that I
was an American, said, " But I suppose you
have now been in England some time?" He
meant, finding me not absolutely a savage,
that I must have been caught a good while
ago. . . .

The next morning I went into the city, the
hotel being on its outskirts, and rambled along
in search of the cathedral. Some church-bells
were chiming and clashing for a wedding or other
festal occasion, and I followed the sound, supposing that it might proceed from the cathedral, but this was not the case. It was not till
I had got to a bridge over the Severn, quite

out of the town, that I saw again its tower, and knew how to shape my course towards it.

I did not see much that was strange or interesting in Gloucester. It is old, with a good many of those antique Elizabethan houses with two or three peaked gables on a line together; several old churches, which always cluster about a cathedral, like chickens round a hen; a hospital for decayed tradesmen; another for blue-coat boys; a great many butcher's shops, scattered in all parts of the town, open in front, with a counter or dresser on which to display the meat, just in the old fashion of Shakespeare's house. It is a large town, and has a good deal of liveliness and bustle, in a provincial way. In short, judging by the sheep, cattle, and horses, and the people of agricultural aspect that I saw about the streets, I should think it must have been market-day. I looked here and there for the old Bell Inn, because, unless I misremember, Fielding brings Tom Jones to this inn, while he and Partridge were travelling together. It is still extant; for, on my arrival the night before, a runner from it had asked me to go thither; but I forgot its celebrity at the moment. I saw nothing of it in my rambles about Gloucester, but at last I found the cathedral, though I found no point from which a good view of the exterior can be seen.

It has a very beautiful and rich outside, how-

Gloucester

ever, and a lofty tower, very large and ponderous, but so finished off, and adorned with pinnacles, and all manner of architectural devices,
— wherewith these old builders knew how to
alleviate their massive structures, — that it seems
to sit lightly in the air.   The porch was open,
and some workmen were trundling barrows into
the nave; so I followed, and found two young
women sitting just within the porch, one of
whom offered to show me round the cathedral.
There was a great dust in the nave, arising from
the operations of the workmen.   They had been
laying a new pavement, and scraping away the
plaster, which had heretofore been laid over the
pillars and walls.   The pillars come out from
the process as good as new, — great, round, massive columns, not clustered like those of most
cathedrals; they are twenty-one feet in circum-
ference, and support semicircular arches.   I think
there are seven of these columns, on each side
of the nave, which did not impress me as very
spacious; and the dust and racket of the work-
people quite destroyed the effect which should
have been produced by the aisles and arches;
so that I hardly stopped to glance at this part,
though I saw some mural monuments and recumbent statues along the walls.

The choir is separated from the nave by the
usual screen, and now by a sail-cloth or something of that kind, drawn across, in order to

keep out the dust, while the repairs are going on. When the young woman conducted me hither, I was at once struck by the magnificent eastern window, the largest in England, which fills, or looks vast enough to fill, all that end of the cathedral, — a most splendid window, full of old painted glass, which looked as bright as sunshine, though the sun was not really shining through it. The roof of the choir is of oak and very fine, and as much as ninety feet high. There are chapels opening from the choir, and within them the monuments of the eminent people who built them, and of benefactors or prelates, or of those otherwise illustrious in their day. My recollection of what I saw here is very dim and confused; more so than I anticipated. I remember somewhere within the choir the tomb of Edward II. with his effigy upon the top of it, in a long robe, with a crown on his head, and a ball and sceptre in his hand; likewise a statue of Robert, son of the Conqueror, carved in Irish oak and painted. He lolls in an easy posture on his tomb, with one leg crossed lightly over the other, to denote that he was a Crusader. There are several monuments of mitred abbots who formerly presided over the cathedral. A Cavalier and his wife, with the dress of the period elaborately represented, lie side by side in excellent preservation; and it is remarkable that, though their noses are very

prominent, they have come down from the past
without any wear and tear. The date of the
Cavalier's death is 1637, and I think his statue
could not have been sculptured until after the
Restoration, else he and his dame would hardly
have come through Cromwell's time unscathed.
Here, as in all the other churches in England, Cromwell is said to have stabled his horses,
and broken the windows, and belabored the old
monuments.

There is one large and beautiful chapel, styled
the Lady's Chapel, which is, indeed, a church
by itself, being ninety feet long and comprising
everything that appertains to a place of worship.
Here, too, there are monuments, and on the
floor are many old bricks and tiles with inscriptions on them, or Gothic devices, and flat tombstones with coats of arms sculptured on them;
as, indeed, there are everywhere else, except in
the nave, where the new pavement has obliterated them. After viewing the choir and the
chapels, the young woman led me down into
the crypts below, where the dead persons who
are commemorated in the upper regions were
buried. The low ponderous pillars and arches
of these crypts are supposed to be older than
the upper portions of the building. They are
about as perfect, I suppose, as when new, but
very damp, dreary, and darksome; and the
arches intersect one another so intricately, that,

if the girl had deserted me, I might easily have
got lost there. These are chapels where masses
used to be said for the souls of the deceased;
and my guide said that a great many skulls and
bones had been dug up here. No doubt a vast
population has been deposited in the course of
a thousand years. I saw two white skulls, in a
niche, grinning, as skulls always do, though it
is impossible to see the joke. These crypts, or
crypts like these, are doubtless what Congreve
calls the "aisles and monumental caves of
Death," in that passage which Dr. Johnson admired so much. They are very singular, —
something like a dark shadow or dismal repetition of the upper church below ground.

Ascending from the crypts, we went next to
the cloisters, which are in a very perfect state,
and form an unbroken square about the green
grass-plot, enclosed within. Here also it is said
Cromwell stabled his horses; but if so, they
were remarkably quiet beasts, for tombstones,
which form the pavement, are not broken, nor
cracked, nor bear any hoof-marks. All around
the cloisters, too, the stone tracery that shuts
them in like a closed curtain, carefully drawn,
remains as it was in the days of the monks, insomuch that it is not easy to get a glimpse of
the green enclosure. Probably there used to be
painted glass in the larger apertures of this stonework; otherwise it is perfect. These cloisters

are very different from the free, open, and airy
ones of Salisbury; but they are more in accordance with our notions of monkish habits; and
even at this day, if I were a canon of Gloucester, I would put that dim ambulatory to a good
use.   The library is adjacent to the cloisters,
and I saw some rows of folios and quartos.   I
have nothing else to record about the cathedral,
though if I were to stay there a month, I suppose it might then begin to be understood.   It
is wicked to look at these solemn old churches
in a hurry.   By the bye, it was not built in a
hurry; but in full three hundred years, having
been begun in 1188 and only finished in 1498,
not a great many years before Papistry began to
go out of vogue in England.

From Gloucester I took the rail for Basing-
stoke before noon.   The first part of the journey was through an uncommonly beautiful tract
of country, hilly, but not wild; a tender and
graceful picturesqueness, — fine single trees and
clumps of trees, and sometimes wide woods, scattered over the landscape, and filling the nooks
of the hills with luxuriant foliage.   Old villages
scattered frequently along our track, looking
very peaceful, with the peace of past ages lingering about them; and a rich, rural verdure of
antique cultivation everywhere.   Old country-
seats — specimens of the old English hall or
manor-house — appeared on the hillsides, with

park-scenery surrounding the mansions; and
the gray churches rose in the midst of all the
little towns.   The beauty of English scenery
makes me desperate, it is so impossible to describe it, or in any way to record its impression,
and such a pity to leave it undescribed; and,
moreover, I always feel that I do not get from
it a hundredth or a millionth part of the enjoyment that there really is in it, hurrying past it
thus.   I was really glad when we rumbled into
a tunnel, piercing for a long distance through a
hill; and emerging on the other side, we found
ourselves in a comparatively level and uninteresting tract of country, which lasted till we
reached Southampton.   English scenery, to be
appreciated and to be reproduced with pen and
pencil, requires to be dwelt upon long, and to
be wrought out with the nicest touches. A coarse
and hasty brush is not the instrument for such
work.

July 6. — Monday, June 30th, was a warm
and beautiful day, and my wife and I took a
cab from Southampton and drove to Netley
Abbey, about three or four miles. The remains
of the Abbey stand in a sheltered place, but
within view of Southampton Water; and it is
a most picturesque and perfect ruin, all ivy-
grown, of course, and with great trees where
the pillars of the nave used to stand, and also

in the refectory and the cloister court ; and so
much soil on the summit of the broken walls,
that weeds flourish abundantly there, and grass
too ; and there was a wild rosebush, in full
bloom, as much as thirty or forty feet from
the ground. Sophia and I ascended a winding-
stair, leading up within a round tower, the steps
much footworn, — and, reaching the top, we
came forth at the height where a gallery had
formerly run round the church, in the thickness
of the wall. The upper portions of the edifice
were now chiefly thrown down ; but I followed
a footpath, on the top of the remaining wall,
quite to the western entrance of the church.
Since the time when the Abbey was taken from
the monks, it has been private property ; and
the possessor, in Henry VIII.'s days, or subse-
quently, built a residence for himself within its
precincts out of the old materials. This has
now entirely disappeared, all but some unsightly
old masonry, patched into the original walls.
Large portions of the ruin have been removed,
likewise, to be used as building materials elsewhere ; and this is the Abbey mentioned, I
think, by Dr. Watts, concerning which a Mr.
William Taylor had a dream while he was con-
templating pulling it down. He dreamed that
a part of it fell upon his head ; and, sure enough,
a piece of the wall did come down and crush
him. In the nave I saw a large mass of con-

glomerated stone that had fallen from the wall
between the nave and cloisters, and thought
that perhaps this was the very mass that killed
poor Mr. Taylor.

The ruins are extensive and very interesting;
but I have put off describing them too long, and
cannot make a distinct picture of them now.
Moreover, except to a spectator skilled in architecture, all ruined abbeys are pretty much alike.
As we came away, we noticed some women
making baskets at the entrance, and one of them
urged us to buy some of her handiwork; for that
she was the gypsy of Netley Abbey, and had
lived among the ruins these thirty years.   So I
bought one for a shilling.   She was a woman
with a prominent nose, and weather tanned, but
not very picturesque or striking.

On the 6th July we left the Villa, with our
enormous luggage, and took our departure from
Southampton by the noon train.   The main
street of Southampton, though it looks pretty
fresh and bright, must be really antique, there
being a great many projecting windows, in the
old-time style, and these make the vista of the
street very picturesque.   I have no doubt that
I missed seeing many things more interesting
than the few that I saw.   Our journey to London was without any remarkable incident, and
at the Waterloo station we found one of Mr.
Bennoch's clerks, under whose guidance we took

two cabs for the East Kent station at London Bridge, and there railed to Blackheath, where we arrived in the afternoon.

.   .   .   .

On Thursday I went into London by one of the morning trains, and wandered about all day, — visiting the Exhibition of the Royal Academy, and Westminster Abbey and St. Paul's, the two latter of which I have already written about in former journals. On Friday, Sophia, Julian, and I walked over the heath, and through the Park to Greenwich, and spent some hours in the Hospital. The painted hall struck me much more than at my first view of it ; it is very beautiful indeed, and the effect of its frescoed ceiling most rich and magnificent, the assemblage of glowing hues producing a general result of splendor. . . .

In the evening I went with Mr. and Mrs. —— to a conversazione at Mrs. Newton Crosland's, who lives on Blackheath. . . . I met with one person who interested me, — Mr. Bailey, the author of Festus ; and I was surprised to find myself already acquainted with him. It is the same Mr. Bailey whom I met a few months ago, when I first dined at Mr. ——'s, — a dark, handsome, rather picturesque-looking man, with a gray beard, and dark hair a little dimmed with gray. He is of quiet and very agreeable deportment, and I liked him and

believed in him. . . . There is sadness glooming out of him, but no unkindness nor asperity.
Mrs. Crosland's conversazione was enriched
with a supper, and terminated with a dance, in
which Mr. —— joined with heart and soul, but
Mrs. —— went to sleep in her chair, and I
would gladly have followed her example if I
could have found a chair to sit upon.   In the
course of the evening I had some talk with a
pale, nervous young lady, who has been a noted
spiritual medium.

Yesterday I went into town by the steamboat from Greenwich to London Bridge, with a
nephew of Mr. ——'s, and, calling at his place
of business, he procured us an order from his
wine merchants, by means of which we were
admitted into the wine vaults of the London
docks.   We there found parties, with an acquaintance who was going, with two French
gentlemen, into the vaults.   It is a good deal
like going down into a mine, each visitor being
provided with a lamp at the end of a stick; and
following the guide along dismal passages, running beneath the streets and extending away
interminably, — roughly arched overhead with
stone, from which depend festoons of a sort of
black fungus, caused by the exhalations of the
wine.   Nothing was ever uglier than this fungus.
It is strange that the most ethereal effervescence
of rich wine can produce nothing better.

The first series of vaults which we entered were filled with port wine, and occupied a space variously estimated at from eleven to sixteen acres, — which I suppose would hold more port wine than ever was made.   At any rate, the pipes and butts were so thickly piled that in some places we could hardly squeeze past them. We drank from two or three vintages; but I was not impressed with any especial excellence in the wine.   We were not the only visitors, for, far in the depths of the vault, we passed a gentleman and two young ladies, wandering about like the ghosts of defunct winebibbers in a Tophet specially prepared for them.   People employed here sometimes go astray, and, their lamps being extinguished, they remain long in this everlasting gloom.   We went likewise to the vaults of sherry wine, which have the same characteristics as those just described, but are less extensive.

It is no guaranty for the excellence or even for the purity of the wine, that it is kept in these cellars, under the lock and key of the government; for the merchants are allowed to mix different vintages, according to their own pleasure, and to adulterate it as they like.   Very little of the wine probably comes out as it goes in, or is exactly what it pretends to be.   I went back to Mr. ——'s office, and we drove together to make some calls jointly and separately.   I went alone to Mrs. Heywood's; afterwards with Mr. —— to the American minister's, whom we found at home; and I requested of him, on the part of the Americans at Liverpool, to tell me the facts about the American gentleman being refused admittance to the Levee. The ambassador did not seem to me to make his point good for having withdrawn with the rejected guest.

. . . .

July 9. (Our wedding-day.) — We were invited yesterday evening to Mrs. S. C. Hall's, where Jenny Lind was to sing; so we left Blackheath at about eight o'clock in a brougham, and reached Ashley Place as the dusk was gathering, after nine. The Halls reside in a handsome suite of apartments, arranged on the new system of flats, each story constituting a separate tenement, and the various families having an entrance hall in common. The plan is borrowed from the Continent, and seems rather alien to the traditionary habits of the English; though, no doubt, a good degree of seclusion is compatible with it. Mr. Hall received us with the greatest cordiality before we entered the drawing-room. Mrs. Hall, too, greeted us with most kindly warmth. Jenny Lind had not yet arrived; but I found Dr. Mackay there, and I was introduced to Miss Catherine Sinclair, who is a literary lady, though none of her works happen to be known to me. Soon the servant announced Madam Goldschmidt, and this famous lady made her appearance, looking quite different from what I expected. Mrs. Hall established her in the inner drawing-room, where was a piano and a harp; and shortly after, our hostess came to me, and said that Madam Goldschmidt wished to be introduced to me. There was a gentle peremptoriness in the summons, that made it something like being commanded into the presence of a princess; a great favor, no doubt, but yet a little humbling to the recipient. However, I acquiesced with due gratitude, and was presented accordingly. She made room for me on the sofa, and I sat down, and began to talk.

Jenny Lind is rather tall, — quite tall, for a woman, — certainly no beauty, but with sense and self-reliance in her aspect and manners. She was suffering under a severe cold, and seemed worn down besides, so probably I saw her under disadvantages. Her conversation is quite simple, and I should have great faith in her sincerity; and there is about her the manner of a person who knows the world, and has conquered it. She said something or other about The Scarlet Letter; and, on my part, I paid her such compliments as a man could pay who had never heard her sing. . . . Her conversational voice is an agreeable one, rather deep, and not particularly smooth.   She talked about America, and of our unwholesome modes of life, as to eating and exercise, and of the ill health especially of our women ; but I opposed this view as far as I could with any truth, insinuating my opinion that we are about as healthy as other people, and affirming for a certainty that we live longer. In good faith, so far as I have any knowledge of the matter, the women of England are as generally out of health as those of America; always something has gone wrong with them ; and as for Jenny Lind, she looks wan and worn enough to be an American herself. This charge of ill health is almost universally brought forward against us nowadays, — and, taking the whole country together, I do not believe the statistics will bear it out.

. . . .

The rooms, which were respectably filled when we arrived, were now getting quite full.   I saw Mr. Stevens, the American man of libraries, and had some talk with him ; and Durham the sculptor ; and Mr. and Mrs. Hall introduced me to various people, some of whom were of note, — for instance, Sir Emerson Tennent, a man of the world, of some parliamentary distinction, wearing a star ; Mr. Samuel Lover, a most good-natured, pleasant Irishman, with a shining and twinkling visage ; Miss Jewsbury, whom I found very conversable.   She is known in literature, but not to me. We talked about Emerson, whom she seems to have been well acquainted with while he was in England; and she mentioned that Miss Martineau had given him a lock of hair; it was not her own hair, but a mummy's.

After our return, Mrs. —— told us that Miss Jewsbury had written, among other things, three histories, and as she asked me to introduce her to Sophia, and means to cultivate our acquaintance, it would be well to know something of them. We were told that she is now employed in some literary undertaking of Lady Morgan's, who, at the age of ninety, is still circulating in society, and is as brisk in faculties as ever. I should like to see her ladyship, that is, I should not be sorry to see her; for distinguished people are so much on a par with others socially, that it would be foolish to be overjoyed at seeing anybody whomsoever.

Leaving out the illustrious Jenny Lind, I suspect that I was myself the greatest lion of the evening; for a good many persons sought the felicity of knowing me, and had little or nothing to say when that honor and happiness was conferred on them. It is surely very wrong and ill mannered in people to ask for an introduction unless they are prepared to make talk; it throws too great an expense and trouble on the wretched lion, who is compelled, on the spur of the mo-

ment, to convert a conversable substance out of
thin air, perhaps for the twentieth time that
evening.   I am sure I did not say — and I think
I did not hear said — one rememberable word
in the course of this visit; though nevertheless
it was a rather agreeable one.   In due season
ices and jellies were handed about; and some
ladies and gentlemen — professional, perhaps —
were kind enough to sing songs, and play on
the piano and harp, while persons in remote corners went on with whatever conversation they
had in hand.   Then came supper; but there
were so many people to go into the supper-room
that we could not all crowd thither together, and,
coming late, I got nothing but some sponge-
cake and a glass of champagne, neither of which
I care for.   After supper, Mr. Lover sang some
Irish songs, his own in music and words, with
rich humorous effect to which the comicality of
his face contributed almost as much as his voice
and words.   The Lord Mayor looked in for
a little while, and, though a hard-featured Jew
enough, was the most picturesque person there.

July 12. — Mrs. Heywood had invited me
to dinner last evening. . . . Her house is very
finely situated, overlooking Hyde Park, and not
a great way from where Tyburn tree used to
stand.   When I arrived there were no guests
but Mr. and Mrs. D——, but by and by came

Mr. Monckton Milnes and a lady, the Bishop of
Lichfield, Mr. Tom Taylor, Mr. Ewart, M. P.,
Sir Somebody Somerville, Mr. and Mrs. Musgrave, and others.   Mr. Milnes, whom I had
not seen for more than a year, greeted me very
cordially, and so did Mr. Taylor.   I took Mrs.
Musgrave in to dinner.   She is an Irish lady,
and Mrs. Heywood had recommended her to
me as being very conversable ; but I had a good
deal more talk with Mrs. M——, with whom
I was already acquainted, than with her.   Mrs.
M—— is of noble blood, and therefore not
snobbish, — quite unaffected, gentle, sweet, and
easy to get on with, reminding me of the best-
mannered American women.   But how can anything characteristic be said or done among a
dozen people sitting at table in full dress ?
Speaking of full dress, the Bishop wore small-
clothes and silk stockings, and entered the drawing-room with a three-cornered hat, which he
kept flattened out under his arm.   He asked
the briefest blessing possible, and, sitting at the
ultra end of the table, I heard nothing further
from him till he officiated as briefly before the
cloth was withdrawn.   Mrs. M—— talked
about Tennyson, with whom her husband was
at the University, and whom he continues to
know intimately.   She says that he considers
Maud his best poem.   He now lives in the
Isle of Wight, spending all the year round there,

and has recently bought the place on which he resides. She was of opinion that he would have been gratified by my calling on him, which I had wished to do while we were at Southampton ; but this is a liberty which I should hardly venture upon with a shy man like Tennyson, — more especially as he might perhaps suspect me of doing it on the score of my own literary character. But I should like much to see him. . . . Mr. Tom Taylor, during dinner, made some fun for the benefit of the ladies on either side of him. I liked him very well this evening.

.   .   .   .

When the ladies had not long withdrawn, and after the wine had once gone round, I asked Mr. Heywood to make my apologies to Mrs. Heywood, and took leave ; all London lying betwixt me and the London Bridge station, where I was to take the rail homeward. At the station I found Mr. Bennoch, who had been dining with the Lord Mayor to meet Sir William Williams, and we railed to Greenwich, and reached home by midnight. Mr. and Mrs. Bennoch have set out on their Continental Journey to-day, — leaving us, for a little space, in possession of what will be more like a home than anything that we shall hereafter find in England.

This afternoon I had taken up the fourth volume of Jerdan's Autobiography, — wretched twaddle, though it records such constant and apparently intimate intercourse with distinguished people, — and was reading it, between asleep and awake, on the sofa, when Mr. Jerdan himself was announced. I saw him in company with Mr. Bennoch, nearly three years ago, at Rock Park, and wondered then what there was in so uncouth an individual to get him so freely into polished society. He now looks rougher than ever, — time-worn, but not reverend ; a thatch of gray hair on his head ; an imperfect set of false teeth ; a careless apparel, checked trousers, and a stick, for he had walked a mile or two from his own dwelling.

I suspect — and long practice at the Consulate has made me keen sighted — that Mr. Jerdan contemplated some benefit from my purse ; and, to the extent of a sovereign or so, I would not mind contributing to his comfort. He spoke of a secret purpose of Mr. —— and himself to obtain me a degree or diploma in some Literary Institution, — what one I know not, and did not ask ; but the honor cannot be a high one, if this poor old fellow can do aught towards it. I am afraid he is a very disreputable senior, but certainly not the less to be pitied on that account ; and there was something very touching in his stiff and infirm movement, as he resumed his stick and took leave, waving me a courteous farewell, and turning upon me a smile, grim with age, as he went down the

steps. In that gesture and smile I fancied some
trace of the polished man of society, such as he
may have once been; though time and hard
weather have roughened him, as they have the
once polished marble pillars which I saw so
rude in aspect at Netley Abbey.

Speaking of Dickens last evening, Mr. ——
mentioned his domestic tastes, — how he pre-
ferred home enjoyments to all others, and did
not willingly go much into society. Mrs. ——,
too, the other day told us of his taking on himself all possible trouble as regards his domestic
affairs. . . . There is a great variety of testimony, various and varied, as to the character of
Dickens. I must see him before I finally leave
England.

July 13. — On Friday morning (11th), at
nine o'clock, I took the rail into town to breakfast with Mr. Milnes. As he had named a
little after ten as the hour, I could not immediately proceed to his house, and so walked
moderately over London Bridge and into the
city, meaning to take a cab from Charing Cross,
or thereabouts. Passing through some street
or other, contiguous to Cheapside, I saw in a
courtyard the entrance to the Guildhall, and
stepped in to look at it. It is a spacious hall,
about one hundred and fifty feet long and perhaps half as broad, paved with flagstones which

look worn and some of them cracked across;
the roof is very lofty and was once vaulted, but
has been shaped anew in modern times.   There
is a vast window partly filled with painted glass,
extending quite along each end of the hall, and
a row of arched windows on either side, throwing their light from far above downward upon
the pavement.   This fashion of high windows,
not reaching within twenty or thirty feet of the
floor, serves to give great effect to the large enclosed space of an antique hall.   Against the
walls are several marble monuments; one to
the Earl of Chatham, a statue of white marble,
with various allegorical contrivances, fronting an
obelisk or pyramid of dark marble; and another
to his son, William Pitt, of somewhat similar
design and of equal size; each of them occupying the whole space, I believe, between pavement and ceiling.   There is likewise a statue of
Beckford, a famous Lord Mayor, — the most
famous except Whittington, and that one who
killed Wat Tyler; and like those two, his fame
is perhaps somewhat mythological, though he
lived and bustled within less than a century.
He is said to have made a bold speech to the
King; but this I will not believe of any Englishman — at least, of any plebeian Englishman
— until I hear it.   But there stands his statue
in the Guildhall in the act of making his speech,
as if the monstrous attempt had petrified him.

Lord Nelson, too, has a monument, and so, I think, has some other modern worthy. At one end of the hall, under one of the great painted windows, stand three or four old statues of mediæval kings, whose identities I forget; and in the two corners of the opposite end are two gigantic absurdities of painted wood, with grotesque visages, whom I quickly recognized as Gog and Magog. They stand each on a pillar, and seem to be about fifteen feet high, and look like enormous playthings for the children of giants; and it is strange to see them in this solemn old hall, among the memorials of dead heroes and statesmen. There is an annual banquet in the Guildhall, given by the Lord Mayor and sheriffs, and I believe it is the very acme of civic feasting.

After viewing the hall, as it still lacked something of ten, I continued my walk through that entanglement of city streets, and quickly found myself getting beyond my reckoning. I cannot tell whither I went, but I passed through a very dirty region, and I remember a long, narrow, evil-odored street, cluttered up with stalls, in which were vegetables and little bits of meat for sale; and there was a frowzy multitude of buyers and sellers. Still I blundered on, and was getting out of the density of the city into broader streets, but still shabby ones, when, looking at my watch, I found it to be past ten, and

no cab-stand within sight. It was a quarter
past when I finally got into one; and the driver
told me that it would take half an hour to go
from thence to Upper Brook Street; so that I
was likely to exceed the license implied in Mr.
Milnes's invitation.   Whether I was quite beyond rule I cannot say; but it did not lack
more than ten minutes of eleven when I was
ushered upstairs, and I found all the company
assembled.   However, it is of little consequence, except that if I had come early, I
should have been introduced to many of the
guests whom now I could only know across
the table.   Mrs. Milnes greeted me very kindly,
and Mr. Milnes came towards me with an
elderly gentleman in a blue coat and gray pantaloons, — with a long, rather thin, homely visage, exceedingly shaggy eyebrows, though no
great weight of brow, and thin gray hair, and
introduced me to the Marquis of Lansdowne.
The Marquis had his right hand wrapped up
in a black silk handkerchief; so he gave me his
left, and, from some awkwardness in meeting
it, when I expected the right, I gave him only
three of my fingers, — a thing I never did before to any person, and it is droll that I should
have done it to a Marquis.   He addressed me
with great simplicity and natural kindness, com-
plimenting me on my works, and speaking
about the society of Liverpool in former days.

Lord Lansdowne was the friend of Moore, and has about him the aroma communicated by the memories of many illustrious people with whom he has associated.

Mr. Ticknor, the Historian of Spanish Literature, now greeted me. Mr. Milnes introduced me to Mrs. Browning, and assigned her to me to conduct into the breakfast-room. She is a small, delicate woman, with ringlets of dark hair, a pleasant, intelligent, and sensitive face, and a low, agreeable voice. She looks youthful and comely, and is very gentle and lady-like. And so we proceeded to the breakfast-room, which is hung round with pictures; and in the middle of it stood a large round table, worthy to have been King Arthur's, and here we seated ourselves without any question of precedence or ceremony. On one side of me was an elderly lady, with a very fine countenance, and in the course of breakfast I discovered her to be the mother of Florence Nightingale. One of her daughters (not Florence) was likewise present. Mrs. Milnes, Mrs. Browning, Mrs. Nightingale, and her daughter were the only ladies at table; and I think there were as many as eight or ten gentlemen, whose names — as I came so late — I was left to find out for myself, or to leave unknown.

It was a pleasant and sociable meal, and, thanks to my cold beef and coffee at home, I had no occasion to trouble myself much about the fare; so I just ate some delicate chicken, and a very small cutlet, and a slice of dry toast, and thereupon surceased from my labors. Mrs. Browning and I talked a good deal during breakfast, for she is of that quickly appreciative and responsive order of women with whom I can talk more freely than with any man; and she has, besides, her own originality, wherewith to help on conversation, though, I should say, not of a loquacious tendency. She introduced the subject of spiritualism, which, she says, interests her very much; indeed, she seems to be a believer. Mr. Browning, she told me, utterly rejects the subject, and will not believe even in the outward manifestations, of which there is such overwhelming evidence. We also talked of Miss Bacon; and I developed something of that lady's theory respecting Shakespeare, greatly to the horror of Mrs. Browning, and that of her next neighbor, — a nobleman, whose name I did not hear. On the whole, I like her the better for loving the man Shakespeare with a personal love. We talked, too, of Margaret Fuller, who spent her last night in Italy with the Brownings; and of William Story, with whom they have been intimate, and who, Mrs. Browning says, is much stirred about spiritualism. Really, I cannot help wondering that so fine a spirit as hers should not reject the matter.

till, at least, it is forced upon her. I like her very much.

Mrs. Nightingale had been talking at first with Lord Lansdowne, who sat next her, but by and by she turned to me, and began to speak of London smoke. . . . Then, there being a discussion about Lord Byron on the other side of the table, she spoke to me about Lady Byron, whom she knows intimately, characterizing her as a most excellent and exemplary person, high principled, unselfish, and now devoting herself to the care of her two grandchildren, — their mother, Byron's daughter, being dead. Lady Byron, she says, writes beautiful verses. Somehow or other, all this praise, and more of the same kind, gave me an idea of an intolerably irreproachable person ; and I asked Mrs. Nightingale if Lady Byron were warm hearted. With some hesitation, or mental reservation, — at all events, not quite outspokenly, — she answered that she was.

I was too much engaged with these personal talks to attend much to what was going on elsewhere ; but all through breakfast I had been more and more impressed by the aspect of one of the guests, sitting next to Milnes. He was a man of large presence, — a portly personage, gray haired, but scarcely as yet aged ; and his face had a remarkable intelligence, not vivid nor sparkling, but conjoined with great quietude, — and if it gleamed or brightened at one time more than another, it was like the sheen over a broad surface of sea. There was a somewhat careless self-possession, large and broad enough to be called dignity; and the more I looked at him, the more I knew that he was a distinguished person, and wondered who. He might have been a minister of state; only there is not one of them who has any right to such a face and presence. At last, — I do not know how the conviction came, — but I became aware that it was Macaulay, and began to see some slight resemblance to his portraits. But I have never seen any that is not wretchedly unworthy of the original. As soon as I knew him, I began to listen to his conversation, but he did not talk a great deal, — contrary to his usual custom; for I am told he is apt to engross all the talk to himself. Probably he may have been restrained by the presence of Ticknor and Mr. Palfrey, who were among his auditors and interlocutors; and as the conversation seemed to turn much on American subjects, he could not well have assumed to talk them down. I am glad to have seen him, — a face fit for a scholar, a man of the world, a cultivated intelligence.

After we left the table, and went into the library, Mr. Browning introduced himself to me, — a younger man than I expected to see, handsome, with brown hair. He is very simple and agreeable in manner, gently impulsive, talking as if his heart were uppermost. He spoke of his pleasure in meeting me, and his appreciation of my books; and — which has not often happened to me — mentioned that The Blithedale Romance was the one he admired most. I wonder why. I hope I showed as much pleasure at his praise as he did at mine; for I was glad to see how pleasantly it moved him. After this I talked with Ticknor and Milnes, and with Mr. Palfrey, to whom I had been introduced very long ago by George Hillard, and had never seen him since. We looked at some autographs, of which Mr. Milnes has two or three large volumes. I recollect a leaf from Swift's Journal to Stella; a letter from Addison; one from Chatterton, in a most neat and legible hand; and a characteristic sentence or two and signature of Oliver Cromwell, written in a religious book. There were many curious volumes in the library, but I had not time to look at them.

I liked greatly the manners of almost all, — yes, as far as I observed, all the people at this breakfast, and it was doubtless owing to their being all people either of high rank or remarkable intellect, or both. An Englishman can hardly be a gentleman, unless he enjoy one or other of these advantages; and perhaps the surest way to give him good manners is to make a lord of him, or rather of his grandfather or great-grandfather. In the third generation, scarcely sooner, he will be polished into simplicity and elegance, and his deportment will be all the better for the homely material out of which it is wrought and refined. The Marquis of Lansdowne, for instance, would have been a very commonplace man in the common ranks of life; but it has done him good to be a nobleman. Not that his tact is quite perfect. In going up to breakfast, he made me precede him; in returning to the library, he did the same, although I drew back, till he impelled me up the first stair, with gentle persistence. By insisting upon it, he showed his sense of condescension much more than if, when he saw me unwilling to take precedence, he had passed forward, as if the point were not worth either asserting or yielding. Heaven knows, it was in no humility that I would have trodden behind him. But he is a kind old man; and I am willing to believe of the English aristocracy generally that they are kind, and of beautiful deportment; for certainly there never can have been mortals in a position more advantageous for becoming so. I hope there will come a time when we shall be so; and I already know a few Americans, whose noble and delicate manners may compare well with any I have seen.

I left the house with Mr. Palfrey. He has come to England to make some researches in the State Paper Office, for the purposes of a work which he has in hand. He mentioned to me a letter which he had seen, written from New England in the time of Charles II. and referring to the order sent by the minister of that day for the appearance of Governor Bellingham and my ancestor on this side of the water. The signature of this letter is an anagram of my ancestor's name. The letter itself is a very bold and able one, controverting the propriety of the measure above indicated; and Mr. Palfrey feels certain that it was written by my aforesaid ancestor. I mentioned my wish to ascertain the place in England whence the family emigrated; and Mr. Palfrey took me to the Record Office, and introduced me to Mr. Joseph Hunter, — a venerable and courteous gentleman, of antiquarian pursuits. The office was odorous of musty parchments, hundreds of years old. Mr. Hunter received me with great kindness, and gave me various old records and rolls of parchment, in which to seek for my family name; but I was perplexed with the crabbed characters, and soon grew weary and gave up the quest. He says that it is very seldom that an American family, springing from the early settlers, can be satisfactorily traced back to their English ancestry.

July 16. — Monday morning I took the rail

from Blackheath to London. It is a very pleasant place, Blackheath, and far more rural than
one would expect, within five or six miles of
London, — a great many trees, making quite a
mass of foliage in the distance; green enclos-
ures; pretty villas, with their nicely kept lawns,
and gardens, with grass-plots and flower borders;
and village streets, set along the sidewalks with
ornamental trees; and the houses standing a
little back, and separated one from another, —
all this within what is called the Park, which has
its gateways, and the sort of semi-privacy with
which I first became acquainted at Rock Park.

.   .   .   .

From the London Bridge station I took a cab
for Paddington, and then had to wait above two
hours before a train started for Birkenhead.
Meanwhile I walked a little about the neighborhood, which is very dull and uninteresting; made
up of crescents and terraces, and rows of houses
that have no individuality, and second-rate shops,
— in short, the outskirts of the vast city, when
it begins to have a kind of village character but
no rurality or sylvan aspect, as at Blackheath.
My journey, when at last we started, was quite
unmarked by incident, and extremely tedious;
it being a slow train, which plods on without
haste and without rest. At about ten o'clock
we reached Birkenhead, and there crossed the
familiar and detestable Mersey, which, as usual,

had a cloudy sky brooding over it. Mrs. Blodgett received me most hospitably, but was impelled, by an overflow of guests, to put me into
a little back room, looking into the court, and
formerly occupied by my predecessor, General
Armstrong. . . . She expressed a hope that I
might not see his ghost, — nor have I, as yet.

Speaking of ghosts, Mr. H. A. B—— told
me a singular story to-day of an apparition that
haunts the Times Office, in Printing-House
Square. A Mr. W—— is the engineer of the
establishment, and has his residence in the edifice, which is built, I believe, on the site of
Merchant Taylor's school, — an old house that
was no longer occupied for its original purpose,
and, being supposed haunted, was left unten-
anted. The father-in-law of Mr. W——, an
old sea captain, came on a visit to him and his
wife, and was put into their guest-chamber,
where he passed the night. The next morning,
assigning no very satisfactory reason, he cut his
visit short and went away. Shortly afterwards,
a young lady came to visit the W——'s; but
she too went away the next morning, — going
first to make a call, as she said, to a friend, and
sending thence for her trunks. Mrs. W——
wrote to this young lady, asking an explanation.
The young lady replied, and gave a singular
account of an apparition, — how she was awakened in the night by a bright light shining

through the window which was parallel to the bed ; then, if I remember rightly, her curtains were withdrawn, and a shape looked in upon her, — a woman's shape, she called it ; but it was a skeleton, with lambent flames playing about its bones, and in and out among the ribs. Other persons have since slept in this chamber, and some have seen the shape, others not. Mr. W—— has slept there himself without seeing anything. He has had investigations by scientific people, apparently under the idea that the phenomenon might have been caused by some of the Times work-people, playing tricks on the magic-lantern principle ; but nothing satisfactory has thus far been elucidated. Mr. B—— had this story from Mrs. Gaskell. . . . Supposing it a ghost, nothing else is so remarkable as its choosing to haunt the precincts of the Times newspaper.

July 29. — On Saturday, 26th, I took the rail from the Lime Street station for London, via the Trent Valley, and reached Blackheath in the evening. . . .

Sunday morning my wife and I, with Julian, railed into London, and drove to the Essex Street Chapel, where Mr. Channing was to preach. The Chapel is the same where Priestley and Belsham used to preach, — one of the plainest houses of worship I was ever in, as

simple and undecorated as the faith there incul-
cated.   They retain, however, all the form and
ceremonial of the English Established Church,
though so modified as to meet the doctrinal
views of the Unitarians.   There may be good
sense in this, inasmuch as it greatly lessens the
ministerial labor to have a stated form of prayer,
instead of a necessity for extempore outpour-
ings ; but it must be, I should think, excessively tedious to the congregation, especially
as, having made alterations in these prayers,
they cannot attach much idea of sanctity to
them.

[Here follows a long record of Mr. Hawthorne's visit to Miss Bacon, — condensed in
Our Old Home, in the paper called Recollec-
tions of a Gifted Woman.]

August 2. — On Wednesday (30th July) we
went to Marlborough House to see the Vernon
gallery of pictures.   They are the works, almost
entirely, of English artists of the last and present century, and comprise many famous paintings ; and I must acknowledge that I had more
enjoyment of them than of those portions of
the National Gallery which I had before seen,
— including specimens of the grand old masters.   My comprehension has not reached their
height.   I think nothing pleased me more than
a picture by Sir David Wilkie, — The Parish

Beadle, with a vagrant boy and a monkey in custody ; it is exceedingly good and true throughout, and especially the monkey's face is a wonderful production of genius, condensing within itself the whole moral and pathos of the picture.

Marlborough House was the residence of the Great Duke, and is to be that of the Prince of Wales, when another place is found for the pictures.   It adjoins St. James's Palace.   In its present state it is not a very splendid mansion, the rooms being small, though handsomely shaped, with vaulted ceilings and carved white marble fireplaces.   I left Sophia here after an hour or two, and walked forth into the hot and busy city with Julian. . . . I called at Routledge's book shop, in hopes to make an arrangement with him about Miss Bacon's business. But Routledge himself is making a journey in the north, and neither of the partners was there, so that I shall have to go thither some other day.   Then we stepped into St. Paul's Cathedral to cool ourselves, and it was delightful so to escape from the sunny, sultry turmoil of Fleet Street and Ludgate, and find ourselves at once in this remote, solemn, shadowy seclusion, marble-cool.   O that we had cathedrals in America, were it only for the sensuous luxury ! We strolled round the cathedral, and I delighted Julian much by pointing out the monuments of three British generals, who were slain in America in the last war, — the naughty and bloodthirsty little man! We then went to Guildhall, where I thought Julian would like to see Gog and Magog; but he had never heard of those illustrious personages, and took no interest in them. . . . But truly I am grateful to the piety of former times for raising this vast, cool canopy of marble [St. Paul's] in the midst of the feverish city. I wandered quite round it, and saw, in a remote corner, a monument to the officers of the Coldstream Guards, slain in the Crimea. It was a mural tablet, with the names of the officers on an escutcheon; and two privates of the Guards, in marble bas-relief, were mourning over them. Over the tablet hung two silken banners, new and glossy, with the battles in which the regiment has been engaged inscribed on them, — not merely Crimean but Peninsular battles. These banners will hang there till they drop away in tatters.

After thus refreshing myself in the cathedral, I went again to Routledge's in Farringdon Street, and saw one of the firm. He expressed great pleasure at seeing me, as indeed he might, having published and sold, without any profit on my part, uncounted thousands of my books. I introduced the subject of Miss Bacon's work; and he expressed the utmost willingness to do everything in his power towards bringing it before the world, but thought that his firm — it being their business to publish for the largest circle of readers — was not the most eligible for the publication of such a book. Very likely this may be so. At all events, however, I am to send him the manuscript, and he will at least give me his advice and assistance in finding a publisher. He was good enough to express great regret that I had no work of my own to give him for publication; and, truly, I regret it too, since, being a resident in England, I could now have all the publishing privileges of a native author. He presented me with a copy of an illustrated edition of Longfellow's Poems, and I took my leave.

Thence I went to the Picture Gallery at the British Institution, where there are three rooms full of paintings by the first masters, the property of private persons. Every one of them, no doubt, was worth studying for a long, long time; and I suppose I may have given, on an average, a minute to each. What an absurdity it would seem, to pretend to read two or three hundred poems, of all degrees between an epic and a ballad, in an hour or two! And a picture is a poem, only requiring the greater study to be felt and comprehended; because the spectator must necessarily do much for himself towards that end. I saw many beautiful things, — among them some landscapes by Claude, which to the eye were like the flavor of a rich, ripe melon to the palate.

.   .   .   .

August 7. — Yesterday we took the rail for London, it being a fine, sunny day, though not so very warm as many of the preceding days have been. . . . We went along Piccadilly as far as the Egyptian Hall. It is quite remarkable how comparatively quiet the town has become, now that the season is over. One can see the difference in all the region west of Temple Bar; and indeed, either the hot weather or some other cause seems to have operated in assuaging the turmoil in the city itself. I never saw London Bridge so little thronged as yesterday. At the Egyptian Hall, or in the same edifice, there is a gallery of pictures, the property of Lord Ward, who allows the public to see them, five days of the week, without any trouble or restriction, — a great kindness on his Lordship's part, it must be owned. It is a very valuable collection, I presume, containing specimens of many famous old masters; some of the early and hard pictures by Raphael, and his master and fellow pupils, — very curious, and nowise beautiful; a perfect, sunny glimpse of Venice, by Canaletto; and saints, and Scriptural, allegorical, and mythological people, by Titian, Guido, Correggio, and many more names than I can remember. There is likewise a dead Magdalen by Canova, and a Venus by the same, very pretty, and with a vivid light of joyous expression in her face ; . . . also Powers's Greek Slave, in which I see little beauty or merit; and two or three other statues.

.   .   .   .

We then drove to Ashley Place, to call on Mrs. S. C. Hall, whom we found at home. In fact, Wednesday is her reception-day ; although, as now everybody is out of town, we were the only callers. She is an agreeable and kindly woman. She told us that her husband and herself propose going to America next year, and I heartily wish they may meet with a warm and friendly reception. I have been seldom more assured of the existence of a heart than in her ; also a good deal of sentiment. She had been visiting Bessie, the widow of Moore, at Sloperton, and gave Sophia a rose from his cottage. Such things are very true and unaffected in her. The only wonder is that she has not lost such girlish freshness of feeling as prompts them. We did not see Mr. Hall, he having gone to the Crystal Palace.

Taking our leave, we returned along Victoria Street — a new street, penetrating through what was recently one of the worst parts of the town, and now bordered with large blocks of buildings, in a dreary, half-finished state, and left so for want of funds — till we came to Westminster Abbey. We went in and spent an hour there, wandering all round the nave and aisles, admiring the grand old edifice itself, but finding more to smile at than to admire in the monuments. . . . The interior view of the Abbey is better than can be described; the heart aches, as one gazes at it, for lack of power and breadth enough to take its beauty and grandeur in. The effect was heightened by the sun shining through the painted window in the western end, and by the bright sunshine that came through the open portal, and lay on the pavement, — that space so bright, the rest of the vast floor so solemn and sombre. At the western end, in a corner from which spectators are barred out, there is a statue of Wordsworth, which I do not recollect seeing at any former visit. Its only companion in the same nook is Pope's friend, Secretary Craggs.

Downing Street, that famous official precinct, took its name from Sir George Downing, who was proprietor or lessee of property there. He was a native of my own old native town, and his descendants still reside there, — collateral descendants, I suppose, — and follow the dry-goods business (drapers).

August 10. — I journeyed to Liverpool via

Chester. . . . One sees a variety of climate, temperature, and season in a ride of two hundred miles, north and south, through England. Near London, for instance, the grain was reaped, and stood in sheaves in the stubble-fields, over which girls and children might be seen gleaning; farther north the golden, or greenish - golden, crops were waving in the wind. In one part of our way the atmosphere was hot and dry; at another point it had been cooled and refreshed by a heavy thunder-shower, the pools of which still lay along our track. It seems to me that local varieties of weather are more common in this island, and within narrower precincts, than in America. . . . I never saw England of such a dusky and dusty green before, — almost sunbrowned, indeed. Sometimes the green hedges formed a marked framework to a broad sheet of golden grain-field. As we drew near Oxford, just before reaching the station I had a good view of its domes, towers, and spires, — better, I think, than when Julian and I rambled through the town a month or two ago.

Mr. Frank Scott Haydon, of the Record Office, London, writes me that he has found a " Henry Atte Hawthorne," on a roll which he is transcribing, of the first Edward III. He belonged to the parish of Aldremeston, in the hundred of Blakenhurste, Worcester County.

August 21. — Yesterday, at twelve o'clock, I took the steamer for Runcorn, from the pier-head. In the streets I had noticed that it was a breezy day; but on the river there was a very stiff breeze from the northeast, right ahead, blowing directly in our face the whole way; and truly this river Mersey is never without a breeze, and generally in the direction of its course, — an evil-tempered, unkindly, blustering wind, that you cannot meet without being exasperated by it. As it came straight against us, it was impossible to find a shelter anywhere on deck, except it were behind the stove-pipe; and, besides, the day was overcast and threatening rain. I have undergone very miserable hours on the Mersey, where, in the space of two years, I voyaged thousands of miles, — and this trip to Runcorn reminded me of them, though it was less disagreeable after more than a twelvemonth's respite. We had a good many passengers on board, most of whom were of the second class, and congregated on the forward deck; more women than men, I think, and some of them with their husbands and children. Several produced lunch and bottles, and refreshed themselves very soon after we started. By and by the wind became so disagreeable that I went below, and sat in the cabin, only occasionally looking out, to get a peep at the shores of the river, which I had never before seen above

Eastham.   However, they are not worth looking at; level and monotonous, without trees or
beauty of any kind, — here and there a village,
and a modern church, on the low ridge behind;
perhaps a windmill, which the gusty day had
set busily to work.   The river continues very
wide — no river, indeed, but an estuary — during almost the whole distance to Runcorn; and
nearly at the end of our voyage we approached
some abrupt and prominent hills, which, many
a time, I have seen on my passages to Rock
Ferry, looking blue and dim, and serving for
prophets of the weather; for when they can be
distinctly seen adown the river, it is a token of
coming rain.   We met many vessels, and passed
many which were beating up against the wind,
and which keeled over, so that their decks must
have dipped, — schooners and vessels that come
from the Bridgewater Canal.   We shipped a sea
ourselves, which gave the fore-deck passengers
a wetting.

Before reaching Runcorn we stopped to land
some passengers at another little port, where
there was a pier and a lighthouse, and a church
within a few yards of the river-side, — a good
many of the river-craft, too, in dock, forming
quite a crowd of masts.   About ten minutes'
further steaming brought us to Runcorn, where
were two or three tall manufacturing chimneys,
with a pennant of black smoke from each; two

vessels of considerable size on the stocks; a church or two; and a meagre, uninteresting, shabby, brick-built town, rising from the edge of the river, with irregular streets, — not village-like, but paved, and looking like a dwarfed, stunted city.   I wandered through it till I came to a tall, high-pedestalled windmill on the outer verge, the vans of which were going briskly round.   Thence retracing my steps, I stopped at a poor hotel and took lunch, and, finding that I was in time to take the steamer back, I hurried on board, and we set sail (or steam) before three.   I have heard of an old castle at Runcorn, but could discover nothing of it.   It was well that I returned so promptly, for we had hardly left the pier before it began to rain, and there was a heavy downfall throughout the voyage homeward.   Runcorn is fourteen miles from Liverpool, and is the farthest point to which a steamer runs.   I had intended to come home by rail, — a circuitous route, — but the advice of the landlady of the hotel, and the aspect of the weather, and a feeling of general discouragement, prevented me.

An incident in S. C. Hall's Ireland, of a stone cross, buried in Cromwell's time, to prevent its destruction by his soldiers.   It was forgotten, and became a mere doubtful tradition, but one old man had been told by his father,

and he by his father, etc., that it was buried
near a certain spot; and at last, two hundred
years after the cross was buried, the vicar of the
parish dug in that spot and found it. In my
(English) romance, an American might bring
the tradition from over the sea, and so discover
the cross, which had been altogether forgotten.

August 24. — Day before yesterday I took the
rail for Southport, — a cool, generally overcast
day, with glimmers of faint sunshine. The ride
is through a most uninteresting tract of country, — at first, glimpses of the river, with the
thousands of masts in the docks; the dismal
outskirts of a great town, still spreading onward, with beginnings of streets, and insulated
brick buildings and blocks; farther on, a wide
monotony of level plain, and here and there a
village and a church; almost always a windmill
in sight, there being plenty of breeze to turn its
vans on this windy coast. The railway skirts
along the sea the whole distance, but is shut out
from the sight of it by the low sand-hills, which
seem to have been heaped up by the waves.
There are one or two lighthouses on the shore.
I have not seen a drearier landscape, even in
Lancashire.

Reaching Southport at three, I rambled about,
with a view to discover whether it be a suitable
residence for my family during September. It

is a large village, or rather more than a village, which seems to be almost entirely made up of lodging-houses, and, at any rate, has been built up by the influx of summer visitors, — a sandy soil, level, and laid out with well-paved streets, the principal of which are enlivened with bazars, markets, shops, hotels of various degrees, and a showy vivacity of aspect.   There are a great many donkey-carriages, — large vehicles, drawn by a pair of donkeys ; bath-chairs, with invalid ladies ; refreshment-rooms in great numbers, — a place where everybody seems to be a transitory guest, nobody at home.   The main street leads directly down to the seashore, along which there is an elevated embankment, with a promenade on the top, and seats, and the toll of a penny. The shore itself, the tide being then low, stretched out interminably seaward, a wide waste of glistening sands ; and on the dry border people were riding on donkeys, with the drivers whipping behind; and children were digging with their little wooden spades ; and there were donkey-carriages far out on the sands, — a pleasant and breezy drive.   A whole city of bathing-machines was stationed near the shore, and I saw others in the seaward distance.   The sea air was refreshing and exhilarating, and if Sophia needs a seaside residence, I should think this might do as well as any other.

I saw a large brick edifice, enclosed within a

wall, and with somewhat the look of an alms-house or hospital; and it proved to be an in-firmary, charitably established for the reception of poor invalids, who need sea air and cannot afford to pay for it. Two or three of such per-sons were sitting under its windows. I do not think that the visitors of Southport are gene-rally of a very opulent class, but of the middle rank, from Manchester and other parts of this northern region. The lodging-houses, how-ever, are of sufficiently handsome style and ar-rangement.

[Mr. Hawthorne extracted from his recorded Oxford experiences his excursion to Blen-heim, but left his observations of the town it-self untouched, — and these I now transcribe. — S. H.]

Oxford, *August* 31. — . . . Yesterday we took the rail for London, and drove across the city to the Paddington Station, where we met Ben-noch, and set out with him for Oxford. I do not quite understand the matter, but it appears that we were expected guests of Mr. Spiers, a very hospitable gentleman, and ex-Mayor of Oxford, and a friend of Bennoch and of the Halls. Mr. S. C. Hall met us at the Oxford Station, and under his guidance we drove to a quiet, comfortable house in St. Giles Street, where rooms had been taken for us. Durham, the sculptor, is likewise of the party.

After establishing ourselves at these lodgings, we walked forth to take a preliminary glimpse of the city, and Mr. Hall, being familiar with the localities, served admirably as a guide. If I remember aright, I spoke very slightingly of the exterior aspect of Oxford, as I saw it with Julian during an hour or two's stay here, on my way to Southampton (to meet Sophia on her return from Lisbon). I am bound to say that my impressions are now very different; and that I find Oxford exceedingly picturesque and rich in beauty and grandeur and in antique stateliness. I do not remember very particularly what we saw, — time-worn fronts of famous colleges and halls of learning everywhere about the streets, and arched entrances ; passing through which, we saw bits of sculpture from monkish hands, — the most grotesque and ludicrous faces, as if the slightest whim of these old carvers took shape in stone, the material being so soft and manageable by them ; an ancient stone pulpit in the quadrangle of Maudlin College (Magdalen), one of only three now extant in England ; a splendid, — no, not splendid, but dimly magnificent — chapel, belonging to the same College, with painted windows of rare beauty, not brilliant with diversified hues, but of a sombre tint. In this chapel there is an alabaster monument, — a recumbent figure of the founder's father, as large as life, — which, though several centuries old, is as well preserved as if fresh from the chisel.

In the High Street, which, I suppose, is the noblest old street in England, Mr. Hall pointed out the Crown Inn, where Shakespeare used to spend the night, and was most hospitably welcomed by the pretty hostess (the mother of Sir William Davenant), on his passage between Stratford and London. It is a three-story house, with other houses contiguous, — an old timber mansion, though now plastered and painted of a yellowish hue. The ground floor is occupied as a shoe shop; but the rest of the house is still kept as a tavern. . . .

It is not now term time, and Oxford loses one of its most characteristic features by the absence of the gownsmen; but still there is a good deal of liveliness in the streets. We walked as far as a bridge beyond Maudlin College, and then drove homeward.

At six we went to dine with the hospitable ex-Mayor, across the wide, tree-bordered street; for his house is nearly opposite our lodgings. He is an intelligent and gentlemanly person, and was Mayor two years ago, and has done a great deal to make peace between the University and the town, heretofore bitterly inimical. His house is adorned with pictures and drawings, and he has an especial taste for art. . . . The dinner-table was decorated with pieces of plate, vases, and other things, which were presented to him as tokens of public or friendly regard and approbation of his action in the Mayoralty. After dinner, too, he produced a large silver snuff-box, which had been given him on the same account; in fact, the inscription affirmed that it was one of five pieces of plate so presented. The vases are really splendid, — one of them two feet high, and richly ornamented. It will hold five or six bottles of wine, and he said that it had been filled, and, I believe, sent round as a loving-cup at some of his entertainments. He cordially enjoys these things, and his genuine benevolence produces all this excellent hospitality. . . . But Bennoch proposed a walk, and we set forth. We rambled pretty extensively about the streets, sometimes seeing the shapes of old edifices dimly and doubtfully, it being an overcast night; or catching a partial view of a gray wall, or a pillar, or a Gothic archway, by lamplight. . . . The clock had some time ago struck eleven, when we were passing under a long extent of antique wall and towers, which were those of Balliol College. Mr. D—— led us into the middle of the street, and showed us a cross, which was paved into it, on a level with the rest of the road. This was the spot where Latimer and Ridley and another

Bishop were martyred in Bloody Mary's time.
There is a memorial to them in another street;
but this, where I set my foot at nearly midnight,
was the very spot where their flesh burned to
ashes, and their bones whitened. It has been a
most beautiful morning, and I have seen few
pleasanter scenes than this street in which we
lodge, with its spacious breadth, its two rows
of fine old trees, with sidewalks as wide as the
whole width of some streets; and, on the opposite side, the row of houses, some of them ancient, with picturesque gables, partially disclosed
through the intervening foliage. . . . From our
window we have a slantwise glimpse to the right
of the walls of St. John's College, and the general aspect of St. Giles. It is of an antiquity
not to shame those mediæval halls. Our own
lodgings are in a house that seems to be very
old, with panelled walls and beams across the
ceilings, lattice-windows in the chambers, and
a musty odor such as old houses inevitably
have. Nevertheless, everything is extremely
neat, clean, and comfortable; and in term time
our apartments are occupied by a Mr. Stebbing,
whose father is known in literature by some
critical writings, and who is a graduate and an
admirable scholar. There is a bookcase of five
shelves, containing his books, mostly standard
works, and indicating a safe and solid taste.

After lunch to-day we (that is, Mrs. Hall,

her adopted daughter, Sophia, and I, with the ex-Mayor) set forth, in an open barouche, to see the remarkables of Oxford, while the rest of the guests went on foot.   We first drew up at New College (a strange name for such an old place, but it was new some time since the Conquest), and went through its quiet and sunny quadrangles, and into its sunny and shadowy gardens.   I am in despair about the architecture and old edifices of these Oxford colleges, it is so impossible to express them in words.   They are themselves — as the architect left them, and as Time has modified and improved them — the expression of an idea which does not admit of being otherwise expressed, or translated into anything else.   Those old battlemented walls around the quadrangles ; many gables ; the windows with stone pavilions, so very antique, yet some of them adorned with fresh flowers in pots, — a very sweet contrast ; the ivy mantling the gray stone ; and the infinite repose, both in sunshine and shadow, — it is as if half a dozen by-gone centuries had set up their rest here, and as if nothing of the present time ever passed through the deeply recessed archway that shuts in the College from the street.   Not but what people have very free admittance ; and many parties of young men and girls and children came into the gardens while we were there.

These gardens of New College are indescrib-
ably beautiful, — not gardens in an American
sense, but lawns of the richest green and softest
velvet grass, shadowed over by ancient trees,
that have lived a quiet life here for centuries,
and have been nursed and tended with such
care, and so sheltered from rude winds, that
certainly they must have been the happiest of
all trees.   Such a sweet, quiet, sacred, stately
seclusion — so age-long as this has been, and,
I hope, will continue to be — cannot exist anywhere else.   One side of the garden wall is
formed by the ancient wall of the city, which
Cromwell's artillery battered, and which still
retains its pristine height and strength.   At intervals, there are round towers that formed the
bastions ; that is to say, on the exterior they are
round towers, but within, in the garden of the
College, they are semicircular recesses, with iron
garden-seats arranged round them.   The loop-
holes through which the archers and muske-
teers used to shoot still pierce through deep
recesses in the wall, which is here about six feet
thick.   I wish I could put into one sentence
the whole impression of this garden, but it could
not be done in many pages.

We looked also at the outside of the wall,
and Mr. Parker, deeply skilled in the antiquities of the spot, showed us a weed growing, —
here in little sprigs, there in large and heavy

festoons, hanging plentifully downward from a shallow root. It is called the Oxford plant, being found only here, and not easily, if at all, introduced anywhere else. It bears a small and pretty blue flower, not altogether unlike the forget-me-not, and we took some of it away with us for a memorial. We went into the chapel of New College, which is in such fresh condition that I think it must be modern; and yet this cannot be, since there are old brasses inlaid into tombstones in the pavement, representing mediæval ecclesiastics and college dignitaries; and busts against the walls, in antique garb; and old painted windows, unmistakable in their antiquity. But there is likewise a window, lamentable to look at, which was painted by Sir Joshua Reynolds, and exhibits strikingly the difference between the work of a man who performed it merely as a matter of taste and business, and what was done religiously and with the whole heart; at least, it shows that the artists and public of the last age had no sympathy with Gothic art. In the chancel of this church there are more painted windows, which I take to be modern, too, though they are in much better taste, and have an infinitely better effect, than Sir Joshua's. At any rate, with the sunshine through them, they looked very beautiful, and tinted the high altar and the pavement with brilliant hues.

The sacristan opened a tall and narrow little recess in the wall of the chancel, and showed it entirely filled with the crosier of William of Wickham. It appears to be made of silver gilt, and is a most rich and elaborate relic, at least six feet high. Modern art cannot, or does not, equal the chasing and carving of this splendid crosier, which is enriched with figures of saints and apostles, and various Gothic devices, — very minute, but all executed as faithfully as if the artist's salvation had depended upon every notch he made in the silver. . . .

Leaving New College, Bennoch and I, under Mr. Parker's guidance, walked round Christ Church meadows, part of our way lying along the banks of the Cherwell, which unites with the Isis to form the Thames, I believe. The Cherwell is a narrow and remarkably sluggish stream ; but is deep in spots, and capriciously so, — so that a person may easily step from knee-deep to fifteen feet in depth. A gentleman present used a queer expression in reference to the drowning of two college men ; he said " it was an *awkward* affair." I think this is equal to Longfellow's story of the Frenchman who avowed himself very much " displeased " at the news of his father's death. At the confluence of the Cherwell and Isis we saw a good many boats, belonging to the students of the various colleges ; some of them being

very large and handsome barges, capable of
accommodating a numerous party, with room
on board for dancing and merrymaking.   Some
of them are calculated to be drawn by horses,
in the manner of canal-boats ; others are pro-
pellable by oars.   It is practicable to perform
the voyage between Oxford and London — a
distance of about one hundred and thirty miles
— in three days.   The students of Oxford are
famous boatmen ; there is a constant rivalship,
on this score, among the different colleges ; and
annually, I believe, there is a match between
Oxford and Cambridge.   The Cambridge men
beat the Oxonians in this year's trial.

On our return into the city, we passed through
Christ Church, which, as regards the number
of students, is the most considerable college of
the University.   It has a stately dome ; but my
memory is confused with battlements, towers,
gables, and Gothic staircases and cloisters.   If
there had been nothing else in Oxford but this
one establishment, my anticipations would not
have been disappointed.   The bell was tolling
for worship in the chapel ; and Mr. Parker told
us that Dr. Pusey is a canon, or in some sort
of dignity, in Christ Church, and would soon
probably make his appearance in the quadrangle, on his way to chapel ; so we walked to and
fro, waiting an opportunity to see him.   A gouty
old dignitary, in a white surplice, came hob-

bling along from one extremity of the court; and by and by, from the opposite corner, appeared Dr. Pusey, also in a white surplice and with a lady by his side. We met him, and I stared pretty fixedly at him, as I well might; for he looked on the ground, as if conscious that he would be stared at.   He is a man past middle life, of sufficient breadth and massiveness, with a pale, intellectual, manly face.   He was talking with the lady, and smiled, but not jollily.   Mr. Parker, who knows him, says that he is a man of kind and gentle affections. The lady was his niece.

Thence we went through High Street and Broad Street, and passing by Balliol College, — a most satisfactory pile and range of old towered and gabled edifices, — we came to the cross on the pavement, which is supposed to mark the spot where the bishops were martyred.   But Mr. Parker told us the mortifying fact, that he had ascertained that this could not possibly have been the genuine spot of martyrdom, which must have taken place at a point within view, but considerably too far off to be moistened by any tears that may be shed here. It is too bad.   We concluded the rambles of the day by visiting the gardens of St. John's College; and I desire, if possible, to say even more in admiration of them than of those of New College, — such beautiful lawns, with tall, an-

cient trees, and heavy clouds of foliage, and
sunny glimpses through archways of leafy
branches, where, to-day, we could see parties
of girls, making cheerful contrast with the sombre walls and solemn shade. The world, surely,
has not another place like Oxford; it is a despair to see such a place and ever to leave it,
for it would take a lifetime and more than one,
to comprehend and enjoy it satisfactorily.

At dinner to-day, the golden vases were all
ranged on the table, the largest and central one
containing a most magnificent bouquet of dah-
lias and other bright-hued flowers.

.   .   .   .

On Tuesday our first visit was to Christ
Church, where we saw the large and stately hall,
above a hundred feet long by forty wide, and
fifty to the top of its carved oaken roof, which
is ornamented with festoons, as it were, and
pendants of solid timber. The walls are panelled with oak, perhaps halfway upward, and
above are the rows of arched windows on each
side; but, near the upper end, two great windows come nearly to the floor. There is a dais,
where the great men of the College and the distinguished guests sit at table, and the tables of
the students are arranged along the length of
the hall. All around, looking down upon those
who sit at meat, are the portraits of a multitude
of illustrious personages who were members of

the learned fraternity in times past; not a portrait being admitted there (unless it be a king,
and I remember only Henry VIII.) save those
who were actually students on the foundation,
receiving the eleemosynary aid of the College.
Most of them were divines; but there are likewise many statesmen, eminent during the last
three hundred years, and, among many earlier
ones, the Marquis of Wellesley and Canning.
It is an excellent idea, for their own glory and
as examples to the rising generations, to have
this multitude of men, who have done good and
great things, before the eyes of those who ought
to do as well as they, in their own time. Archbishops, prime ministers, poets, deep scholars,
— but doubtless an outward success has generally been their claim to this position, and
Christ Church may have forgotten a better man
than the best of them. It is not, I think, the
tendency of English life, nor of the education
of their colleges, to lead young men to high
moral excellence, but to aim at illustrating themselves in the sight of mankind.

.   .   .   .

Thence we went into the kitchen, which is
arranged very much as it was three centuries
ago, with two immense fireplaces. There was
likewise a gridiron, which, without any exagger-
ation, was large enough to have served for the
martyrdom of St. Lawrence. The college din-

ners are good, but plain, and cost the students one shilling and eleven pence each, being rather cheaper than a similar one could be had at an inn.   There is no provision for breakfast or supper in commons ; but they can have these meals sent to their rooms from the buttery, at a charge proportioned to the dishes they order. There seems to be no necessity for a great expenditure on the part of Oxford students.

From the kitchen we went to the chapel, which is the cathedral of Oxford, and well worth seeing, if there had not been so many other things to see. It is now under repair, and there was a great heap of old woodwork and panelling lying in one of the aisles, which had been stripped away from some of the ancient pillars, leaving them as good as new. There is a shrine of a saint, with a wooden canopy over it ; and some painted glass, old and new ; and a statue of Cyril Jackson, with a face of shrewdness and insight ; and busts, as mural monuments.

Our next visit was to Merton College, which, though not one of the great colleges, is as old as any of them, and looks exceedingly venerable. We were here received by a friend of Mr. Spiers, in his academic cap but without his gown, which is not worn except in term time. He is a very civil gentleman, and showed us some antique points of architecture, — such as a Norman archway, with a passage over it, through which the Queen of Charles I. used to go to chapel; and an edifice of the thirteenth century, with a stone roof, which is considered to be very curious.

How ancient is the aspect of these college quadrangles! so gnawed by time as they are, so crumbly, so blackened, and so gray where they are not black, — so quaintly shaped, too, with here a line of battlement and there a row of gables; and here a turret, with probably a winding stair inside; and lattice windows, with stone mullions, and little panes of glass set in lead; and the cloisters, with a long arcade, looking upon the green or pebbled enclosure. The quality of the stone has a great deal to do with the apparent antiquity. It is a stone found in the neighborhood of Oxford, and very soon begins to crumble and decay superficially when exposed to the weather; so that twenty years do the work of a hundred, so far as appearances go. If you strike one of the old walls with a stick, a portion of it comes powdering down. The effect of this decay is very picturesque, and is especially striking, I think, on edifices of classic architecture, such as some of the Oxford colleges are, greatly enriching the Grecian columns, which look so cold when the outlines are hard and distinct. The Oxford people, however, are tired of this crumbly stone, and when repairs are necessary, they use a more durable material, which does not well assort with the antiquity into which it is intruded.

Mr. E—— showed us the library of Merton College. It occupies two sides of an old building, and has a very delightful fragrance of ancient books. The halls containing it are vaulted, and roofed with oak, not carved and ornamented, but laid flat, so that they look very like a grand and spacious old garret. All along there is a row of alcoves on each side, with rude benches and reading-desks, in the simplest style, and nobody knows how old. The books look as old as the building. The more valuable were formerly chained to the bookcases; and a few of them have not yet broken their chains. It was a good emblem of the dark and monkish ages, when learning was imprisoned in their cloisters, and chained in their libraries, in the days when the schoolmaster had not yet gone abroad. Mr. E—— showed us a very old copy of the Bible; and a vellum manuscript, most beautifully written in black letter, and illuminated, of the works of Duns Scotus, who was a scholar of Merton College.

He then showed us the chapel, a large part of which has been renewed and ornamented with pictured windows and other ecclesiastical splendor, and paved with encaustic tiles, according to the Puseyite taste of the day; for Merton

248

has adopted the Puseyite doctrines, and is one of their chief strongholds in Oxford. If they do no other good, they at least do much for preservation and characteristic restoration of the old English churches; but perhaps, even here, there is as much antiquity spoiled as retained. In the portion of the chapel not yet restored we saw the rude old pavement, inlaid with gravestones, in some of which were brasses, with the figures of the college dignitaries whose dust slumbered beneath; and I think it was here that I saw the tombstone of Anthony-à-Wood, the gossiping biographer of the learned men of Oxford.

From the chapel we went into the college gardens, which are very pleasant, and possess the advantage of looking out on the broad verdure of Christ Church meadows and the river beyond. We loitered here awhile, and then went to Mr. E——'s rooms, to which the entrance is by a fine old staircase. They had a very comfortable aspect, — a wainscoted parlor and bedroom, as nice and cosy as a bachelor could desire, with a good collection of theological books; and on a peg hung his gown, with a red border about it, denoting him to be a pro-proctor. He was kind enough to order a lunch, consisting of bread and cheese, college ale, and a certain liquor called "Archdeacon." . . . We ate and drank, . . . and, bidding farewell to

good Mr. E——, we pursued our way to the
Ratcliffe Library.

This is a very handsome edifice, of a circular
shape; the lower story consisting altogether of
arches, open on all sides, as if to admit anybody
to the learning here stored up. I always see
great beauty and lightsomeness in these classic
and Grecian edifices, though they seem cold and
intellectual, and not to have had their mortar
moistened with human life-blood, nor to have
the mystery of human life in them, as Gothic
structures do. The library is in a large and
beautiful room, in the story above the basement, and, as far as I saw, consisted chiefly or
altogether of scientific works. I saw Silliman's
Journal on one of the desks, being the only
trace of American science, or American learning
or ability, in any department, which I discovered in the University of Oxford. After seeing
the library, we went to the top of the building,
where we had an excellent view of Oxford and
the surrounding country. Then we went to the
Convocation Hall, and afterwards to the theatre, where Sophia sat down in the Chancellor's
chair, which is very broad, and ponderously
wrought of oak. I remember little here, except
the amphitheatre of benches, and the roof, which
seems to be supported by golden ropes, and
on the wall, opposite the door, some full-length
portraits, among which one of that ridiculous

coxcomb, George IV., was the most prominent. These kings thrust themselves impertinently forward by bust, statue, and picture, on all occasions, and it is not wise in them to show their shallow foreheads among men of mind.

Mr. Spiers tried to get us admittance to the Bodleian Library; but this is just the moment when it is closed for the purpose of being cleaned; so we missed seeing the principal halls of this library, and were only admitted into what was called the Picture Gallery. This, however, satisfied all my desires, so far as the backs of books are concerned, for they extend through a gallery, running round three sides of a quadrangle, making an aggregate length of more than four hundred feet, — a solid array of bookcases, full of books, within a protection of open iron-work. Up and down the gallery there are models of classic temples; and about midway in its extent stands a brass statue of Earl Pembroke, who was Chancellor of the University in James I.'s time, not in scholarly garb, however, but in plate and mail, looking indeed like a thunderbolt of war. I rapped him with my knuckles, and he seemed to be solid metal, — though, I should imagine, hollow at heart. A thing which interested me very much was the lantern of Guy Fawkes. It was once tinned, no doubt, but is now nothing but rusty iron, partly broken. As this is called the Picture

Gallery, I must not forget the pictures, which are ranged in long succession over the book-cases, and include almost all Englishmen whom the world has ever heard of, whether in states-manship or literature. I saw a canvas on which had once been a lovely and unique portrait of Mary of Scotland; but it was consigned to a picture cleaner to be cleansed, and, discovering that it was painted over another picture, he had the curiosity to clean poor Mary quite away, — thus revealing a wishy-washy woman's face, which now hangs in the gallery. I am so tired of seeing notable things that I almost wish that whatever else is remarkable in Oxford could be obliterated in some similar manner.

From the Bodleian we went to the Taylor Institute, which was likewise closed; but the woman who had it in charge had formerly been a servant of Mr. Spiers, and he so over-persuaded her that she finally smiled and admitted us. It would truly have been a pity to miss it; for here, on the basement floor, are the original mod-els of Chantrey's busts and statues, great and small; and in the rooms above are a far richer treasure, — a large collection of original draw-ings by Raphael and Michel Angelo. These are far better for my purpose than their fin-ished pictures, — that is to say, they bring me much closer to the hands that drew them and the minds that imagined them. It is like look-

ing into their brains, and seeing the first con-
ception before it took shape outwardly (I have
somewhere else said about the same thing of
such sketches). I noticed one of Raphael's
drawings, representing the effect of eloquence;
it was a man speaking in the centre of a group,
between whose ears and the orator's mouth connecting lines were drawn. Raphael's idea must
have been to compose his picture in such a way
that their auricular organs should not fail to be
in a proper relation with the eloquent voice;
and though this relation would not have been
individually traceable in the finished picture, yet
the general effect — that of deep and entranced
attention — would have been produced.

In another room there are some copies of
Raphael's cartoons, and some queer mediæval
pictures, as stiff and ugly as can well be conceived, yet successful in telling their own story.
We looked a little while at these, and then,
thank Heaven! went home and dressed for dinner. I can write no more to-day. Indeed,
what a mockery it is to write at all!

[Here follows the drive to Cumnor Place,
Stanton Harcourt, Nuneham Courtney, God-
stowe, etc., — already published in Our Old
Home. — S. H.]

September 9. — The morning after our excursion on the Thames was as bright and beau-

tiful as many preceding ones had been.   After breakfast Sophia and I walked a little about the town, and bought Thomas à Kempis, in both French and English, for Una. . . . Mr. De la Motte, the photographer, had breakfasted with us, and Mr. Spiers wished him to take a photograph of our whole party.   So, in the first place, before the rest were assembled, he made an experimental group of such as were there ; and I did not like my own aspect very much. Afterwards, when we were all come, he arranged us under a tree in the garden, — Mr. and Mrs. Spiers, with their eldest son, Mr. and Mrs. Hall and Fanny, Mr. Addison, my wife, and me, — and stained the glass with our figures and faces in the twinkling of an eye ; not Sophia's face, however, for she turned it away, and left only a portion of her bonnet and dress, — and Mrs. Hall, too, refused to countenance the proceeding.   But all the rest of us were caught to the life, and I was really a little startled at recognizing myself so apart from myself, and done so quickly too.

This was the last important incident of our visit to Oxford, except that Mr. Spiers was again most hospitable at lunch.   Never did anybody attend more faithfully to the comfort of his friends than does this good gentleman.   But he has shown himself most kind in every possible way, and I shall always feel truly grateful.

No better way of showing our sense of his hospitality, and all the trouble he has taken for us (and our memory of him), has occurred to us, than to present him with a set of my Tales and Romances; so, by the next steamer, I shall write to Ticknor & Fields to send them, elegantly bound, and Sophia will emblazon his coat of arms in each volume. He accompanied us and Mr. and Mrs. Hall to the railway station, and we left Oxford at two o'clock.

It had been a very pleasant visit, and all the persons whom we met were kind and agreeable, and disposed to look at one another in a sunny aspect. I saw a good deal of Mr. Hall. He is a thoroughly genuine man, of kind heart and true affections, a gentleman of taste and refinement, and full of humor.

On the Saturday after our return to Blackheath we went to Hampton Court, about which, as I have already recorded a visit to it, I need say little here. But I was again impressed with the stately grandeur of Wolsey's great Hall, with its great window at each end, and one side window descending almost to the floor, and a row of windows on each side, high towards the roof, and throwing down their many-colored light on the stone pavement, and on the Gobelin tapestry, which must have been gorgeously rich when the walls were first clothed with it. I fancied, then, that no modern architect could produce so fine a room; but oddly enough, in the great entrance hall of the Euston station, yesterday, I could not see how this last fell very much short of Wolsey's Hall in grandeur. We were quite wearied in passing through the endless suites of rooms in Hampton Court and gazing at the thousands of pictures; it is too much for one day, — almost enough for one life, in such measure as life can be bestowed on pictures. It would have refreshed us had we spent half the time in wandering about the grounds, which, as we glimpsed at them from the windows of the Palace, seemed very beautiful, though laid out with an antique formality of straight lines and broad gravelled paths. Before the central window there is a beautiful sheet of water, and a fountain upshooting itself and plashing into it, with a continuous and pleasant sound. How beautifully the royal robe of a monarchy is embroidered! Palaces, pictures, parks! They do enrich life; and kings and aristocracies cannot keep these things to themselves; they merely take care of them for others. Even a king, with all the glory that can be shed around him, is but the liveried and bedizened footman of his people, and the toy of their delight. I am very glad that I came to this country while the English are still playing with such a toy.

Yesterday Julian and I left Blackheath, and

reached Liverpool last night. The rest of my family will follow in a few days; and so finishes our residence in Bennoch's house, where I, for my part, have spent some of the happiest hours that I have known since we left our American home. It is a strange, vagabond, gypsy sort of life, — this that we are leading; and I know not whether we shall finally be spoiled for any other, or shall enjoy our quiet Wayside, as we never did before, when once we reach it again.

.   .   .   .

The evening set in misty and obscure; and it was dark almost when Julian and I arrived at the landing stage on our return. I was struck with the picturesque effect of the high tower and tall spire of St. Nicholas, rising upward, with dim outline, into the duskiness; while midway of its height the dial plates of an illuminated clock blazed out, like two great eyes of a giant.

September 13. — On Saturday my wife, with all her train, arrived at Mrs. B——'s; and on Tuesday — vagabonds as we are — we again struck our tent, and set out for Southport.

I do not know what sort of character it will form in the children, — this unsettled, shifting, vagrant life, with no central home to turn to, except what we carry in ourselves. It was a windy day, and, judging by the look of the trees, on the way to Southport, it must be almost always windy, and with the blast in one prevailing direction; for invariably their branches, and the whole contour and attitude of the tree, turn from seaward, with a strangely forlorn aspect. Reaching Southport, we took an omnibus, and under the driver's guidance came to our tall stone house, fronting on the sands, and styled " Brunswick Terrace." . . .

The English system of lodging-houses has its good points; but it is, nevertheless, a contrivance for bearing the domestic cares of home about with you whithersoever you go; and immediately you have to set about producing your own bread and cheese. However, Fanny took most of this trouble off our hands, though there was inevitably the stiffness and discomfort of a new housekeeping on the first day of our arrival; besides that, it was cool, and the wind whistled and grumbled and eddied into the chinks of the house.

Meanwhile, in all my experience of Southport, I have never yet seen the sea, but only an interminable breadth of sands, looking pooly or plashy in some places, and barred across with dryer reaches of sand, but no expanse of water. It must be miles and miles, at low water, to the veritable seashore. We are about twenty miles

north of Liverpool, on the border of the Irish
Sea; and Ireland, and, I suppose, the Isle of
Man intervene betwixt us and the ocean, not
much to our benefit; for the air of the English
coast, under ocean influences, is said to be milder
than when it comes across the land, — milder,
therefore, above or below Ireland, because then
the Gulf Stream ameliorates it.

Betimes, the forenoon after our arrival, I had
to take the rail to Liverpool, but returned, a little after five, in the midst of a rain, — still low
water and interminable sands; still a dreary,
howling blast. We had a cheerful fireside, however, and should have had a pleasant evening,
only that the wind on the sea made us excessively drowsy. This morning we awoke to hear
the wind still blustering, and blowing up clouds
with fitful little showers, and soon blowing them
away again, and letting the brightest of sunshine
fall over the plashy waste of sand. We have
already walked forth on the shore with Julian
and Rose, who pick up shells, and dig wells in
the sand with their little wooden spades: but
soon we saw a rainbow on the western sky, and
then a shower came spattering down upon us
in good earnest. We first took refuge under
the bridge that stretches between the two portions of the promenade; but as there was a chill
draught there, we made the best of our way
home. The sun has now again come out brightly,

though the wind is still tumbling a great many clouds about the sky.

.   .   .   .

Evening. — Later I walked out with Una, and, looking seaward, we saw the foam and spray of the advancing tide, tossed about on the verge of the horizon, — a long line, like the crests and gleaming helmets of an army. In about half an hour we found almost the whole waste of sand covered with water, and white waves breaking out all over it; but, the bottom being so nearly level, and the water so shallow, there was little of the spirit and exultation of the sea in a strong breeze. Of the long line of bathing-machines, one after another was hitched to a horse, and trundled forth into the water, where, at a long distance from shore, the bathers found themselves hardly middle deep.

September 19. — The wind grumbled and made itself miserable all last night, and this morning it is still howling as ill naturedly as ever, and roaring and rumbling in the chimneys. The tide is far out, but, from an upper window, I fancied at intervals that I could see the plash of the surf-wave on the distant limit of the sand; perhaps, however, it was only a gleam on the sky. Constantly there have been sharp spatters of rain, hissing and rattling against the windows,

while a little before or after, or perhaps simultaneously, a rainbow, somewhat watery of tex-
ture, paints itself on the western clouds. Gray,
sullen clouds hang about the sky, or sometimes
cover it with a uniform dulness; at other times
the portions towards the sun gleam almost light-
somely; now there may be an airy glimpse of
clear blue sky in a fissure of the clouds; now
the very brightest of sunshine comes out all of a
sudden, and gladdens everything. The breadth
of sands has a various aspect, according as there
are pools, or moisture enough to glisten, or a
dryer tract; and where the light gleams along a
yellow ridge or bar, it is like sunshine itself.
Certainly the temper of the day shifts; but the
smiles come far the seldomest, and its frowns
and angry tears are most reliable. By seven
o'clock pedestrians began to walk along the
promenade, close-buttoned against the blast;
later, a single bathing-machine got under way,
by means of a horse, and travelled forth seaward; but within what distance it finds the invisible margin I cannot say, — at all events, it looks
like a dreary journey. Just now I saw a sea-
gull wheeling on the blast, close in towards the
promenade.

September 21. — Yesterday morning was
bright, sunny and windy, and cool and exhilarating. I went to Liverpool at eleven, and, re-

turning at five, found the weather still bright and cool. The temperature, methinks, must soon diminish the population of Southport, which, judging from appearances, must be mainly made up of temporary visitors. There is a newspaper, The Southport Visitor, published weekly, and containing a register of all the visitants in the various hotels and lodging-houses. It covers more than two sides of the paper, to the amount of some hundreds. The guests come chiefly from Liverpool, Manchester, and the neighboring country towns, and belong to the middle classes. It is not a fashionable watering-place. Only one nobleman's name, and those of two or three baronets, now adorn the list. The people whom we see loitering along the beach and the promenade have, at best, a well-to-do tradesmanlike air. I do not find that there are any public amusements; nothing but strolling on the sands, donkey-riding, or drives in donkey-carts; and solitary visitors must find it a dreary place. Yet one or two of the streets are brisk and lively, and, being well thronged, have a holiday aspect. There are no carriages in town save donkey-carts; some of which are drawn by three donkeys abreast, and are large enough to hold a whole family. These conveyances will take you far out on the sands through wet and dry. The beach is haunted by The Flying Dutchman, — a sort of boat on wheels, schooner-rigged with sails, and which sometimes makes pretty good speed with a fair wind.

This morning we have been walking with Julian and Rose out over the "ribbed sea sands," a good distance from shore. Throughout the week the tides will be so low as not to cover the shallow basin of this bay, if a bay it be. The weather was sullen, with now and then a faint gleam of sunshine, lazily tracing our shadows on the sand; the wind rather quieter than on preceding days. . . . In the sunshine the sands seem to be frequented by great numbers of gulls, who begin to find the northern climate too wintry. You see their white wings in the sunlight, but they become almost or quite invisible in the shade. We shall soon have an opportunity of seeing how a watering-place looks when the season is quite over; for we have concluded to remain here till December, and everybody else will take flight in a week or two.

A short time ago, in the evening, in a street of Liverpool, I saw a decent man, of the lower orders, taken much aback by being roughly brushed against by a rowdy fellow. He looked after him, and exclaimed indignantly, " Is that a Yankee? " It shows the kind of character we have here.

October 7. — On Saturday evening I gave a dinner to Bennoch, at the Adelphi Hotel. The

chief point or characteristic of English customs
was that Mr. Radley, our landlord, himself attended at table, and officiated as chief waiter.
He has a fortune of £100,000, — half a mil-
lion of dollars, — and is an elderly man of good
address and appearance. In America, such a
man would very probably be in Congress ; at
any rate he would never conceive the possibility
of changing plates, or passing round the table
with hock and champagne. Some of his hock
was a most rich and imperial wine, such as can
hardly be had on the Rhine itself. There were
eight gentlemen besides Bennoch.

A donkey, the other day, stubbornly refusing
to come out of a boat which had brought him
across the Mersey ; at last, after many kicks
had been applied, and other persecutions of that
kind, a man stepped forward, addressing him
affectionately, " Come along, brother," — and
the donkey obeyed at once.

October 26. — On Thursday, instead of taking the rail for Liverpool, I set out, about
eleven, for a long walk. It was an overcast
morning, such as in New England would have
boded rain ; but English clouds are not nearly
so portentous as American in that respect. Accordingly, the sun soon began to peep through
crevices, and I had not gone more than a mile

or two when it shone a little too warmly for comfort, yet not more than I liked. It was very much like our pleasant October days at home ; indeed, the climates of the two countries more nearly coincide during the present month than at any other season of the year. The air was almost perfectly still; but once in a while it stirred, and breathed coolly in my face ; it is very delightful, this latent freshness, in a warm atmosphere.

The country about Southport has as few charms as it is possible for any region to have. In the close neighborhood of the shore, it is nothing but sand-hillocks, covered with coarse grass ; and this is the original nature of the whole site on which the town stands, although it is now paved, and has been covered with soil enough to make gardens, and to nourish here and there a few trees. A little farther inland the surface seems to have been marshy, but has been drained by ditches across the fields and along the roadside; and the fields are embanked on all sides with parapets of earth which appear as if intended to keep out inundations. In fact, Holland itself cannot be more completely on a level with the sea. The only dwellings are the old, whitewashed stone cottages, with thatched roofs, on the brown straw of which grow various weeds and mosses, brightening it with green patches, and sprouting along the ridgepole, —

the homeliest hovels that ever mortals lived in, and which they share with pigs and cows at one end. Hens, too, run in and out of the door. One or two of these hovels bore signs, " Licensed to sell beer, ale, and tobacco," and generally there were an old woman and some children visible. In all cases there was a ditch full of water close at hand, stagnant, and often quite covered with a growth of water-weeds, — very unwholesome, one would think, in the neighborhood of a dwelling; and, in truth, the children and grown people did look pale.

In the fields, along the roadside, men and women were harvesting their carrots and other root-crops, especially digging potatoes, — the pleasantest of all farm labor, in my opinion, there being such a continual interest in opening the treasures of each hill. As I went on, the country began to get almost imperceptibly less flat, and there was some little appearance of trees. I had determined to go to Omskirk, but soon got out of the way, and came to a little hamlet that looked antique and picturesque, with its small houses of stone and brick, built with the one material and repaired with the other perhaps ages afterwards. Here I inquired my way of a woman, who told me, in broad Lancashire dialect, " that I maun go back, and turn to my left, till I came to a finger-post;" and so I did, and found another little

hamlet, the principal object in which was a
public-house, with a large sign representing a
dance round a May-pole. It was now about
one o'clock ; so I entered, and, being ushered
into what, I suppose, they called the coffee-
room, I asked for some cold meat and ale.
There was a jolly, round, rather comely woman
for a hostess, with a free, hospitable, yet rather
careless manner.

The coffee-room smelt rather disagreeably of
bad tobacco-smoke, and was shabbily furnished
with an old sofa and flag-bottomed chairs, and
adorned with a print of " Old Billy," a horse
famous for a longevity of about sixty years ;
and also with colored engravings of old-fashioned hunting-scenes, conspicuous with scarlet
coats. There was a very small bust of Milton
on the mantelpiece. By and by the remains
of an immense round of beef, three quarters
cut away, were put on the table ; then some
smoking-hot potatoes ; and finally the hostess
told me that their own dinner was just ready,
and so she had brought me in some hot chops,
thinking I might prefer them to the cold meat.
I did prefer them ; and they were stewed or
fried chops, instead of broiled, and were very
savory. There was household bread too, and
rich cheese, and a pint of ale, home brewed, not
very mighty but good to quench thirst, and, by
way of condiment, some pickled cabbage ; so,

instead of a lunch, I made quite a comfortable dinner. Moreover, there was a cold pudding on the table, and I called for a clean plate, and helped myself to some of it. It was of rice, and was strewn over, rather than intermixed, with some kinds of berries, the nature of which I could not exactly make out.

I then set forth again. It was still sunny and warm, and I walked more slowly than before dinner; in fact, I did little more than lounge along, sitting down at last on the stone parapet of a bridge.

The country grew more pleasant, more sylvan, and, though still of a level character, not so drearily flat. Soon appeared the first symptom that I had seen of a gentleman's residence, — a lodge at a park gate, then a long stretch of wall, with a green lawn, and afterwards an extent of wooded land; then another gateway, with a neat lodge on each side of it, and lastly another extent of wood. The Hall or Mansion-house, however, was nowhere apparent, being doubtless secluded deep and far within its grounds. I inquired of a boy who was the owner of the estate, and he answered, " Mr. Scarybrick ;" and no doubt it is a family of local eminence.

Along the road, — an old inn; some aged stone houses, built for merely respectable occupants; a canal, with two canal-boats, heaped up with a cargo of potatoes ; two little girls, who were watching lest some cows should go astray, and had their two little chairs by the roadside and their dolls and other playthings, and so followed the footsteps of the cows all day long.   I met two boys, coming from Omskirk, mounted on donkeys, with empty panniers, on which they had carried vegetables to market.   Finally, between two and three o'clock, I saw the great tower of Omskirk Church, with its spire, — not rising out of the tower, but sprouting up close beside it ; and, entering the town, I directed my steps first to this old church.

It stands on a gentle eminence, sufficient to give it a good site, and has a pavement of flat gravestones in front.   It is doubtless, as regards its foundation, a very ancient church, but has not exactly a venerable aspect, being in too good repair, and much restored in various parts ; not ivy-grown, either, though green with moss here and there.   The tower is square and immensely massive, and might have supported a very lofty spire ; so that it is the more strange that what spire it has should be so oddly stuck beside it, springing out of the church wall.   I should have liked well enough to enter the church, as it is the burial place of the Earls of Derby, and perhaps may contain some interesting monuments; but as it was all shut up, and even the iron gates of the churchyard closed and locked, I merely looked at the outside.

From the church, a street leads to the market-place, in which I found a throng of men and women, it being market-day; wares of various kinds, tin, earthen, and cloth, set out on the pavements; droves of pigs; ducks and fowls; baskets of eggs; and a man selling quack medicines, recommending his nostrums as well as he could. The aspect of the crowd was very English, — portly and ruddy women; yeomen with small-clothes and broad-brimmed hats, all very quiet and heavy and good-humored. Their dialect was so provincial that I could not readily understand more than here and there a word.

But after all, there were few traits that could be made a note of. I soon grew weary of the scene, and so I went to the railway station, and waited there nearly an hour for the train to take me to Southport. Omskirk is famous for its gingerbread, which women sell to the railway passengers at a sixpence for a rouleau of a dozen little cakes.

November 30. — A week ago last Monday, Herman Melville came to see me at the Consulate, looking much as he used to do, and with his characteristic gravity and reserve of manner. . . . We soon found ourselves on pretty much

our former terms of sociability and confidence.
. . . He is thus far on his way to Constanti-
nople. I do not wonder that he found it necessary to take an airing through the world,
after so many years of toilsome pen-labor, following upon so wild and adventurous a youth
as his was. I invited him to come and stay
with us at Southport, as long as he might remain in this vicinity, and accordingly he did
come the next day. . . . On Wednesday we
took a pretty long walk together, and sat down
in a hollow among the sand-hills, sheltering
ourselves from the high cool wind. Melville,
as he always does, began to reason of Providence
and futurity, and of everything else that lies
beyond human ken. . . . He has a very high
and noble nature, and is better worth immor-
tality than the most of us. . . . On Saturday
we went to Chester together. I love to take
every opportunity of going to Chester ; it being
the one only place, within easy reach of Liverpool, which possesses any old English interest.

.   .   .   .

We went to the cathedral. Its gray nave
impressed me more than at any former visit.
Passing into the cloisters, an attendant took
possession of us, and showed us about.

Within the choir there is a profusion of very
rich oaken carving, both on the screen that
separates it from the nave, and on the seats and

walls ; very curious and most elaborate, and
lavished (one would say) most wastefully, where
nobody would think of looking for it, — where,
indeed, amid the dimness of the cathedral, the
exquisite detail of the elaboration could not
possibly be seen.   Our guide lighted some of the
gas-burners, of which there are many hundreds,
to help us see them ; but it required close scru-
tiny even then.   It must have been out of the
question, when the whole means of illumination
were only a few smoky torches or candles. There
was a row of niches, where the monks used to
stand for four hours together, in the performance of some of their services ; and to relieve
them a little, they were allowed partially to sit
on a projection of the seats, which were turned
up in the niche for that purpose ; but if they
grew drowsy, so as to fail to balance themselves,
the seat was so contrived as to slip down, thus
bringing the monk to the floor.   These projections on the seats are each and all of them
carved with curious devices, no two alike.   The
guide showed us one, representing, apparently,
the first quarrel of a new-married couple, wrought
with wonderful expression.   Indeed, the artist
never failed to bring out his idea in the most
striking manner, — as, for instance, Satan under
the guise of a lion, devouring a sinner bodily ;
and again in the figure of a dragon with a man
halfway down his gullet, the legs hanging out.

The carver may not have seen anything grotesque in this, nor intended it at all by way of
joke; but certainly there would appear to be a
grim mirthfulness in some of the designs.   One
does not see why such fantasies should be strewn
about the holy interior of a cathedral, unless it
were intended to contain everything that belongs
to the heart of man, both upward and downward.

In a side aisle of the choir we saw a tomb,
said to be that of the Emperor Henry IV. of
Germany, though on very indistinct authority.
This is an oblong tomb, carved, and, on one
side, painted with bright colors and gilded.   During a very long period it was built and plastered
into the wall, and the exterior side was whitewashed; but, on being removed, the inner side
was found to have been ornamented with gold
and color, in the manner in which we now see it.
If this were customary with tombs, it must have
added vastly to the gorgeous magnificence, to
which the painted windows and polished pillars
and ornamented ceilings contributed so much.
In fact, a cathedral in its fresh estate seems to
have been like a pavilion of the sunset, all pur-
ple and gold; whereas now it more resembles
deepest and grayest twilight.

Afterwards we were shown into the ancient
refectory, now used as the city grammar school,
and furnished with the usual desks and seats

for the boys.   In one corner of this large room
was the sort of pulpit or elevated seat, with a
broken staircase of stone ascending to it, where
one of the monks used to read to his brethren,
while sitting at their meals.   The desks were
cut and carved with the scholars' knives, just as
they used to be in the school-rooms where I
was a scholar.   Thence we passed into the
chapter-house, but, before that, we went through
a small room, in which Melville opened a cup-
board, and discovered a dozen or two of wine-
bottles ; but our guide told us that they were
now empty, and never were meant for jollity,
having held only sacramental wine.   In the
chapter-house we saw the library, some of the
volumes of which were antique folios.   There
were two dusty and tattered banners hanging
on the wall, and the attendant promised to make
us laugh by something that he would tell us
about them.   The joke was that these two banners had been in the battle of Bunker Hill ; and
our countrymen, he said, always smiled on hearing this.   He had discovered us to be Americans by the notice we took of a mural tablet in
the choir, to the memory of a Lieutenant-Gov-
ernor Clarke, of New York, who died in Chester
before the Revolution.   From the chapter-house
he ushered us back into the nave, ever and anon
pointing out some portion of the edifice more
ancient than the rest, and when I asked him

how he knew this, he said that he had learnt it
from the archæologists, who could read off such
things like a book. This guide was a lively,
quick-witted man, who did his business less by
rote, and more with a vivacious interest, than
any guide I ever met.

After leaving the cathedral we sought out the
Yacht Inn, near the water-gate. This was, for
a long period of time, the principal inn of Chester, and was the house at which Swift once put
up, on his way to Holyhead, and where he invited the clergy to come and sup with him. We
sat down in a small snuggery, conversing with
the landlord. The Chester people are, according to my experience, very affable, and fond of
talking with strangers about the antiquities and
picturesque characteristics of their town. It
partly lives, the landlord told us, by its visitors,
and many people spend the summer here on
account of the antiquities and the good air. He
showed us a broad, balustraded staircase, leading into a large, comfortable, old-fashioned parlor, with windows looking on the street and on
the Custom House that stood opposite. This
was the room where Swift expected to receive
the clergy of Chester ; and on one of the win-
dow-panes were two acrid lines, written with the
diamond of his ring, satirizing those venerable gentlemen, in revenge, for their refusing his
invitation. The first line begins rather indis-

tinctly; but the writing grows fully legible as it proceeds.

The Yacht Tavern is a very old house, in the gabled style. The timbers and framework are still perfectly sound. In the same street is the Bishop's house (so called as having been the residence of a prelate long ago), which is covered with curious sculpture, representing Scriptural scenes. And in the same neighborhood is the county court, accessible by an archway, through which we penetrated, and found ourselves in a passage, very ancient and dusky, overlooked from the upper story by a gallery, to which an antique staircase ascended, with balustrades and square landing-places. A printer saw us here, and asked us into his printing-office, and talked very affably; indeed, he could have hardly been more civil, if he had known that both Melville and I have given a good deal of employment to the brethren of his craft.

December 15. — An old gentleman has recently paid me a good many visits, — a Kentucky man, who has been a good deal in England and Europe generally without losing the freshness and unconventionality of his earlier life. He was a boatman, and afterwards captain of a steamer on the Ohio and Mississippi; but has gained property, and is now the owner of mines of coal and iron, which he is endeavoring to dispose of here in England. A plain, respectable, well-to-do-looking personage of more than seventy years; very free of conversation, and beginning to talk with everybody as a matter of course; tall, stalwart, a dark face, with white curly hair and keen eyes; and an expression shrewd, yet kindly and benign. He fought through the whole War of 1812, beginning with General Harrison at the battle of Tippecanoe, which he described to me. He says that at the beginning of the battle, and for a considerable time, he heard Tecumseh's voice, loudly giving orders. There was a man named Wheatley in the American camp, a strange, incommunicative person, — a volunteer, making war entirely on his own hook, and seeking revenge for some relatives of his, who had been killed by the Indians. In the midst of the battle this Wheatley ran at a slow trot past R—— (my informant), trailing his rifle, and making towards the point where Tecumseh's voice was heard. The fight drifted around, and R—— along with it; and by and by he reached a spot where Wheatley lay dead, with his head on Tecumseh's breast. Tecumseh had been shot with a rifle, but, before expiring, appeared to have shot Wheatley with a pistol, which he still held in his hand. R—— affirms that Tecumseh was flayed by the Kentucky men on the spot, and his skin converted into razor-

strops.   I have left out the most striking point
of the narrative, after all, as R—— told it, viz.,
that soon after Wheatley passed him, he suddenly ceased to hear Tecumseh's voice ringing
through the forest, as he gave his orders.   He
was at the battle of New Orleans, and gave me
the story of it from beginning to end; but I
remember only a few particulars in which he
was personally concerned.   He confesses that
his hair bristled upright — every hair in his head
— when he heard the shouts of the British soldiers before advancing to the attack.   His uncomfortable sensations lasted till he began to
fire, after which he felt no more of them.   It
was in the dusk of the morning, or a little before sunrise, when the assault was made ; and
the fight lasted about two hours and a half, during which R—— fired twenty-four times ; and,
said he, "I saw my object distinctly each time,
and I was a good rifle-shot."   He was raising
his rifle to fire the twenty-fifth time, when an
American officer, General Carroll, pressed it
down, and bade him fire no more.   " Enough
is enough," quoth the General.   For there
needed no more slaughter, the British being in
utter rout and confusion.   In this retreat many
of the enemy would drop down among the dead,
then rise, run a considerable distance, and drop
again, thus confusing the riflemen's aim.   One
fellow had thus got about four hundred and

fifty yards from the American line, and, thinking himself secure, he made a derisive gesture.
" I 'll have a shot at him, anyhow," cried a rifle-
man; so he fired, and the poor devil dropped.

R—— himself, with one of his twenty-four
shots, hit a British officer, who fell forward on
his face, about thirty paces from our line, and
as the enemy were then retreating (they advanced and were repelled two or three times)
R—— ran out, and turned him over on his
back. The officer was a man about thirty-eight,
tall and fine-looking; his eyes were wide open,
clear, and bright, and were fixed full on R——
with a somewhat stern glance, but there was the
sweetest and happiest smile over his face that
could be conceived. He seemed to be dead;
— at least, R—— thinks that he did not really
see him, fixedly as he appeared to gaze. The
officer held his sword in his hand, and R——
tried in vain to wrest it from him, until suddenly the clutch relaxed. R—— still keeps the
sword hung up over his mantelpiece. I asked
him how the dead man's aspect affected him.
He replied that he felt nothing at the time;
but that ever since, in all trouble, in uneasy
sleep, and whenever he is out of tune, or wak-
ing early, or lying awake at night, he sees this
officer's face, with the clear bright eyes and the
pleasant smile, just as distinctly as if he were
bending over him. His wound was in the

breast, exactly on the spot that R—— had aimed at, and bled profusely. The enemy advanced in such masses, he says, that it was impossible not to hit them unless by purposely firing over their heads.

After the battle R—— leaped over the rampart, and took a prisoner who was standing unarmed in the midst of the slain, having probably dropped down during the heat of the action, to avoid the hailstorm of rifle-shots. As he led him in the prisoner paused, and pointed to an officer who was lying dead beside his dead horse, with his foot still in the stirrup. " There lies our General," said he. The horse had been killed by a grapeshot, and Pakenham himself, apparently, by a six-pounder ball, which had first struck the earth, covering him from head to foot with mud and clay, and had then entered his side, and gone upward through his breast. His face was all besmirched with the moist earth. R—— took the slain general's foot out of the stirrup, and then went to report his death.

Much more he told me, being an exceedingly talkative old man, and seldom, I suppose, finding so good a listener as myself. I like the man, — a good-tempered, upright, bold and free old fellow ; of a rough breeding, but sufficiently smoothed by society to be of pleasant intercourse. He is as dogmatic as possible, having formed his own opinions, often on very disputable grounds, and hardened in them; taking queer views of matters and things, and giving shrewd and not ridiculous reasons for them; but with a keen, strong sense at the bottom of his character.

.   .   .   .

A little while ago I met an Englishman in a railway carriage, who suggests himself as a kind of contrast to this warlike and vicissitudinous backwoodsman. He was about the same age as R——, but had spent, apparently, his whole life in Liverpool, and has long occupied the post of Inspector of Nuisances, — a rather puffy and consequential man; gracious, however, and affable, even to casual strangers like myself. The great contrast betwixt him and the American lies in the narrower circuit of his ideas; the latter talking about matters of history of his own country and the world: glancing over the whole field of politics, propounding opinions and theories of his own, and showing evidence that his mind had operated for better or worse on almost all conceivable matters; while the Englishman was odorous of his office, strongly flavored with that, and otherwise most insipid. He began his talk by telling me of a dead body which he had lately discovered in a house in Liverpool, where it had been kept about a fortnight by the relatives, partly from want of funds for the burial, and partly in expectation of the arrival of some friends from Glasgow.   There was a plate of glass in the coffin-lid, through which the Inspector of Nuisances, as he told me, had looked and seen the dead man's face in an ugly state of decay, which he minutely described.   However, his conversation was not altogether of this quality; for he spoke about larks, and how abundant they are just now, and what a good pie they make — only they must be skinned, else they will have a bitter taste.   We have since had a lark-pie ourselves, and I believe it was very good in itself; only the recollection of the Nuisance-man's talk was not a very agreeable flavor. A very racy and peculiarly English character might be made out of a man like this, having his life-concern wholly with the disagreeables of a great city.   He seemed to be a good and kindly person, too, but earthy, — even as if his frame had been moulded of clay impregnated with the draining of slaughter-houses.

.   .   .   .

December 21.— On Thursday evening I dined for the first time with the new Mayor at the Town Hall.   I wish to preserve all the characteristic traits of such banquets, because, being peculiar to England, these municipal feasts may do well to picture in a novel.   There was a big old silver tobacco-box, nearly or quite as large round as an ordinary plate, out of which the dignitaries of Liverpool used to fill their pipes, while sitting in council or after their dinners. The date " 1690 " was on the lid. It is now used as a snuff-box, and wends its way from guest to guest round the table. We had turtle, and, among other good things, American canvas-back ducks. . . . These dinners are certainly a good institution, and likely to be promotive of good feeling ; the Mayor giving them often, and inviting in their turn all the respectable and eminent citizens of whatever political bias. About fifty gentlemen were present that evening ; I had the post of honor at the Mayor's right hand ; and France, Turkey, and Austria were toasted before the Republic, for, as the Mayor whispered me, he must first get his allies out of the way. The Turkish Consul and the Austrian both made better English speeches than any Englishman, during the evening ; for it is inconceivable what shapeless and ragged utterances Englishmen are content to put forth, without attempting anything like a wholeness ; but inserting a patch here and a patch there, and finally getting out what they wish to say, indeed, but in most disorganized guise. . . . I can conceive of very high enjoyment in making a speech ; one is in such a curious sympathy with his audience, feeling instantly how every sentence affects them, and wonderfully excited and encouraged by the sense that it has gone to the right spot. Then, too, the imminent emergency, when a man is overboard, and must sink or swim, sharpens, concentrates, and invigorates the mind, and causes matters of thought and sentiment to assume shape and expression, though, perhaps, it seemed hopeless to express them, just before you rose to speak. Yet I question much whether public speaking tends to elevate the orator, intellectually or morally; the effort, of course, being to say what is immediately received by the audience, and to produce an effect on the instant. I don't quite see how an honest man can be a good and successful orator; but I shall hardly undertake to decide the question on my merely post-prandial experience.

The Mayor toasted his guests by their professions, — the merchants, for instance, the bankers, the solicitors, — and while one of the number responded, his brethren also stood up, each in his place, thus giving their assent to what he said. I think the very worst orator was a major of artillery, who spoke in a meek little nervous voice, and seemed a good deal more discomposed than probably he would have been in the face of the enemy. The first toast was " The Ladies," to which an old bachelor responded.

December 31. — Thus far we have come
through the winter, on this bleak and blasty
shore of the Irish Sea, where, perhaps, the
drowned body of Milton's friend Lycidas might
have been washed ashore more than two centuries ago.   This would not be very likely, however, so wide a tract of sands, never deeply
covered by the tide, intervening betwixt us and
the sea.   But it is an excessively windy place,
especially here on the Promenade; always a
whistle and a howl, — always an eddying gust
through the corridors and chambers, — often a
patter of hail or rain or snow against the windows; and in the long evenings the sounds
outside are very much as if we were on shipboard in mid-ocean, with the waves dashing
against the vessel's sides.   I go to town almost
daily, starting at about eleven, and reaching
Southport again at a little past five; by which
time it is quite dark, and continues so till
nearly eight in the morning.

Christmas time has been marked by few
characteristics.   For a week or two previous to
Christmas Day, the newspapers contained rich
details respecting market-stalls and butchers'
shops, — what magnificent carcasses of prize
oxen and sheep they displayed. . . .

The Christmas Waits came to us on Christmas Eve, and on the day itself, in the shape of
little parties of boys or girls, singing wretched

doggerel rhymes, and going away well pleased with the guerdon of a penny or two. Last evening came two or three older choristers at pretty near bedtime, and sang some carols at our door. They were psalm tunes, however. Everybody with whom we have had to do, in any manner of service, expects a Christmas-box; but, in most cases, a shilling is quite a satisfactory amount. We have had holly and mistletoe stuck up on the gas-fixtures and elsewhere about the house.

On the mantelpiece in the coroner's court the other day, I saw corked and labelled phials, which it may be presumed contained samples of poisons that have brought some poor wretches to their deaths, either by murder or suicide. This court might be wrought into a very good and pregnant description, with its grimy gloom illuminated by a conical skylight constructed to throw daylight down on corpses; its greasy Testament covered over with millions of perjured kisses; the coroner himself, whose life is fed on all kinds of unnatural death; its subordinate officials, who go about scenting murder, and might be supposed to have caught the scent in their own garments; its stupid, brutish juries, settling round corpses like flies; its criminals, whose guilt is brought face to face with them here, in closer contact than at the subsequent trial.

O—— P——, the famous Mormonite, called on me a little while ago, — a short, black-haired, dark-complexioned man ; a shrewd, intelligent, but unrefined countenance, excessively unprepossessing ; an uncouth gait and deportment ; the aspect of a person in comfortable circumstances, and decently behaved, but of a vulgar nature and destitute of early culture. I think I should have taken him for a shoemaker, accustomed to reflect in a rude, strong, evil-disposed way on matters of this world and the next, as he sat on his bench. He said he had been residing in Liverpool about six months ; and his business with me was to ask for a letter of introduction that should gain him admittance to the British Museum, he intending a visit to London. He offered to refer me to respectable people for his character ; but I advised him to apply to Mr. Dallas, as the proper person for his purpose.

March 1, 1857. — On the night of last Wednesday week, our house was broken into by robbers. They entered by the back window of the breakfast-room, which is the children's school-room, breaking or cutting a pane of glass, so as to undo the fastening. I have a dim idea of having heard a noise through my sleep ; but if so, it did not more than slightly disturb me. Una heard it, she being at watch with

Rose; and Julian, having a cold, was also wakeful, and thought the noise was of servants moving about below. Neither did the idea of robbers occur to Una. Julian, however, hearing Una at her mother's door, asking for medicine for Rose, called out for medicine for his cold, and the thieves probably thought we were bestirring ourselves, and so took flight. In the morning the servants found the hall door and the breakfast-room window open; some silver cups and some other trifles of plate were gone from the sideboard, and there were tokens that the whole lower part of the house had been ransacked; but the thieves had evidently gone off in a hurry, leaving some articles which they would have taken, had they been more at leisure.

We gave information to the police, and an inspector and constable soon came to make investigations, taking a list of the missing articles, and informing themselves as to all particulars that could be known. I did not much expect ever to hear any more of the stolen property; but on Sunday a constable came to request my presence at the police office to identify the lost things. The thieves had been caught in Liverpool, and some of the property found upon them, and some of it at a pawnbroker's where they had pledged it. The police office is a small dark room, in the basement story of the Town

Hall of Southport; and over the mantelpiece, hanging one upon another, there are innumerable advertisements of robberies in houses, and on the highway, — murders, too, and garrotings; and offences of all sorts, not only in this district, but wide away, and forwarded from other police stations. Being thus aggregated together, one realizes that there are a great many more offences than the public generally takes note of. Most of these advertisements were in pen and ink, with minute lists of the articles stolen; but the more important were in print; and there, too, I saw the printed advertisement of our own robbery, not for public circulation, but to be handed about privately, among the police officers and pawnbrokers. A rogue has a very poor chance in England, the police being so numerous, and their system so well organized.

In a corner of the police office stood a contrivance for precisely measuring the heights of prisoners; and I took occasion to measure Julian, and found him four feet seven inches and a half high. A set of rules for the self-government of police officers was nailed on the door, between twenty and thirty in number, and composing a system of constabulary ethics. The rules would be good for men in almost any walk of life; and I rather think the police officers conform to them with tolerable strictness.

They appear to be subordinated to one another on the military plan. The ordinary constable does not sit down in the presence of his inspector, and this latter seems to be half a gentleman; at least, such is the bearing of our Southport inspector, who wears a handsome uniform of green and silver, and salutes the principal inhabitants, when meeting them in the street, with an air of something like equality. Then again there is a superintendent, who certainly claims the rank of a gentleman, and has perhaps been an officer in the army. The superintendent of this district was present on this occasion.

The thieves were brought down from Liverpool on Tuesday, and examined in the Town Hall. I had been notified to be present, but, as a matter of courtesy, the police officers refrained from calling me as a witness, the evidence of the servants being sufficient to identify the property. The thieves were two young men not much over twenty, — James and John Macdonald, terribly shabby, dirty, jail-bird like, yet intelligent of aspect and one of them handsome. The police knew them already, and they seemed not much abashed by their position. There were half a dozen magistrates on the bench, — idle old gentlemen of Southport and the vicinity, who lounged into the court, more as a matter of amusement than anything else, and lounged out again at their own pleasure;

for these magisterial duties are a part of the
pastime of the country gentlemen of England.
They wore their hats on the bench.   There
were one or two of them more active than their
fellows ; but the real duty was done by the
Clerk of the Court.   The seats within the bar
were occupied by the witnesses, and around the
great table sat some of the more respectable
people of Southport ; and without the bar were
the commonalty in great numbers ; for this is
said to be the first burglary that has occurred
here within the memory of man, and so it has
caused a great stir.

There seems to be a strong case against the
prisoners.   A boy attached to the railway testified to having seen them at Birchdale on
Wednesday afternoon, and directed them on
their way to Southport ; Peter Pickup recognized
them as having applied to him for lodgings in
the course of that evening ; a pawnbroker swore
to one of them as having offered my top-coat
for sale or pledge in Liverpool ; and my boots
were found on the feet of one of them, — all
this in addition to other circumstances of pregnant suspicion.   So they were committed for
trial at the Liverpool assizes, to be holden some
time in the present month.   I rather wished
them to escape.

February 27. — Coming along the promenade a little before sunset, I saw the mountains of the Welsh coast shadowed very distinctly against the horizon. Mr. Channing told me that he had seen these mountains once or twice during his stay at Southport; but, though constantly looking for them, they have never before greeted my eyes in all the months that we have spent here. It is said that the Isle of Man is likewise discernible occasionally ; but as the distance must be between sixty and seventy miles, I should doubt it. How misty is England ! I have spent four years in a gray gloom. And yet it suits me pretty well.

April 10. — At Skipton. My wife, Julian, and I left Southport to-day for a short tour to York and its neighborhood. The weather has been exceedingly disagreeable for weeks past, but yesterday and to-day have been pleasant, and we take advantage of the first glimpses of spring - like weather. We came by Preston, along a road that grew rather more interesting as we proceeded to this place, which is about sixty miles from Southport, and where we arrived between five and six o'clock. First of all, we got some tea ; and then, as it was a pleasant sunset, we set forth from our old-fashioned inn to take a walk.

Skipton is an ancient town, and has an ancient though well-repaired aspect, the houses being

built of gray stone, but in no picturesque shapes;
the streets well paved; the site irregular and
rising gradually towards Skipton Castle, which
overlooks the town, as an old lordly castle ought
to overlook the feudal village which it protects.
The castle was built shortly after the Conquest
by Robert de Romeli, and was afterwards the
property and residence of the famous Cliffords.
We met an honest man, as we approached the
gateway, who kindly encouraged us to apply for
admittance, notwithstanding it was Good Friday; telling us how to find the housekeeper,
who would probably show us over the castle.
So we passed through the gate, between two
embattled towers; and in the castle court we
met a flock of young damsels, who had been
rambling about the precincts.   They likewise
directed us in our search for the housekeeper,
and Sophia, being bolder than I in such assaults
on feudal castles, led the way down a dark archway and up an exterior stairway, and, knocking
at a door, immediately brought the housekeeper
to a parley.

She proved to be a nowise awful personage,
but a homely, neat, kindly, intelligent, and middle-aged body.   She seemed to be all alone in
this great old castle, and at once consented to
show us about, — being, no doubt, glad to see
any Christian visitors.   The castle is now the
property of Sir R. Tufton; but the present

family do not make it their permanent residence,
and have only occasionally visited it.   Indeed,
it could not well be made an eligible or comfortable residence, according to modern ideas; the
rooms occupying the several stories of large
round towers, and looking gloomy and sombre,
if not dreary, — not the less so for what has
been done to modernize them; for instance,
modern paper-hangings, and, in some of the
rooms, marble fireplaces.   They need a great
deal more light and higher ceilings; and I rather
imagine that the warm, rich effect of glowing
tapestry is essential to keep one's spirit cheerful
in these ancient rooms.   Modern paper-hangings are too superficial and wishy-washy for the
purpose.   Tapestry, it is true, there is now,
completely covering the walls of several of the
rooms, but all faded into ghastliness; nor could
some of it have been otherwise than ghastly
even in its newness, for it represented persons
suffering various kinds of torture, with crowds
of monks and nuns looking on.   In another
room there was the story of Solomon and the
Queen of Sheba, and other subjects not to be
readily distinguished in the twilight that was
gathering in these antique chambers.   We saw,
too, some very old portraits of the Cliffords
and the Thanets, in black frames, and the pictures themselves sadly faded and neglected. The
famous Countess Anne of Pembroke, Dorset,

and Montgomery was represented on one of the leaves of a pair of folding doors, and one of her husbands, I believe, on the other leaf. There was the picture of a little idiot lordling, who had choked himself to death; and a portrait of Oliver Cromwell, who battered this old castle, together with almost every other English or Welsh castle that I ever saw or heard of. The housekeeper pointed out the grove of trees where his cannon were planted during the siege. There was but little furniture in the rooms — amongst other articles, an antique chair, in which Mary Queen of Scots is said to have rested.

The housekeeper next took us into the part of the castle which has never been modernized since it was repaired, after the siege of Cromwell. This is a dismal series of cellars above ground, with immensely thick walls, letting in but scanty light, and dim staircases of stone; and a large hall, with a vast fireplace, where every particle of heat must needs have gone up chimney, — a chill and heart-breaking place enough. Quite in the midst of this part of the castle is the courtyard, — a space of some thirty or forty feet in length and breadth, open to the sky, but shut completely in on every side by the buildings of the castle, and paved over with flat stones. Out of this pavement, however, grows a yew-tree, ascending to the tops of the towers, and completely filling, with its branches and foliage, the whole open space between them. Some small birds — quite a flock of them — were twittering and fluttering among the upper branches. We went upward, through two or three stories of dismal rooms, — among others, through the ancient guard-room, — till we came out on the roof of one of the towers, and had a very fine view of an amphitheatre of ridgy hills which shut in and seclude the castle and the town. The upper foliage was within our reach, close to the parapet of the tower; so we gathered a few twigs as memorials. The house-keeper told us that the yew-tree is supposed to be eight hundred years old, and, comparing it with other yews that I have seen, I should judge that it must measure its antiquity by centuries, at all events. It still seems to be in its prime.

Along the base of the castle, on the opposite side to the entrance, flows a stream, sending up a pleasant murmur from among the trees. The housekeeper said it was not a stream, but only a "wash," whatever that may be; and I conjecture that it creates the motive power of some factory-looking edifices, which we saw on our first arrival at Skipton.

We now took our leave of the housekeeper, and came homeward to our inn, where I have written the foregoing pages by a bright fire;

but I think I write better descriptions after letting the subject lie in my mind a day or two.
It is too new to be properly dealt with immediately after coming from the scene.

The castle is not at all crumbly, but in excellent repair, though so venerable. There are
rooks cawing about the shapeless patches of
their nests, in the tops of the trees. In the
castle wall, as well as in the round towers of
the gateway, there seem to be little tenements,
perhaps inhabited by the servants and depen-
dants of the family. They looked in very good
order, with tokens of present domesticity about
them. The whole of this old castle, indeed,
was as neat as a new, small dwelling, in spite
of an inevitable musty odor of antiquity.

April 11. — This morning we took a carriage
and two horses, and set out for Bolton Priory,
a distance of about six miles. The morning was
cool, with breezy clouds, intermingled with sunshine, and, on the whole, as good as are nine
tenths of English mornings. Julian sat beside
the driver, and Sophia and I in the carriage, all
closed but one window. As we drove through
Skipton, the little town had a livelier aspect
than yesterday, when it wore its Good Friday's
solemnity; — but now its market - place was
thronged, principally with butchers, displaying
their meat under little movable pent-houses,

and their customers. The English people really like to think and talk of butcher's meat, and gaze at it with delight ; and they crowd through the avenues of the market-houses and stand enraptured round a dead ox.

We passed along by the castle wall, and noticed the escutcheon of the Cliffords or the Thanets carved in stone over the portal, with the motto *Désormais*, the application of which I do not well see ; these ancestral devices usually referring more to the past than to the future. There is a large old church, just at the extremity of the village, and just below the castle, on the slope of the hill. The gray wall of the castle extends along the road a considerable distance, in good repair, with here and there a buttress and the semicircular bulge of a tower.

The scenery along the road was not particularly striking, — long slopes, descending from ridges ; a generally hard outline of country, with not many trees, and those, as yet, destitute of foliage. It needs to be softened with a good deal of wood. There were stone farmhouses, looking ancient, and able to last till twice as old. Instead of the hedges, so universal in other parts of England, there were stone fences of good height and painful construction, made of small stones, which I suppose have been picked up out of the fields through hundreds of years. They reminded me of old Massachusetts, though

very unlike our rude stone walls, which nevertheless last longer than anything else we build.
Another New England feature was the little
brooks, which here and there flowed across our
road, rippling over the pebbles, clear and bright.
I fancied, too, an intelligence and keenness in
some of the Yorkshire physiognomies, akin to
those characteristics in my countrymen's faces.

We passed an ancient, many-gabled inn, large,
low, and comfortable, bearing the name of the
Devonshire House, as does our own hotel, for
the Duke of Devonshire is a great proprietor in
these parts.   A mile or so beyond, we came to
a gateway, broken through what, I believe, was
an old wall of the Priory grounds; and here
we alighted, leaving our driver to take the carriage to the inn.   Passing through this hole in
the wall, we saw the ruins of the Priory at the
bottom of the beautiful valley about a quarter
of a mile off; and, well as the monks knew how
to choose the sites of their establishments, I
think they never chose a better site than this,
— in the green lap of protecting hills, beside
a stream, and with peace and fertility looking
down upon it on every side.   The view down
the valley is very fine, and, for my part, I am
glad that some peaceable and comfort-loving
people possessed these precincts for many hundred years, when nobody else knew how to appreciate peace and comfort.

The old gateway tower, beneath which was formerly the arched entrance into the domain of the Priory, is now the central part of a hunting-seat of the Duke of Devonshire, and the edifice is completed by a wing of recent date on each side. A few hundred yards from this hunting-box are the remains of the Priory, consisting of the nave of the old church, which is still in good repair, and used as the worshipping-place of the neighborhood (being a perpetual curacy of the parish of Skipton), and the old ruined choir, roofless, with broken arches, ivy-grown, but not so rich and rare a ruin as either Melrose, Netley, or Furness. Its situation makes its charm. It stands near the river Wharfe, — a broad and rapid stream, which hurries along between high banks, with a sound which the monks must have found congenial to their slumberous moods. It is a good river for trout, too ; and I saw two or three anglers, with their rods and baskets, passing through the ruins towards its shore. It was in this river Wharfe that the boy of Egremont was drowned, at the Strid, a mile or two higher up the stream.

In the first place, we rambled round the exterior of the ruins ; but, as I have said, they are rather bare and meagre in comparison with other abbeys, and I am not sure that the especial care and neatness with which they are preserved does not lessen their effect on the beholder.   Neglect, wildness, crumbling walls, the climbing and conquering ivy; masses of stone lying where they fell; trees of old date, growing where the pillars of the aisles used to stand, — these are the best points of ruined abbeys.   But everything here is kept with such trimness that it gives you the idea of a petrifaction.   Decay is no longer triumphant; the Duke of Devonshire has got the better of it.   The grounds around the church and the ruins are still used for burial, and there are several flat tombstones and altar tombs, with crosiers engraved or carved upon them, which at first I took to be the memorials of bishops or abbots, and wondered that the sculpture should still be so distinct.   On one, however, I read the date 1850 and the name of a layman; for the tombstones were all modern, the humid English atmosphere giving them their mossy look of antiquity, and the crosier had been assumed only as a pretty device.

Close beside the ruins there is a large, old stone farmhouse, which must have been built on the site of a part of the Priory, — the cells, dormitories, refectory, and other portions pertaining to the monks' daily life, I suppose, and built, no doubt, with the sacred stones.   I should imagine it would be a haunted house, swarming with cowled spectres.   We wished to see the interior of the church, and procured a guide from this farmhouse, — the sexton, probably,

— a gray-haired, ruddy, cheery, and intelligent man, of familiar though respectful address. The entrance of the church was undergoing improvement, under the last of the abbots, when the Reformation occurred; and it has ever remained in an unfinished state, till now it is mossy with age, and has a beautiful tuft of wall-flowers growing on a ledge over the Gothic arch of the doorway. The body of the church is of much anterior date, though the oaken roof is supposed to have been renewed in Henry VIII.'s time. This, as I said before, was the nave of the old Abbey church, and has a one-sided and unbalanced aspect, there being only a single aisle, with its row of sturdy pillars. The pavement is covered with pews of old oak, very homely and unornamental; on the side opposite the aisle there are two or three windows of modern stained glass, somewhat gaudy and impertinent; there are likewise some hatchments and escutcheons over the altar and elsewhere. On the whole, it is not an impressive interior; but, at any rate, it had the true musty odor which I never conceived of till I came to England, — the odor of dead men's decay, garnered up and shut in, and kept from generation to generation; not disgusting nor sickening, because it is so old and of the past.

On one side of the altar there was a small square chapel, — or what had once been a chapel,

— separated from the chancel by a partition about a man's height, if I remember aright. Our guide led us into it, and observed that some years ago the pavement had been taken up in this spot, for burial purposes; but it was found that it had already been used in that way, and that the corpses had been buried upright. Inquiring further, I found that it was the Clapham family, and another that was called Morley, that were so buried; and then it occurred to me that this was the vault Wordsworth refers to in one of his poems, — the burial-place of the Claphams and Mauleverers, whose skeletons, for aught I know, were even then standing upright under our feet. It is but a narrow place, perhaps a square of ten feet. We saw little or nothing else that was memorable, unless it were the signature of Queen Adelaide in a visitors' book.

On our way back to Skipton it rained and hailed, but the sun again shone out before we arrived. We took the train for Leeds at half past ten, and arrived there in the afternoon, passing the ruined Abbey of Kirkstall on our way. The ruins looked more interesting than those of Boiton, though not so delightfully situated, and now in the close vicinity of manufactories, and only two or three miles from Leeds. We took a dish of soup, and spent a miserable hour in and about the railway station of Leeds; whence we

departed at four, and reached York in an hour
or two. We put up at the Black Swan, and before tea went out, on the cool bright edge of
evening, to get a glimpse of the cathedral, which
impressed me more grandly than when I first
saw it, nearly a year ago. Indeed, almost any
object gains upon me at the second sight. I
have spent the evening in writing up my journal, — an act of real virtue.

After walking round the cathedral, we went
up a narrow and crooked street, very old and
shabby, but with an antique house projecting as
much as a yard over the pavement on one side,
— a timber house it seemed to be, plastered over
and stained yellow or buff. There was no external door affording entrance into this edifice;
but about midway of its front we came to a low,
Gothic, stone archway, passing right through
the house; and as it looked much time-worn,
and was sculptured with untraceable devices,
we went through. There was an exceedingly
antique, battered, and shattered pair of oaken
leaves, which used doubtless to shut up the passage in former times, and keep it secure; but
for the last centuries, probably, there has been
free ingress and egress. Indeed, the portal arch
may never have been closed since the Reformation. Within we found a quadrangle, of which
the house upon the street formed one side, the
others being composed of ancient houses, with

gables in a row, all looking upon the paved quadrangle, through quaint windows of various fashion. An elderly, neat, pleasant-looking woman now came in beneath the arch, and as she had a look of being acquainted here, we asked her what the place was; and she told us, that in the old popish times the prebends of the cathedral used to live here, to keep them from doing mischief in the town. The establishment, she said, was now called "The College," and was let in rooms and small tenements to poor people. On consulting the York Guide, I find that her account was pretty correct; the house having been founded in Henry VI.'s time, and called St. William's College, the statue of the patron saint being sculptured over the arch. It was intended for the residence of the parsons and priests of the cathedral, who had formerly caused troubles and scandals by living in the town.

We returned to the front of the cathedral on our way homeward, and an old man stopped us, to inquire if we had ever seen the Fiddler of York. We answered in the negative, and said that we had not time to see him now; but the old gentleman pointed up to the highest pinnacle of the southern front, where stood the Fiddler of York, one of those Gothic quaintnesses which blotch the grandeur and solemnity of this and other cathedrals.

305

April 12. — This morning was bleak and most ungenial; a chilly sunshine, a piercing wind, a prevalence of watery cloud, — April weather, without the tenderness that ought to be half revealed in it.   This is Easter Sunday, and service at the cathedral commenced at half past ten; so we set out betimes and found admittance into the vast nave, and thence into the choir.   An attendant ushered Sophia and Julian to a seat at a distance from me, and then gave me a place in one of the stalls where the monks used to sit or kneel while chanting the services.   I think these stalls are now appropriated to the prebends.   They are of carved oaken wood, much less elaborate and wonderfully wrought than those of Chester Cathedral, where all was done with head and heart, each a separate device, instead of cut by machinery like this.   The whole effect of this carved work, however, lining the choir with its light tracery and pinnacles, is very fine.   The whole choir, from the roof downward, except the old stones of the outer walls, is of modern renovation, it being but a few years since this part of the cathedral was destroyed by fire.   The arches and pillars and lofty roof, however, have been well restored; and there was a vast east window, full of painted glass, which, if it be modern, is wonderfully chaste and Gothic-like.   All the other windows have painted glass, which does not flare

and glare as if newly painted. But the light,
whitewashed aspect of the general interior of
the choir has a cold and dreary effect. There
is an enormous organ, all clad in rich oaken
carving, of similar pattern to that of the stalls.
It was communion day, and near the high altar,
within a screen, I saw the glistening of the gold
vessels wherewith the services were to be performed.

The choir was respectably filled with a pretty
numerous congregation, among whom I saw
some officers in full dress, with their swords by
their sides ; and one old white-bearded warrior,
who sat near me, seemed very devout at his
religious exercises. In front of me and on the
corresponding benches, on the other side of
the choir, sat two rows of white-robed choristers, twenty in all, and these, with some women,
performed the vocal part of the music. It is
not good to see musicians, for they are sometimes coarse and vulgar people, and so the
auditor loses faith in any fine and spiritual tones
that they may breathe forth.

The services of Easter Sunday comprehend
more than the ordinary quantity of singing and
chanting; at all events, nearly an hour and a
half were thus employed, with some intermix-
ture of prayers and reading of Scriptures; and
being almost congealed with cold, I thought it
would never come to an end. The spirit of my

Puritan ancestors was mighty within me, and I
did not wonder at their being out of patience
with all this mummery, which seemed to me
worse than papistry because it was a corruption
of it.   At last a canon gave out the text, and
preached a sermon about twenty minutes long,
— the coldest, dryest, most superficial rubbish ;
for this gorgeous setting of the magnificent
cathedral, the elaborate music, and the rich ceremonies seem inevitably to take the life out of
the sermon, which, to be anything, must be all.
The Puritans showed their strength of mind
and heart by preferring a sermon an hour and
a half long, into which the preacher put his
whole soul, and lopping away all these externals, into which religious life had first leafed
and flowered, and then petrified.

After the service, while waiting for my wife
in the nave, I was accosted by a young gentleman who seemed to be an American, and whom
I have certainly seen before, but whose name I
could not recollect. This, he said, was his first
visit to York, and he was evidently inclined to
join me in viewing the curiosities of the place,
but, not knowing his name, I could not introduce him to my wife, and so made a parting
salute.

After dinner, we set forth and took a promenade along the wall, and a ramble through some
of the crooked streets, noting the old, jutting-

storied houses, story above story, and the old churches, gnawed like a bone by the teeth of Time, till we came suddenly to the Black Swan before we expected it. . . . I rather fancy that I must have observed most of the external peculiarities at my former visit, and therefore need not make another record of them in this journal.

In the course of our walk we saw a procession of about fifty charity-school boys, in flat caps, each with bands under his chin, and a green collar to his coat; all looking unjoyous, and as if they had no home nor parents' love. They turned into a gateway, which closed behind them; and as the adjoining edifice seemed to be a public institution, — at least, not private, — we asked what it was, and found it to be a hospital or residence for Old Maiden ladies, founded by a gentlewoman of York; I know not whether she herself is of the sisterhood. It must be a very singular institution, and worthy of intimate study, if it were possible to make one's way within the portal.

After writing the above Julian and I went out for another ramble before tea; and, taking a new course, we came to a grated iron fence and gateway, through which we could see the ruins of St. Mary's Abbey. They are very extensive, and situated quite in the midst of the city, and the wall and then a tower of the

Abbey seem to border more than one of the streets. Our walk was interesting, as it brought us unexpectedly upon several relics of antiquity, — a loopholed and battlemented gateway; and at various points fragments of the old Gothic stonework, built in among more recent edifices, which themselves were old; grimness intermixed with quaintness and grotesqueness; old fragments of religious or warlike architecture mingled with queer domestic structures, — the general effect sombre, sordid, and grimy; but yet with a fascination that makes us fain to linger about such scenes, and come to them again.

We passed round the cathedral, and saw jackdaws fluttering round the pinnacles, while the bells chimed the quarters, and little children played on the steps under the grand arch of the entrance. It is very stately, very beautiful, this minster; and doubtless would be very satisfactory, could I only know it long and well enough, — so rich as its front is, even with almost all the niches empty of their statues; not stern in its effect, which I suppose must be owing to the elaborate detail with which its great surface is wrought all over, like the chasing of a lady's jewel-box, and yet so grand! There is a dwelling-house on one side, gray with antiquity, which has apparently grown out of it like an excrescence; and though a good-sized edifice,

310

yet the cathedral is so large that its vastness is not in the least deformed by it. If it be a dwelling-house, I suppose it is inhabited by the person who takes care of the cathedral. This morning, while listening to the tedious chanting and lukewarm sermon, I depreciated the whole affair, cathedral and all; but now I do more justice, at least to the latter, and am only sorry that its noble echoes must follow at every syllable, and re-reverberate at the commas and semicolons, such poor discourses as the canon's. But, after all, it was the Puritans who made the sermon of such importance in religious worship as we New-Englanders now consider it; and we are absurd in considering this magnificent church and all those embroidered ceremonies only in reference to it.

Before going back to the hotel, I went again up the narrow and twisted passage of College Street, to take another glance at St. William's College. I underestimated the projection of the front over the street — it is considerably more than three feet, and is about eight or nine feet above the pavement. The little statue of St. William is an alto-relievo over the arched entrance, and has an escutcheon of arms on each side, all much defaced. In the interior of the quadrangle, the houses have not gables nor peaked fronts, but have peaked windows on the red-tiled roofs. The doorway, opposite the entrance-arch, is rather stately; and on one side is a large projecting window, which is said to belong to the room where the printing-press of Charles I. was established in the days of the Parliament.

Monday, April 13. — This morning was chill, and worse, it was showery, so that our purposes to see York were much thwarted. At about ten o'clock, however, we took a cab and drove to the cathedral, where we arrived while service was going on in the choir, and ropes were put up as barriers between us and the nave; so that we were limited to the south transept, and a part of one of the aisles of the choir. It was dismally cold. We crept cheerlessly about within our narrow precincts (narrow, that is to say, in proportion to the vast length and breadth of the cathedral), gazing up into the hollow height of the central tower, and looking at a monumental brass, fastened against one of the pillars, representing a beruffled lady of the Tudor times, and at the canopied tomb of Archbishop de Grey, who ruled over the diocese in the thirteenth century. Then we went into the side aisle of the choir, where there were one or two modern monuments; and I was appalled to find that a sermon was being preached by the ecclesiastic of the day, nor were there any signs of an imminent termination. I am not aware

that there was much pith in the discourse, but
there was certainly a good deal of labor and
earnestness in the preacher's mode of delivery;
although, when he came to a close, it appeared
that the audience was not more than half a
dozen people.

The barriers being now withdrawn, we walked
adown the length of the nave, which did not
seem to me so dim and vast as the recollection
which I have had of it since my visit of a year
ago. But my preimaginations and my memories
are both apt to play me false with all admirable
things, and so create disappointments for me,
while perhaps the thing itself is really far better
than I imagine or remember it. We engaged
an old man, one of the attendants pertaining to
the cathedral, to be our guide, and he showed
us first the stone screen in front of the choir,
with its sculptured kings of England; and then
the tombs in the north transept, — one of a
modern archbishop, and one of an ancient one,
behind which the insane person who set fire to
the church a few years ago hid himself at nightfall. Then our guide unlocked a side door, and
led us into the chapter-house, — an octagonal
hall, with a vaulted roof, a tessellated floor, and
seven arched windows of old painted glass, the
richest that I ever saw or imagined, each looking
like an inestimable treasury of precious stones,
with a gleam and glow even in the sullen light

of this gray morning. What would they be with the sun shining through them? With all their brilliancy, moreover, they were as soft as rose leaves. I never saw any piece of human architecture so beautiful as this chapter-house; at least, I thought so while I was looking at it, and think so still; and it owed its beauty in very great measure to the painted windows; I remember looking at these windows from the outside yesterday, and seeing nothing but an opaque old crust of conglomerated panes of glass; but now that gloomy mystery was radiantly solved.

Returning into the body of the cathedral, we next entered the choir, where, instead of the crimson cushions and draperies which we had seen yesterday, we found everything folded in black. It was a token of mourning for one of the canons, who died on Saturday night. The great east window, seventy-five feet high, and full of old painted glass in many exquisitely wrought and imagined Scriptural designs, is considered the most splendid object in the minster. It is a pity that it is partially hidden from view, even in the choir, by a screen before the high altar; but indeed, the Gothic architects seem first to imagine beautiful and noble things, and then to consider how they may best be partially screened from sight. A certain secrecy and twilight effect belong to their plan.

We next went round the side aisles of the choir, which contain many interesting monuments of prelates, and a specimen of the very common Elizabethan design of an old gentleman in a double ruff and trunk breeches, with one of his two wives on either side of him, all kneeling in prayer; and their conjoint children, in two rows, kneeling in the lower compartments of the tomb. We saw, too, a rich marble monument of one of the Strafford family, and the tombstone of the famous Earl himself, — a flat tombstone in the pavement of the aisle, covering the vault where he was buried, and with four iron rings fastened into the four corners of the stone whereby to lift it.

And now the guide led us into the vestry, where there was a good fire burning in the grate, and it really thawed my heart, which was congealed with the dismal chill of the cathedral. Here we saw a good many curious things, — for instance, two wooden figures in knightly armor, which had stood sentinels beside the ancient clock before it was replaced by a modern one; and, opening a closet, the guide produced an old iron helmet, which had been found in a tomb where a knight had been buried in his armor; and three gold rings and one brass one, taken out of the graves, and off the finger-bones of mediæval archbishops, — one of them with a ruby set in it; and two silver-gilt chalices, also

315

treasures of the tombs; and a wooden head, carved in human likeness, and painted to the life, likewise taken from a grave where an archbishop was supposed to have been buried. They found no veritable skull nor bones, but only this block-head, as if Death had betrayed the secret of what the poor prelate really was. We saw, too, a canopy of cloth, wrought with gold threads, which had been borne over the head of King James I., when he came to York, on his way to receive the English Crown. There were also some old brass dishes, in which pence used to be collected in monkish times. Over the door of this vestry were hung two banners of a Yorkshire regiment, tattered in the Peninsular wars, and inscribed with the names of the battles through which they had been borne triumphantly; and Waterloo was among them. The vestry, I think, occupies that excrescential edifice which I noticed yesterday as having grown out of the cathedral.

After looking at these things we went down into the crypts, under the choir. These were very interesting, as far as we could see them; being more antique than anything above ground, but as dark as any cellar. There is here, in the midst of these sepulchral crypts, a spring of water, said to be very pure and delicious, owing to the limestone through which the rain that feeds its source is filtered. Near it is a stone trough, in which the monks used to wash their hands.

I do not remember anything more that we saw at the cathedral, and at noon we returned to the Black Swan.   The rain still continued, so that Sophia could not share in any more of my rambles, but Julian and I went out again, and discovered the Guildhall.   It is a very ancient edifice of Richard II.'s time, and has a statue over the entrance which looks time-gnawed enough to be of coeval antiquity, although in reality it is only a representation of George II. in his royal robes.   We went in, and found ourselves in a large and lofty hall with an oaken roof and a stone pavement, and the farther end was partitioned off as a court of justice.   In that portion of the hall the Judge was on the bench, and a trial was going forward; but in the hither portion a mob of people, with their hats on, were lounging and talking, and enjoying the warmth of the stoves.   The window over the judgment-seat had painted glass in it, and so, I think, had some of the hall windows.   At the end of the hall hung a great picture of Paul defending himself before Agrippa, where the Apostle looked like an athlete, and had a remarkably bushy black beard.   Between two of the windows hung an Indian bell from Burmah, ponderously thick and massive.   Both the picture and the bell had been presented to the city as tokens of affectionate remembrance by its children; and it is pleasant to think that such feelings exist in these old stable communities, and that there are permanent localities where such gifts can be kept from generation to generation.

At four o'clock we left the city of York, still in a pouring rain. The Black Swan, where we had been staying, is a good specimen of the old English inn, sombre, quiet, with dark staircases, dingy rooms, curtained beds, — all the possibilities of a comfortable life and good English fare, in a fashion which cannot have been much altered for half a century. It is very homelike when one has one's family about him, but must be prodigiously stupid for a solitary man.

We took the train for Manchester, over pretty much the same route that I travelled last year. Many of the higher hills in Yorkshire were white with snow, which, in our lower region, softened into rain; but as we approached Manchester, the western sky reddened, and gave promise of better weather. We arrived at nearly eight o'clock, and put up at the Palatine Hotel. In the evening I scrawled away at my journal till past ten o'clock; for I have really made it a matter of conscience to keep a tolerably full record of my travels, though conscious that everything good escapes in the process. In the

morning we went out and visited the Manchester Cathedral, a particularly black and grimy
edifice, containing some genuine old wood carvings within the choir. We stayed a good while,
in order to see some people married. One
couple, with their groomsman and bridesmaid,
were sitting within the choir; but when the
clergyman was robed and ready, there entered
five other couples, each attended by groomsman
and bridesmaid. They were all of the lower
orders; one or two respectably dressed, but
most of them poverty-stricken, — the men in
their ordinary loafer's or laborer's attire, the
women with their poor, shabby shawls drawn
closely about them; faded untimely, wrinkled
with penury and care; nothing fresh, virgin-
like, or hopeful about them; joining themselves
to their mates with the idea of making their
own misery less intolerable by adding another's
to it. All the six couples stood up in a row before the altar, with the groomsmen and brides-
maids in a row behind them; and the clergyman
proceeded to marry them in such a way that it
almost seemed to make every man and woman
the husband and wife of every other. However, there were some small portions of the
service directed towards each separate couple;
and they appeared to assort themselves in their
own fashion afterwards, each one saluting his
bride with a kiss. The clergyman, the sexton,

and the clerk all seemed to find something funny in this affair; and the woman who admitted us into the church smiled too, when she told us that a wedding-party was waiting to be married.   But I think it was the saddest thing we have seen since leaving home; though funny enough if one likes to look at it from a ludicrous point of view.   This mob of poor marriages was caused by the fact that no marriage fee is paid during Easter.

This ended the memorable things of our tour; for my wife and Julian left Manchester for Southport, and I for Liverpool, before noon.

April 19. — On the 15th, having been invited to attend at the laying of the corner-stone of Mr. Browne's Free Library, I went to the Town Hall, according to the programme, at eleven o'clock.   There was already a large number of people (invited guests, members of the Historical Society, and other local associations) assembled in the great ball-room, and one of these was delivering an address to Mr. Browne as I entered.   Approaching the outer edge of the circle, I was met and cordially greeted by Monckton Milnes, whom I like, and who always reminds me of Longfellow, though his physical man is more massive.   While we were talking together, a young man approached him with a pretty little expression of surprise and

320

pleasure at seeing him there. He had a slightly
affected or made-up manner, and was rather a
comely person. Mr. Milnes introduced him to
me as Lord ——. Hereupon, of course, I observed him more closely; and I must say that
I was not long in discovering a gentle dignity
and half-imperceptible reserve in his manner;
but still my first impression was quite as real as
my second one. He occupies, I suppose, the
foremost position among the young men of
England, and has the fairest prospects of a high
course before him; nevertheless, he did not impress me as possessing the native qualities that
could entitle him to a high public career. He
has adopted public life as his hereditary profession, and makes the very utmost of all his
abilities, cultivating himself to a determined
end, knowing that he shall have every advantage towards attaining his object. His natural
disadvantages must have been, in some respects,
unusually great; his voice, for instance, is not
strong, and appeared to me to have a more pos-
itive defect than mere weakness. Doubtless he
has struggled manfully against this defect; and
it made me feel a certain sympathy, and, indeed, a friendliness, for which he would not at
all have thanked me had he known it. I felt,
in his person, what a burden it is upon human shoulders, the necessity of keeping up the
fame and historical importance of an illustri-

ous house ; at least, when the heir to its honors has sufficient intellect and sensibility to feel the claim that his country and his ancestors and his posterity all have upon him. Lord —— is fully capable of feeling these claims ; but I would not care, methinks, to take his position, unless I could have considerably more than his strength.

In a little while we formed ourselves into a procession, four in a row, and set forth from the Town Hall, through James Street, Lord Street, Lime Street, all the way through a line of policemen and a throng of people ; and the windows were alive with heads, and I never before was so conscious of a great mass of humanity, though perhaps I may often have seen as great a crowd. But a procession is the best point of view from which to see the crowd that collects together. The day, too, was very fine, even sunshiny, and the streets dry, — a blessing which cannot be overestimated ; for we should have been in a strange trim for the banquet, had we been compelled to wade through the ordinary mud of Liverpool. The procession itself could not have been a very striking object. In America, it would have had a hundred picturesque and perhaps ludicrous features, — the symbols of the different trades, banners with strange devices, flower shows, children, volunteer soldiers, cavalcades, and every suitable and unsuitable contrivance; but we were merely a trail of ordinary-looking individuals, in great-coats, and with precautionary umbrellas. The only characteristic or professional costume, as far as I noticed, was that of the Bishop of Chester, in his flat cap and black silk gown; and that of Sir Henry Smith, the General of the District, in full uniform, with a star and half a dozen medals on his breast. Mr. Browne himself, the hero of the day, was the plainest and simplest man of all, — an exceedingly unpretending gentleman in black; small, white-haired, pale, quiet, and respectable. I rather wondered why he chose to be the centre of all this ceremony; for he did not seem either particularly to enjoy it, or to be at all incommoded by it, as a more nervous and susceptible man might have been.

The site of the projected edifice is on one of the streets bordering on St. George's Hall; and when we came within the enclosure, the corner-stone, a large square of red freestone, was already suspended over its destined place. It has a brass plate let into it, with an inscription, which will perhaps not be seen again till the present English type has grown as antique as black-letter is now. Two or three photographs were now taken of the site, the corner-stone, Mr. Browne, the distinguished guests, and the crowd at large; then ensued a prayer from the Bishop of Chester, and speeches from Mr. Holme, Mr. Browne, Lord ——, Sir John Pakington, Sir Henry Smith, and as many others as there was time for. Lord —— acquitted himself very creditably, though brought out unexpectedly, and with evident reluctance. I am convinced that men, liable to be called on to address the public, keep a constant supply of commonplaces in their minds, which, with little variation, can be adapted to one subject about as well as to another; and thus they are always ready to do well enough, though seldom to do particularly well.

From the scene of the corner-stone we went to St. George's Hall, where a drawing-room and dressing-room had been prepared for the principal guests. Before the banquet, I had some conversation with Sir James Kay Shuttleworth, who had known Miss Brontë very intimately, and bore testimony to the wonderful fidelity of Mrs. Gaskell's life of her. He seemed to have had an affectionate regard for her, and said that her marriage promised to have been productive of great happiness; her husband being not a remarkable man, but with the merit of an exceeding love for her.

Mr. Browne now took me up into the gallery, which by this time was full of ladies; and thence we had a fine view of the noble hall, with the tables laid, in readiness for the banquet. I cannot conceive of anything finer than this hall; it needs nothing but painted windows to make it perfect, and those I hope it may have one day or another.

At two o'clock we sat down to the banquet, which hardly justified that name, being only a cold collation, though sufficiently splendid in its way. In truth, it would have been impossible to provide a hot dinner for nine hundred people in a place remote from kitchens. The principal table extended lengthwise of the hall, and was a little elevated above the other tables, which stretched across, about twenty in all. Before each guest, besides the bill of fare, was laid a programme of the expected toasts, among which appeared my own name, to be proposed by Mr. Monckton Milnes. These things do not trouble me quite as much as they used, though still it sufficed to prevent much of the enjoyment which I might have had if I could have felt myself merely a spectator. My left-hand neighbor was Colonel Campbell, of the Artillery; my right-hand one was Mr. Picton, of the Library Committee; and I found them both companionable men, especially the Colonel, who had served in China and in the Crimea, and owned that he hated the French. We did not make a very long business of the eatables, and then came the usual toasts of ceremony, and afterwards those more peculiar to the occasion, one of the first of which was "The House of Stanley," to which Lord —— responded. It was a noble subject, giving scope for as much eloquence as any man could have brought to bear upon it, and capable of being so wrought out as to develop and illustrate any sort of conservative or liberal tendencies which the speaker might entertain. There could not be a richer opportunity for reconciling and making friends betwixt the old system of society and the new; but Lord —— did not seem to make anything of it. I remember nothing that he said excepting his statement that the family had been five hundred years connected with the town of Liverpool. I wish I could have responded to "The House of Stanley," and his Lordship could have spoken in my behalf. None of the speeches were remarkably good; the Bishop of Chester's perhaps the best, though he is but a little man in aspect, not at all filling up one's idea of a bishop, and the rest were on an indistinguishable level, though, being all practised speakers, they were less hum-y and ha-y than English orators ordinarily are.

I was really tired to death before my own turn came, sitting all that time, as it were, on the scaffold, with the rope round my neck. At last Monckton Milnes was called up and made a speech, of which, to my dismay, I could hardly hear a single word, owing to his being at a considerable distance, on the other side of the chairman, and flinging his voice, which is a bass one, across the hall, instead of adown it, in my direction. I could not distinguish one word of any allusions to my works, nor even when he came to the toast, did I hear the terms on which he put it, nor whether I was toasted on my own basis, or as representing American literature, or as Consul of the United States. At all events, there was a vast deal of clamor; and uprose peers and bishop, general, mayor, knights, and gentlemen, everybody in the hall greeting me with all the honors. I had uprisen, too, to commence my speech, but had to sit down again till matters grew more quiet, and then I got up, and proceeded to deliver myself with as much composure as I ever felt at my own fireside. It is very strange, this self-possession and clear-sightedness which I have experienced when standing before an audience, showing me my way through all the difficulties resulting from my not having heard Monckton Milnes's speech; and on since reading the latter, I do not see how I could have answered it better. My speech certainly was better cheered than any other; especially one passage, where I made a colossus of Mr. Browne, at which the audience grew so tumultuous in their applause that they drowned my figure of speech before it was half out of my mouth.

After rising from table, Lord —— and I talked about our respective oratorical performances; and he appeared to have a perception that he is not naturally gifted in this respect. I like Lord ——, and wish that it were possible that we might know one another better. If a nobleman has any true friend out of his own class, it ought to be a republican. Nothing further of interest happened at the banquet, and the next morning came out the newspapers with vile reports of my speech, attributing to me a variety of forms of ragged nonsense, which, poor speaker as I am, I was quite incapable of uttering.

May 10. — The winter is over, but as yet we scarcely have what ought to be called spring; nothing but cold east winds, accompanied with sunshine, however, as east winds generally are in this country. All milder winds seem to bring rain. The grass has been green for a month, — indeed, it has never been entirely brown, — and now the trees and hedges are beginning to be in foliage. Weeks ago the daisies bloomed, even in the sandy grass-plot bordering on the promenade beneath our front windows; and in the progress of the daisy, and towards its consummation, I saw the propriety of Burns's epithet, " wee, modest, *crimson-tipped* flowers," — its little white petals in the bud being fringed

328

all round with crimson, which fades into pure white when the flower blooms. At the beginning of this month I saw fruit-trees in blossom, stretched out flat against stone walls, reminding me of a dead bird nailed against the side of a barn. But it has been a backward and dreary spring; and I think Southport, in the course of it, has lost its advantage over the rest of the Liverpool neighborhood in point of milder atmosphere. The east wind feels even rawer here than in the city.

Nevertheless, the columns of the Southport Visitor begin to be well replenished with the names of guests, and the town is assuming its aspect of summer life. To say the truth, except where cultivation has done its utmost, there is very little difference between winter and summer in the mere material aspect of Southport; there being nothing but a waste of sand intermixed with plashy pools to seaward, and a desert of sand-hillocks on the land side. But now the brown, weather-hardened donkey-women haunt people that stray along the reaches, and delicate persons face the cold, rasping, ill-tempered blast on the promenade, and children dig in the sands; and, for want of something better, it seems to be determined that this shall be considered spring.

Southport is as stupid a place as I ever lived in; and I cannot but bewail our ill fortune to have been compelled to spend so many months on these barren sands, when almost every other square yard of England contains something that would have been historically or poetically interesting.   Our life here has been a blank.   There was, indeed, a shipwreck, a month or two ago, when a large ship came ashore within a mile from our windows; the larger portion of the crew landing safely on the hither sands, while six or seven betook themselves to the boat, and were lost in attempting to gain the shore, on the other side of the Ribble.   After a lapse of several weeks, two or three of their drowned bodies were found floating in this vicinity, and brought to Southport for burial; so that it really is not at all improbable that Milton's Lycidas floated hereabouts, in the rise and lapse of the tides, and that his bones may still be whitening among the sands.

In the same gale that wrecked the above-mentioned vessel, a portion of a ship's mast was driven ashore, after evidently having been a very long time in and under water; for it was covered with great barnacles and torn seaweed, insomuch that there was scarcely a bare place along its whole length; clusters of sea-anemones were sticking to it, and I know not what strange marine productions besides.   Julian at once recognized the sea-anemones, knowing them by his much reading of Gosse's Aquarium; and

330

though they must now have been two or three days high and dry out of water, he made an extempore aquarium out of a bowl, and put in above a dozen of these strange creatures. In a little while they bloomed out wonderfully, and even seemed to produce young anemones; but, from some fault in his management, they afterwards grew sickly and died. Sophia thinks that the old storm-shattered mast, so studded with the growth of the ocean depths, is a relic of the Spanish Armada which strewed its wrecks along all the shores of England; but I hardly think it would have taken three hundred years to produce this crop of barnacles and sea-anemones. A single summer might probably have done it.

Yesterday we all of us except Rose went to Liverpool to see the performances of an American circus company. I had previously been, a day or two before, with Julian, and had been happy to perceive that the fact of its being an American establishment really induced some slight swelling of the heart within me. It is ridiculous enough, to be sure, but I like to find myself not wholly destitute of this noble weakness, patriotism. As for the circus, I never was fond of that species of entertainment, nor do I find in this one the flash and glitter and whirl which I remember in other American exhibitions.

[Here follow the visits to Lincoln and Boston, printed in Our Old Home. — S. H.]

May 27. — We left Boston by railway at noon, and arrived in Peterborough in about an hour and a quarter, and have put up at the Railway Hotel. After dinner we walked into the town to see the cathedral, of the towers and arches of which we had already had a glimpse from our parlor window.

Our journey from Boston hitherward was through a perfectly level country, — the fens of Lincolnshire, — green, green, and nothing else, with old villages and farmhouses and old church towers; very pleasant and rather wearisomely monotonous. To return to Peterborough. It is a town of ancient aspect; and we passed, on our way towards the market-place, a very ancient looking church with a very far projecting porch, opening in front and on each side through arches of broad sweep. The street by which we approached from our hotel led us into the market-place, which had what looked like an old Guildhall on one side. On the opposite side, above the houses, appeared the towers of the cathedral, and a street leads from the market-place to its front, through an arched gateway which used to be the external entrance to the abbey, I suppose, of which the cathedral was formerly the church. The front of the cathedral is very striking, and unlike any other that I have seen ; being formed by three lofty and majestic arches in a row, with three gable peaks above them, forming a sort of colonnade, within which is the western entrance of the nave. The towers are massive, but low in proportion to their bulk. There are no spires, but pinnacles and statues, and all the rich detail of Gothic architecture, the whole of a venerable gray hue. It is in perfect repair, and has not suffered externally, except by the loss of multitudes of statues, gargoyles, and miscellaneous eccentricities of sculpture, which used to smile, frown, laugh, and weep over the faces of these old fabrics.

We entered through a side portal, and sat down on a bench in the nave, and kept ourselves quiet ; for the organ was sounding, and the choristers were chanting in the choir. The nave and transepts are very noble, with clustered pillars and Norman arches, and a great height under the central tower ; the whole, however, being covered with plaster and whitewash, except the roof, which is of painted oak. This latter adornment has the merit, I believe, of being veritably ancient ; but certainly I should prefer the oak of its native hue, for the effect of the paint is to make it appear as if the ceiling were covered with imitation mosaic-work or an oil-cloth carpet.

After sitting awhile, we were invited by a verger, who came from within the screen, to enter the choir and hear the rest of the service. We found the choristers there in their white garments, and an audience of half a dozen people, and had time to look at the interior of the choir. All the carved woodwork of the tabernacle, the bishop's throne, the prebends' stalls, and whatever else, is modern; for this cathedral seems to have suffered woefully from Cromwell's soldiers, who hacked at the old oak, and hammered and pounded upon the marble tombs, till nothing of the first and very few of the latter remain. It is wonderful how suddenly the English people lost their sense of the sanctity of all manner of externals in religion, without losing their religion too. The French, in their Revolution, underwent as sudden a change; but they became pagans and atheists, and threw away the substance with the shadow.

I suspect that the interior arrangement of the choir and the chancel has been greatly modernized; for it is quite unlike anything that I have seen elsewhere. Instead of one vast eastern window, there are rows of windows lighting the Lady Chapel, and seen through rows of arches in the screen of the chancel; the effect being, whoever is to have the credit of it, very rich and beautiful. There is, I think, no stained glass in the windows of the nave, though in the windows of the chancel there is some of recent date, and from fragments of veritable antique. The effect of the whole interior is grand, expansive, and both ponderous and airy ; not dim, mysterious, and involved, as Gothic interiors often are, the roundness and openness of the arches being opposed to this latter effect.

When the chanting came to a close, one verger took his stand at the entrance of the choir, and another stood farther up the aisle, and then the door of a stall opened, and forth came a clerical dignity of much breadth and substance, aged and infirm, and was ushered out of the choir with a great deal of ceremony. We took him for the bishop, but he proved to be only a canon. We now engaged an attendant to show us through the Lady Chapel and the other penetralia, which it did not take him long to accomplish. One of the first things he showed us was the tombstone, in the pavement of the southern aisle, beneath which Mary Queen of Scots had been originally buried, and where she lay for a quarter of a century, till borne to her present resting-place in Westminster Abbey. It is a plain marble slab, with no inscription. Near this, there was a Saxon monument of the date 870, with sculpture in relief upon it, — the memorial of an Abbot Hedda, who was killed by the Danes when they destroyed the monastery that preceded the abbey and church. I remember, likewise, the recumbent figure of the prelate, whose face has been quite obliterated by Puritanic violence; and I think that there is not a single tomb older than the parliamentary wars, which has not been in like manner battered and shattered, except the Saxon abbot's just mentioned.   The most pretentious monument remaining is that of a Mr. Deacon, a gentleman of George I.'s time, in wig and breeches, leaning on his elbow, and resting one hand upon a skull.   In the north aisle, precisely opposite to that of Queen Mary, the attendant pointed out to us the slab beneath which lie the ashes of Catharine of Aragon, the divorced queen of Henry VIII.

In the nave there was an ancient font, a venerable and beautiful relic, which has been repaired not long ago, but in such a way as not to lessen its individuality.   This sacred vessel suffered especial indignity from Cromwell's soldiers; insomuch that if anything could possibly destroy its sanctity, they would have effected that bad end.   On the eastern wall of the nave, and near the entrance, hangs the picture of old Scarlett, the sexton who buried both Mary of Scotland and Catharine of Aragon, and not only these two queens, but everybody else in Peterborough, twice over.   I think one feels a sort of enmity and spite against these grave-diggers, who live so long, and seem to contract a kindred and partnership with Death, being boon companions with him, and taking his part against mankind.

In a chapel or some side apartment, there were two pieces of tapestry wretchedly faded, the handiwork of two nuns, and copied from two of Raphael's cartoons.

.   .   .   .

We now emerged from the cathedral, and walked round its exterior, admiring it to our utmost capacity, and all the more because we had not heard of it beforehand, and expected to see nothing so huge, majestic, grand, and gray. And of all the lovely closes that I ever beheld, that of Peterborough Cathedral is to me the most delightful; so quiet it is, so solemnly and nobly cheerful, so verdant, so sweetly shadowed, and so presided over by the stately minster, and surrounded by ancient and comely habitations of Christian men. The most enchanting place, the most enviable as a residence in all this world, seemed to me that of the Bishop's secretary, standing in the rear of the cathedral, and bordering on the churchyard; so that you pass through hallowed precincts in order to come at it, and find it a Paradise, the holier and sweeter for the dead men who sleep so near. We looked through the gateway into the lawn, which really seemed hardly to belong to this world, so bright and soft the sunshine was, so fresh the grass, so lovely the trees, so trained and refined and mellowed down was the whole nature of the spot, and so shut in and guarded from all intrusion. It is in vain to write about it; nowhere but in England can there be such a spot, nor anywhere but in the close of Peterborough Cathedral.

May 28. — I walked up into the town this morning, and again visited the cathedral. On the way I observed the Falcon Inn, a very old-fashioned hostelry, with a thatched roof, and what looked like the barn door or stable door in a side front. Very likely it may have been an inn ever since Queen Elizabeth's time. The Guildhall, as I supposed it to be, in the market-place, has a basement story entirely open on all sides, but from its upper story it communicates with a large old house in the rear. I have not seen an older-looking town than Peterborough; but there is little that is picturesque about it, except within the domain of the cathedral. It was very fortunate for the beauty and antiquity of these precincts that Henry VIII. did not suffer the monkish edifices of the abbey to be overthrown and utterly destroyed, as was the case with so many abbeys, at the Reformation; but, converting the abbey church into a cathedral, he preserved much of the other arrangement of the buildings connected with it. And so it happens that to this day we have the massive and stately gateway, with its great pointed arch, still keeping out the world from those who have inherited the habitations of the old monks; for though the gate is never closed, one feels himself in a sacred seclusion the instant he passes under the archway. And everywhere there are old houses that appear to have been adapted from the monkish residences, or from their spacious offices, and made into convenient dwellings for ecclesiastics, or vergers, or great or small people connected with the cathedral; and with all modern comfort they still retain much of the quaintness of the olden time, — arches, even rows of arcades, pillars, walls, beautified with patches of Gothic sculpture, not wilfully put on by modern taste, but lingering from a long past; deep niches, let into the fronts of houses, and occupied by images of saints; a growth of ivy, overspreading walls, and just allowing the windows to peep through, — so that no novelty, nor anything of our hard, ugly, and actual life comes into these limits, through the defences of the gateway, without being mollified and modified. Except in some of the old colleges of Oxford, I have not seen any other place that impressed me in this way; and the grounds of Peterborough Cathedral have the advantage over even the Oxford colleges, insomuch that the life is here domestic, — that of the family, that of the affections, — a natural life, which one deludes himself with imagining may be made into something sweeter and purer in this beautiful spot than anywhere else.   Doubtless the inhabitants find it a stupid and tiresome place enough, and get morbid and sulky, and heavy and obtuse of head and heart, with the monotony of their life.   But still I must needs believe that a man with a full mind, and objects to employ his affection, ought to be very happy here.   And perhaps the forms and appliances of human life are never fit to make people happy until they cease to be used for the purposes for which they were directly intended, and are taken, as it were, in a sidelong application.   I mean that the monks, probably, never enjoyed their own edifices while they were a part of the actual life of the day, so much as these present inhabitants now enjoy them when a new use has grown up apart from the original one.

Towards noon we all walked into the town again, and on our way went into the old church with the projecting portal, which I mentioned yesterday.   A woman came hastening with the keys when she saw us looking up at the door. The interior had an exceeding musty odor, and was very ancient, with side aisles opening by a row of pointed arches into the nave, and a gallery of wood on each side, and built across the

two rows of arches.   It was paved with tombstones, and I suppose the dead people contributed to the musty odor.   Very naked and un-
adorned it was, except with a few mural monuments of no great interest.   We stayed but a
little while, and amply rewarded the poor woman
with a sixpence.   Thence we proceeded to the
cathedral, pausing by the way to look at the
old Guildhall, which is no longer a Guildhall,
but a butter-market; and then we bought some
prints of exterior and interior views of the minster, of which there are a great variety on note-
paper, letter-sheets, large engravings and litho-
graphs.   It is very beautiful ; there seems to be
nothing better than to say this over again.   We
found the doors most hospitably open, and every
part entirely free to us, — a kindness and liber-
ality which we have nowhere else experienced
in England, whether as regards cathedrals or
any other public buildings.   My wife sat down
to draw the font, and I walked through the
Lady Chapel meanwhile, pausing over the empty
bed of Queen Mary, and the grave of Queen
Catharine, and looking at the rich and sumptu-
ous roof, where a fountain, as it were, of groins
of arches spouts from numberless pilasters,
intersecting one another in glorious intricacy.
Under the central tower, opening to either transept, to the nave, and to the choir, are four majestic arches, which I think must equal in height

341

those of which I saw the ruins, and one, all but perfect, at Furness Abbey. They are about eighty feet high.

I may as well give up Peterborough here, though I hate to leave it undescribed even to the tufts of yellow flowers, which grow on the projections high out of reach, where the winds have sown their seeds in soil made by the aged decay of the edifice. I could write a page, too, about the rooks or jackdaws that flit and clamor about the pinnacles, and dart in and out of the eyelet-holes, the piercings, — whatever they are called, — in the turrets and buttresses. On our way back to the hotel, Julian saw an advertisement of some knights in armor that were to tilt to-day; so he and I waited, and by and by a procession appeared, passing through the antique market-place and in front of the abbey gateway, which might have befitted the same spot three hundred years ago. They were about twenty men-at-arms on horseback, with lances and banners. We were a little too near for the full enjoyment of the spectacle; for, though some of the armor was real, I could not help observing that other suits were made of silver paper or gold tinsel. A policeman (a queer anomaly in reference to such a mediæval spectacle) told us that they were going to joust and run at the ring, in a field a little beyond the bridge.

May 28. — We left Peterborough this afternoon, and, however reluctant to leave the cathedral, we were glad to get away from the hotel; for, though outwardly pretentious, it is a wretched and uncomfortable place, with scanty table, poor attendance, and enormous charges. The first stage of our journey to-day was to Grantham, through a country the greater part of which was as level as the Lincolnshire landscapes have been, throughout our experience of them. We saw several old villages, gathered round their several churches; and one of these little communities, "Little Byforth," had a very primitive appearance, — a group of twenty or thirty dwellings of stone and thatch, without a house among them that could be so modern as a hundred years. It is a little wearisome to think of people living from century to century in the same spot, going in and out of the same doors, cultivating the same fields, meeting the same faces, and marrying one another over and over again; and going to the same church, and lying down in the same churchyard, — to appear again, and go through the same monotonous round in the next generation.

At Grantham, our route branches off from the main line; and there was a delay of about an hour, during which we walked up into the town, to take a nearer view of a tall gray steeple which we saw from the railway station. The

streets that led from the station were poor and
commonplace ; and indeed, a railway seems to
have the effect of making its own vicinity
mean. We noticed nothing remarkable until
we got to the market-place, in the centre of
which there is a cross, doubtless of great antiquity, though it is in too good condition not
to have been recently repaired. It consists of an
upright pillar, with a pedestal of half a dozen
stone steps, which are worn hollow by the many
feet that have scraped their hobnailed shoes
upon them. Among these feet, it is highly probable, may have been those of Sir Isaac Newton,
who was a scholar of the free school of this
town ; and when Julian scampered up the steps,
we told him so. Visible from the market-
place also stands the Angel Inn, which seems
to be a wonderfully old inn, being adorned with
gargoyles and other antique sculpture, with projecting windows, and an arched entrance, and
presenting altogether a frontispiece of so much
venerable state that I feel curious to know its
history. Had I been aware that the chief hotel
of Grantham were such a time-honored establishment, I should have arranged to pass the night
there, especially as there were interesting objects
enough in the town to occupy us pleasantly.
The church — the steeple of which is seen over
the market-place, but is removed from it by a
street or two — is very fine ; the tower and

spire being adorned with arches, canopies, and niches, — twelve of the latter for the twelve Apostles, all of whom have now vanished, — and with fragments of other Gothic ornaments. The jackdaws have taken up their abodes in the crevices and crannies of the upper half of the steeple.

We left Grantham at nearly seven, and reached Nottingham just before eight. The castle, situated on a high and precipitous rock, directly over the edge of which look the walls, was visible, as we drove from the station to our hotel. We followed the advice of a railway attendant in going first to the May Pole, which proved to be a commercial inn, with the air of a drinking-shop, in a by-alley ; and, furthermore, they could not take us in. So we drove to the George the Fourth, which seems to be an excellent house , and here I have remained quiet, the size of the town discouraging me from going out in the twilight which was fast coming on after tea. These are glorious long days for travel ; daylight fairly between four in the morning and nine at night, and a margin of twilight on either side.

May 29. — After breakfast this morning, I wandered out and lost myself ; but at last found the post-office, and a letter from Mr. Wilding, with some perplexing intelligence.

Nottingham is an unlovely and uninteresting town. The castle I did not see; but I happened upon a large and stately old church, almost cathedralic in its dimensions. On returning to the hotel, we deliberated on the mode of getting to Newstead Abbey, and we finally decided upon taking a fly; in which conveyance, accordingly, we set out before twelve. It was a slightly overcast day, about half intermixed of shade and sunshine, and rather cool, but not so cool that we could exactly wish it warmer. Our drive to Newstead lay through what was once a portion of Sherwood forest, though all of it, I believe, has now become private property, and is converted into fertile fields, except where the owners of estates have set out plantations. We have now passed out of the fen-country, and the land rises and falls in gentle swells, presenting a pleasant, but not striking, character of scenery. I remember no remarkable object on the road, — here and there an old inn, a gentleman's seat of moderate pretension, a great deal of tall and continued hedge, a quiet English greenness and rurality, — till, drawing near Newstead Abbey, we began to see copious plantations, principally of firs, larches, and trees of that order, looking very sombre, though with some intermingling of lighter foliage. It was after one when we reached "The Hut," — a small, modern wayside inn, almost directly across the road from the entrance-gate of Newstead. The post-boy calls the distance ten miles from Nottingham. He also averred that it was forbidden to drive visitors within the gates; so we left the fly at the inn, and set out to walk from the entrance to the house. There is no porter's lodge; and the grounds, in this outlying region, had not the appearance of being very primly kept, but were well wooded with evergreens, and much overgrown with ferns, serving for cover for hares, which scampered in and out of their hiding-places. The road went winding gently along, and, at the distance of nearly a mile, brought us to a second gate, through which we likewise passed and walked onward a good way farther, seeing much wood, but as yet nothing of the Abbey. At last, through the trees, we caught a glimpse of its battlements, and saw, too, the gleam of water, and then appeared the Abbey's venerable front. It comprises the western wall of the church, which is all that remains of that fabric, — a great central window, entirely empty, without tracery or mullions; the ivy clambering up on the inside of the wall, and hanging over in front. The front of the inhabited part of the house extends along on a line with this church wall, rather low, with battlements along its top, and all in good keeping with the ruinous remnant. We met a servant,

who replied civilly to our inquiries about the
mode of gaining admittance, and bade us ring a
bell at the corner of the principal porch. We
rang accordingly, and were forthwith admitted into a low, vaulted basement, ponderously
wrought with intersecting arches, dark and rather
chilly, just like what I remember to have seen
at Battle Abbey ; and, after waiting here a little
while, a respectable elderly gentlewoman appeared, of whom we requested to be shown
round the Abbey. She courteously acceded,
first presenting to us a book in which to in-
scribe our names.

I suppose ten thousand people, three fourths
of them Americans, have written descriptions
of Newstead Abbey ; and none of them, so far
as I have read, give any true idea of the place ;
neither will my description, if I write one. In
fact, I forget very much that I saw, and especially in what order the objects came. In the
basement was Byron's bath, — a dark and cold
and cellar-like hole, which it must have required
good courage to plunge into ; in this region, too,
or near it, was the chapel, which Colonel Wildman has decorously fitted up, and where service
is now regularly performed, but which was used
as a dog's kennel in Byron's time.

After seeing this, we were led to Byron's own
bedchamber, which remains just as when he
slept in it, — the furniture and all the other

348

arrangements being religiously preserved. It was in the plainest possible style, homely, indeed, and almost mean, — and ordinary paper-hanging, and everything so commonplace that it was only the deep embrasure of the window that made it look unlike a bedchamber in a middling-class lodging-house. It would have seemed difficult, beforehand, to fit up a room in that picturesque old edifice so that it should be utterly void of picturesqueness ; but it was effected in this apartment, and I suppose it is a specimen of the way in which old mansions used to be robbed of their antique character, and adapted to modern tastes, before mediæval antiquities came into fashion. Some prints of the Cambridge colleges, and other pictures indicating Byron's predilections at the time, and which he himself had hung there, were on the walls. This, the housekeeper told us, had been the Abbot's chamber, in the monastic time. Adjoining it is the haunted room, where the ghostly monk, whom Byron introduces into Don Juan, is said to have his lurking place. It is fitted up in the same style as Byron's, and used to be occupied by his valet or page. No doubt, in his Lordship's day, these were the only comfortable bedrooms in the Abbey ; and by the housekeeper's account of what Colonel Wildman has done, it is to be inferred that the place must have been in a most wild, shaggy, tumbledown condition, inside and out, when he bought it.

It is very different now. After showing us these two apartments of Byron and his servant, the housekeeper led us from one to another and another magnificent chamber fitted up in antique style, with oak panelling, and heavily carved bedsteads, of Queen Elizabeth's time or of the Stuarts, hung with rich tapestry curtains of similar date, and with beautiful old cabinets of carved wood, sculptured in relief, or tortoiseshell and ivory. The very pictures and realities, these rooms were, of stately comfort; and they were called by the name of kings, — King Edward's, King Charles II.'s, King Henry VII.'s chamber; and they were hung with beautiful pictures, many of them portraits of these kings. The chimney-pieces were carved and emblazoned; and all, so far as I could judge, was in perfect keeping, so that if a prince or noble of three centuries ago were to come to lodge at Newstead Abbey, he would hardly know that he had strayed out of his own century. And yet he might have known by some token, for there are volumes of poetry and light literature on the tables in these royal bedchambers, and in that of Henry VII. I saw The House of the Seven Gables and The Scarlet Letter, in Routledge's edition.

Certainly the house is admirably fitted up;

and there must have been something very excellent and comprehensive in the domestic arrangements of the monks, since they adapt themselves so well to a state of society entirely different from that in which they originated. The library is a very comfortable room, and provocative of studious ideas, though lounging and luxurious. It is long and rather low, furnished with soft couches, and on the whole, though a man might dream of study, I think he would be most likely to read nothing but novels there. I know not what the room was in monkish times, but it was waste and ruinous in Lord Byron's. Here, I think, the housekeeper unlocked a beautiful cabinet, and took out the famous skull which Lord Byron transformed into a drinking-goblet. It has a silver rim and stand, but still the ugly skull is bare and evident, and the naked inner bone receives the wine. I should think it would hold at least a quart, — enough to overpower any living head into which this death's-head should transfer its contents; and a man must be either very drunk or very thirsty, before he would taste wine out of such a goblet. I think Byron's freak was outdone by that of a cousin of my own, who once solemnly assured me that he had a spittoon made out of the skull of his enemy. The ancient coffin in which the goblet-skull was found was shown us in the basement of the Abbey.

There was much more to see in the house than I had any previous notion of; but except the two chambers already noticed, nothing remained the least as Byron left it.   Yes, another place there was, — his own small dining-room with a table of moderate size, where, no doubt, the skull-goblet has often gone its rounds.   Colonel Wildman's dining-room was once Byron's shooting-gallery, and the original refectory of the monks.   It is now magnificently arranged, with a vaulted roof, a music-gallery at one end, suits of armor and weapons on the walls, and mailed arms extended, holding candelabras. There are one or two painted windows, commemorative of the Peninsular War, and the battles in which the Colonel and his two brothers fought, — for these Wildmen seem to have been mighty troopers, and Colonel Wildman is represented as a fierce-looking, mustachioed hussar at two different ages.   The housekeeper spoke of him affectionately, but says that he is now getting into years, and that they fancy him failing.   He has no children.   He appears to have been on good terms with Byron, and had the latter ever returned to England, he was under promise to make his first visit to his old home, and it was in such an expectation that Colonel Wildman had kept Byron's private apartments in the same condition in which he found them.   Byron was informed of all the

Colonel's fittings up and restorations, and when he introduces the Abbey in Don Juan, the poet describes it, not as he himself left it, but as Colonel Wildman has restored it. There is a beautiful drawing-room, and all these apartments are adorned with pictures, the collection being especially rich in portraits by Sir Peter Lely, — that of Nell Gwynn being one, who is one of the few beautiful women whom I have seen on canvas.

We parted with the housekeeper, and I with a good many shillings, at the door by which we entered; and our next business was to see the private grounds and gardens. A little boy attended us through the first part of our progress, but soon appeared the veritable gardener, — a shrewd and sensible old man, who has been very many years on the place. There was nothing of especial interest as concerning Byron until we entered the original old monkish garden, which is still laid out in the same fashion as the monks left it, with a large, oblong piece of water in the centre, and terraced banks rising at two or three different stages with perfect regularity around it; so that the sheet of water looks like the plate of an immense looking-glass, of which the terraces form the frame. It seems as if, were there any giant large enough, he might raise up this mirror and set it on end. In the monks' garden there is a marble statue of Pan, which, the gardener told us, was brought by the Wicked Lord (great-uncle of Byron) from Italy, and was supposed by the country people to represent the Devil, and to be the object of his worship, — a natural idea enough, in view of his horns and cloven feet and tail, though this indicates, at all events, a very jolly devil. There is also a female statue, beautiful from the waist upward, but shaggy and cloven-footed below, and holding a little cloven-footed child by the hand. This, the old gardener assured us, was Pandora, wife of the above-mentioned Pan, with her son. Not far from this spot, we came to the tree on which Byron carved his own name and that of his sister, Augusta. It is a.tree of twin stems, — a birch-tree, I think, — growing up side by side. One of the stems still lives and flourishes, but that on which he carved the two names is quite dead, as if there had been something fatal in the inscription that has made it forever famous. The names are still very legible, although the letters had been closed up by the growth of the bark before the tree died. They must have been deeply cut at first.

There are old yew-trees of unknown antiquity in this garden, and many other interesting things; and among them may be reckoned a fountain of very pure water, called the Holy Well, of which we drank. There are several fountains, besides the large mirror in the centre of the garden ; and these are mostly inhabited by carp, the genuine descendants of those which peopled the fish-ponds in the days of the monks. Coming in front of the Abbey, the gardener showed us the oak that Byron planted, now a vigorous young tree ; and the monument which he erected to his Newfoundland dog, and which is larger than most Christians get, being composed of a marble, altar - shaped tomb, surrounded by a circular area of steps, as much as twenty feet in diameter. The gardener said, however, that Byron intended this, not merely as the burial-place of his dog, but for himself too, and his sister. I know not how this may have been, but this inconvenience would have attended his being buried there, that, on transfer of the estate, his mortal remains would have become the property of some other man.

We had now come to the empty space, — a smooth green lawn, where had once been the Abbey church. The length had been sixty-four yards, the gardener said, and within his remembrance there had been many remains of it, but now they are quite removed, with the exception of the one ivy-grown western wall, which, as I mentioned, forms a picturesque part of the present front of the Abbey. Through a door in this wall the gardener now let us out. . . .

In the evening our landlady, who seems to be a very intelligent woman, of a superior class to most landladies, came into our parlor, while I was out, and talked about the present race of Byrons and Lovelaces, who have often been at this house. There seems to be a taint in the Byron blood which makes those who inherit it wicked, mad, and miserable. Even Colonel Wildman comes in for a share of this ill luck, for he has almost ruined himself by his expenditure on the estate, and by his lavish hospitality, especially to the Duke of Sussex, who liked the Colonel, and used often to visit him during his lifetime, and his Royal Highness's gentlemen ate and drank Colonel Wildman almost up. So says our good landlady. At any rate, looking at this miserable race of Byrons, who held the estate so long, and at Colonel Wildman, whom it has ruined in forty years, we might see grounds for believing in the evil fate which is supposed to attend confiscated church property. Nevertheless, I would accept the estate, were it offered me.

. . . Glancing back, I see that I have omitted some items that were curious in describing the house, — for instance, one of the cabinets had been the personal property of Queen Elizabeth. It seems to me that the fashion of modern furniture has nothing to equal these old cabinets for beauty and convenience. In the state apartments, the floors were so highly waxed and polished that we slid

on them as if on ice, and could only make sure
of our footing by treading on strips of carpeting
that were laid down.

June 7. — We left Nottingham a week ago,
and made our first stage to Derby, where we
had to wait an hour or two at a great, bustling,
pell-mell, crowded railway station. It was much
thronged with second and third class passengers
coming and departing in continual trains; for
these were the Whitsuntide holidays, which set
all the lower orders of English people astir.
This time of festival was evidently the origin of
the old Election holidays in Massachusetts; the
latter occurring at the same period of the year,
and being celebrated (so long as they could be
so) in very much the same way, with games,
idleness, merriment of set purpose, and drunkenness. After a weary while we took the train
for Matlock, via Ambergate, and arrived at the
former place late in the afternoon. The village
of Matlock is situated on the banks of the Derwent, in a delightful little nook among the hills,
which rise above it in steeps, and in precipitous
crags, and shut out the world so effectually that
I wonder how the railway ever found it out.
Indeed, it does make its approach to this region
through a long tunnel. It was a beautiful,
sunny afternoon when we arrived, and my present impressions are, that I have never seen

anywhere else such exquisite scenery as that
which surrounds the village. The street itself,
to be sure, is commonplace enough, and hot,
dusty, and disagreeable; but if you look above
it, or on either side, there are green hills descending abruptly down, and softened with
woods, amid which are seen villas, cottages, castles; and beyond the river is a line of crags,
perhaps three hundred feet high, clothed with
shrubbery in some parts from top to bottom,
but in other places presenting a sheer precipice
of rock, over which tumbles, as it were, a cascade of ivy and creeping plants. It is very beautiful, and, I might almost say, very wild; but
it has those characteristics of finish, and of being redeemed from nature, and converted into
a portion of the adornment of a great garden,
which I find in all English scenery. Not that
I complain of this; on the contrary, there is
nothing that delights an American more, in
contrast with the roughness and ruggedness of
his native scenes, — to which, also, he might be
glad to return after a while.

We put up at the old Bath Hotel, — an immense house, with passages of such extent that at
first it seemed almost a day's journey from parlor
to bedroom. The house stands on a declivity,
and after ascending one pair of stairs, we came,
in travelling along the passageway, to a door
that opened upon a beautifully arranged garden,

with arbors and grottoes, and the hillside rising steep above.   During all the time of our
stay at Matlock there was brilliant sunshine,
and, the grass and foliage being in their freshest
and most luxuriant phase, the place has left as
bright a picture as I have anywhere in my
memory.

The morning after our arrival we took a
walk, and, following the sound of a church-
bell, entered what appeared to be a park, and,
passing along a road at the base of a line of
crags, soon came in sight of a beautiful church.
I rather imagine it to be the place of worship
of the Arkwright family, whose seat is in this
vicinity, — the descendants of the famous Arkwright who contributed so much towards turning England into a cotton-manufactory.   We
did not enter the church, but passed beyond
it, and over a bridge, and along a road that
ascended among the hills, and finally brought
us out by a circuit to the other end of Matlock
village, after a walk of three or four miles.   In
the afternoon we took a boat across the Derwent, — a passage which half a dozen strokes
of the oars accomplished, — and reached a very
pleasant seclusion called " The Lovers' Walk."
A ferriage of twopence pays for the transit across
the river, and gives the freedom of these grounds,
which are threaded with paths that meander and
zigzag to the top of the precipitous ridge, amid

trees and shrubbery and the occasional ease of rustic seats. It is a sweet walk for lovers, and was so for us; although Julian, with his scramblings and disappearances, and shouts from above, and headlong scamperings down the precipitous paths, occasionally frightened his mother. After gaining the heights, the path skirts along the precipice, allowing us to see down into the village street, and nearer, the Derwent winding through the valley so close beneath us that we might have flung a stone into it. These crags would be very rude and harsh if left to themselves, but they are quite softened, and made sweet and tender, by the great deal of foliage that clothes their sides, and creeps and clambers over them, only letting a stern face of rock be seen here and there, and with a smile rather than a frown.

The next day, Monday, we went to see the grand cavern. The entrance is high up on the hillside, whither we were led by a guide, of whom there are many, and they all pay tribute to the proprietor of the cavern. There is a small shed by the side of the cavern mouth, where the guide provided himself and us with tallow candles, and then led us into the darksome and ugly pit, the entrance of which is not very imposing, for it has a door of rough pine boards, and is kept under lock and key. This is the disagreeable phase — one of the disagreeable phases — of man's conquest over nature in England, — cavern mouths shut up with cellar doors, cataracts under lock and key, precipitous crags compelled to figure in ornamented gardens, — and all accessible at a fixed amount of shillings or pence. It is not possible to draw a full free breath under such circumstances. When you think of it, it makes the wildest scenery look like the artificial rock-work which Englishmen are so fond of displaying in the little bit of grass-plot under their suburban parlor windows. However, the cavern was dreary enough and wild enough, though in a mean sort of way; for it is but a long series of passages and crevices, generally so narrow that you scrape your elbows, and so low that you hit your head. It has nowhere a lofty height, though sometimes it broadens out into ample space, but not into grandeur, the roof being always within reach, and in most places smoky with the tallow candles that have been held up to it. A very dirty, sordid, disagreeable burrow, more like a cellar gone mad than anything else; but it served to show us how the crust of the earth is moulded. This cavern was known to the Romans, and used to be worked by them as a lead mine. Derbyshire spar is now taken from it; and in some of its crevices the gleam of the tallow candles is faintly reflected from the crystallizations; but, on the whole, I felt like a mole, as I went creeping along, and was glad when we came into the sunshine again. I rather think my idea of a cavern is taken from the one in the Forty Thieves, or in Gil Blas, — a vast, hollow womb, roofed and curtained with obscurity. This reality is very mean.

Leaving the cavern, we went to the guide's cottage, situated high above the village, where he showed us specimens of ornaments and toys manufactured by himself from Derbyshire spar and other materials. There was very pretty mosaic work, flowers of spar, and leaves of malachite, and miniature copies of Cleopatra's Needle, and other Egyptian monuments, and vases of graceful pattern, — brooches, too, and many other things. The most valuable spar is called Blue John, and is only to be found in one spot, where, also, the supply is said to be growing scant. We bought a number of articles, and then came homeward, still with our guide, who showed us, on the way, the Romantic Rocks. These are some crags which have been rent away and stand insulated from the hillside, affording a pathway between it and them ; while the places can yet be seen where the sundered rocks would fit into the craggy hill if there were but a Titan strong enough to adjust them again. It is a very picturesque spot, and the price for seeing it is twopence ; though in our case it was included in the four

shillings which we had paid for seeing the cavern. The representative men of England are
the showmen and the policemen; both very
good people in their way.

Returning to the hotel, Julian and his mother
went through the village to the river, near the
railway, where Julian set himself to fishing, and
caught three minnows. I followed, after a while,
to fetch them back, and we called into one or
two of the many shops in the village, which
have articles manufactured of the spar for sale.
Some of these are nothing short of magnificent. There was an inlaid table, valued at sixty
guineas, and a splendid ornament for any drawing-room; another, inlaid with the squares of a
chessboard. We heard of a table in the possession of the Marquis of Westminster, the
value of which is three hundred guineas. It
would be easy and pleasant to spend a great
deal of money in such things as we saw there,
— but all our purchases in Matlock did not
amount to more than twenty shillings, invested
in brooches, shawl-pins, little vases and toys,
which will be valuable to us as memorials on
the other side of the water. After this we
visited a petrifying cave, of which there are
several hereabouts. The process of petrifaction
requires some months, or perhaps a year or
two, varying with the size of the article to be
operated upon. The articles are placed in the

cave, under the drippings from the roof, and a hard deposit is formed upon them, and sometimes, as in the case of a bird's-nest, causes a curious result, — every straw and hair being immortalized and stiffened into stone. A horse's head was in process of petrifaction; and Julian bought a broken eggshell for a penny, though larger articles are expensive. The process would appear to be entirely superficial, — a mere crust on the outside of things, — but we saw some specimens of petrified oak, where the stony substance seemed to be intimately incorporated with the wood, and to have really changed it into stone. These specimens were immensely ponderous, and capable of a high polish, which brought out beautiful streaks and shades.

One might spend a very pleasant summer in Matlock, and I think there can be no more beautiful place in the world; but we left it that afternoon, and railed to Manchester, where we arrived between ten and eleven at night. The next day I left Sophia to go to the Art Exhibition, and took Julian with me to Liverpool, where I had an engagement that admitted of no delay. Thus ended our tour, in which we had seen but a little bit of England, yet rich with variety and interest. What a wonderful land! It is our forefathers' land; our land, for I will not give up such a precious inheritance. We are now back again in flat and sandy Southport,

which, during the past week, has been thronged
with Whitsuntide people, who crowd the streets,
and pass to and fro along the promenade, with
a universal and monotonous air of nothing to
do, and very little enjoyment.   It is a pity that
poor folks cannot employ their little hour of leisure to better advantage, in a country where the
soil is so veined with gold.

These are delightfully long days.   Last night,
at half past nine, I could read with perfect ease
in parts of the room remote from the window;
and at nearly half past eleven there was a broad
sheet of daylight in the west, gleaming brightly
over the plashy sands.   I question whether there
be any total night at this season.

June 21. — Southport, I presume, is now in
its most vivid aspect; there being a multitude
of visitors here, principally of the middling
classes, and a frequent crowd, whom I take to
be working-people from Manchester and other
factory towns.   It is the strangest place to come
to for the pleasures of the sea, of which we
scarcely have a glimpse from month's end to
month's end, nor any fresh, exhilarating breath
from it, but a lazy, languid atmosphere, brooding over the waste of sands; or even if there be a
sulky and bitter wind blowing along the promenade, it still brings no salt elixir.   I never was
more weary of a place in all my life, and never

felt such a disinterested pity as of the people who come here for pleasure. Nevertheless, the town has its amusements, — in the first place, the daylong and perennial one of donkey-riding along the sands, large parties of men and girls pottering along together ; the Flying Dutchman trundles hither and thither when there is breeze enough ; an archery-man sets up his targets on the beach ; the bathing-houses stand by scores and fifties along the shore, and likewise on the banks of the Ribble, a mile seaward ; the hotels have their billiard-rooms ; there is a theatre every evening ; from morning till night comes a succession of organ-grinders, playing interminably under your window ; and a man with a bassoon and a monkey, who takes your pennies and pulls off his cap in acknowledgment ; and wandering minstrels, with guitar and voice ; and a Highland bagpipe, squealing out a tangled skein of discord, together with a Highland maid, who dances a hornpipe ; and Punch and Judy, — in a word, we have specimens of all manner of vagrancy that infests England. In these long days, and long and pleasant ones, the promenade is at its liveliest about nine o'clock, which is but just after sundown ; and our little Rose finds it difficult to go to sleep amid so much music as comes to her ears from bassoon, bagpipe, organ, guitar, and now and then a military band. One feature of the place is the sick

and infirm people, whom we see dragged along
in bath-chairs, or dragging their own limbs lan-
guidly; or sitting on benches; or meeting in
the streets, and making acquaintance on the
strength of mutual maladies, — pale men leaning on their ruddy wives; cripples, three or four
together in a ring, and planting their crutches in
the centre.   I don't remember whether I have
ever mentioned among the notabilities of Southport the Town Crier, — a meek-looking old
man, who sings out his messages in a most dole-
ful tone, as if he took his title in a literal sense,
and were really going to cry, or crying in the
world's behalf; one other stroller, a foreigner
with a dog, shaggy round the head and shoulders, and closely shaven behind. The poor little beast jumped through hoops, ran about on
two legs of one side, danced on its hind legs, or
on its fore paws with its hind ones straight up
in the air, — all the time keeping a watch on his
master's eye, and evidently mindful of many a
beating.

June 25. — The war steamer Niagara came
up the Mersey a few days since, and day before
yesterday Captain Hudson called at my office,
— a somewhat meagre elderly gentleman, of
simple and hearty manners and address, having
his purser, Mr. Eldredge, with him, who, I think,
rather prides himself upon having a Napoleonic

367

profile. The captain is an old acquaintance of Mrs. Blodgett, and has come ashore principally with a view to calling on her; so, after we had left our cards for the Mayor, I showed these naval gentlemen the way to her house. Mrs. Blodgett and Miss W—— were prodigiously glad to see him; and they all three began to talk of old times and old acquaintances; for when Mrs. Blodgett was a rich lady at Gibraltar, she used to have the whole navy-list at her table, — young midshipmen and lieutenants then, perhaps, but old, gouty, paralytic commodores now, if still even partly alive. It was arranged that Mrs. Blodgett, with as many of the ladies of her family as she chose to bring, should accompany me on my official visit to the ship the next day; and yesterday we went accordingly, — Mrs. Blodgett, Miss W——, and six or seven American captains' wives, their husbands following in another boat. I know too little of ships to describe one, or even to feel any great interest in the details of this or of any other ship; but the nautical people seemed to see much to admire. She lay in the Sloyne, in the midst of a broad basin of the Mersey, with a pleasant landscape of green England, now warm with summer sunshine, on either side, with churches and villa residences and suburban and rural beauty. The officers of the ship are gentlemanly men, externally very well mannered, although not polished and refined to any considerable extent. At least, I have not found naval men so, in general; but still it is pleasant to see Americans who are not stirred by such motives as usually interest our countrymen, — no hope nor desire of growing rich, but planting their claims to respectability on other grounds, and therefore acquiring a certain nobleness, whether it be inherent in their nature or no. It always seems to me they look down upon civilians with quiet and not ill-natured scorn, which one has the choice of smiling or being provoked at. It is not a true life which they lead, but shallow and aimless; and unsatisfactory it must be to the better minds among them; nor do they appear to profit by what would seem the advantages presented to them in their world-wide though not world-deep experience. They get to be very clannish too.

After seeing the ship we landed, all of us, ladies and captain, and went to the gardens of the Rock Ferry Hotel, where Julian and I stayed behind the rest.

June 28. — On the 26th my wife, Julian, and I left Southport, taking the train for Preston, and as we had to stop an hour or two before starting for Carlisle, I walked up into the town. The street through which most of my walk lay was brick - built, lively, bustling, and not particularly noteworthy; but, turning a little way down another street, the town had a more ancient aspect. The day was intensely hot, the sun lying bright and broad as ever I remember it in an American city; so that I was glad to get back again to the shade and shelter of the station. The heat and dust, moreover, made our journey to Carlisle very uncomfortable. It was through very pretty, and sometimes picturesque scenery, being on the confines of the hill country, which we could see on our left, dim and blue; and likewise we had a refreshing breath from the sea in passing along the verge of Morecambe Bay. We reached Carlisle at about five o'clock, and, after taking tea at the Bush Hotel, set forth to look at the town.

The notable objects were a castle and a cathedral; and we first found our way to the castle, which stands on elevated ground, on the side of the city towards Scotland. A broad, well-constructed path winds round the castle at the base of the wall, on the verge of a steep descent to the plain beneath, through which winds the river Eden. Along this path we walked quite round the castle, a circuit of perhaps half a mile, — pleasant, being shaded by the castle's height and by the foliage of trees. The walls have been so much rebuilt and restored that it is only here and there that we see an old buttress, or a few time-worn stones intermixed with the new facing with which the aged substance is overlaid. The material is red freestone, which seems to be very abundant in this part of the country. We found no entrance to the castle till the path had led us from the free and airy country into a very mean part of the town, where the wretched old houses thrust themselves between us and the castle wall, and then, passing through a narrow street, we walked up what appeared like a by-lane, and the portal of the castle was before us. There was a sentry-box just within the gate, and a sentinel was on guard, for Carlisle Castle is a national fortress, and has usually been a depot for arms and ammunition. The sergeant, or corporal of the guard, sat reading within the gateway, and, on my request for admittance, he civilly appointed one of the soldiers to conduct us to the castle. As I recollect, the chief gateway of the castle, with the guard-room in the thickness of the wall, is situated some twenty yards behind the first entrance where we met the sentinel.

It was an intelligent young soldier who showed us round the castle, and very civil, as I always find soldiers to be. He had not anything particularly interesting to show, nor very much to say about it ; and what he did say, so far as it referred to the history of the castle, was probably apocryphal.

The castle has an inner and outer ward on

the descent of the hill, and included within the circuit of the exterior wall. Having been always occupied by soldiers, it has not been permitted to assume the picturesque aspect of a ruin, but the buildings of the interior have either been constantly repaired, as they required it, or have been taken down when past repair. We saw a small part of the tower where Mary Queen of Scots was confined on her first coming to England; these remains consist only of a portion of a winding stone staircase, at which we glanced through a window. The keep is very large and massive, and no doubt old in its inner substance. We ascended to the castle walls, and looked out over the river towards the Scottish hills, which are visible in the distance, — the Scottish border being not more than eight or nine miles off. Carlisle Castle has stood many sieges, and witnessed many battles under its walls. There are now, on its ramparts, only some half a dozen old-fashioned guns, which our soldier told us had gone quite out of use in these days. They were long iron twelve-pounders, with one or two carronades. The soldier was of an artillery regiment, and wore the Crimean medal. He said the garrison now here consists only of about twenty men, all of whom had served in the Crimea, like himself. They seem to lead a very dull and monotonous life, as indeed it must be, without object

or much hope, or any great employment of the
present, like prisoners, as indeed they are.   Our
guide showed us on the rampart a place where
the soldiers had been accustomed to drop themselves down at night, hanging by their hands
from the top of the wall, and alighting on their
feet close beside the path on the outside.   The
height seemed at least that of an ordinary house,
but the soldier said that nine times out of ten
the fall might be ventured without harm ; and
he spoke from experience, having himself got
out of the castle in this manner.   The place
is now boarded up, so as to make egress difficult or impossible.

The castle, after all, was not particularly
worth seeing.   The soldier's most romantic
story was of a daughter of Lord Scroope, a
former governor of the castle, when Mary of
Scotland was confined here.   She attempted to
assist the Queen in escaping, but was shot dead
in the gateway by the warder ; and the soldier
pointed out the very spot where the poor young
lady fell and died, — all which would be very
interesting were there a word of truth in the
story.   But we liked our guide for his intelligence, simplicity, and for the pleasure which he
seemed to take, as an episode of his dull daily
life, in talking to strangers.   He observed that
the castle walls were solid, and indeed, there
was breadth enough to drive a coach and four

along the top; but the artillery of the Crimea
would have shelled them into ruins in a very
few hours. When we got back to the guard-
house, he took us inside, and showed the dismal and comfortless rooms where soldiers are
confined for drunkenness, and other offences
against military laws, telling us that he himself
had been confined there, and almost perished
with cold. I should not much wonder if he
were to get into durance again, through mis-
use of the fee which I put into his hand at
parting.

The cathedral is at no great distance from
the castle; and though the streets are mean and
sordid in the vicinity, the close has the antique
repose and shadowy peace, at once domestic
and religious, which seem peculiar and universal in cathedral closes. The foundation of this
cathedral church is very ancient, it having been
the church portion of an old abbey, the refectory and other remains of which are still seen
around the close. But the whole exterior of the
building, except here and there a buttress, and
one old patch of gray stones, seems to have
been renewed within a very few years with red
freestone; and really I think it is all the more
beautiful for being new, — the ornamental parts
being so sharply cut, and the stone, moreover,
showing various shadings, which will disappear
when it gets weather-worn. There is a very

large and fine east window, of recent construction, wrought with delicate stone tracery. The
door of the south transept stood open, though
barred by an iron grate. We looked in, and saw
a few monuments on the wall, but found nobody to give us admittance. The portal of this
entrance is very lovely with wreaths of stone
foliage and flowers round the arch, recently
carved; yet not so recently but that the swal-
lows have given their sanction to it, as if it were
a thousand years old, and have built their nests
in the deeply carved recesses. While we were
looking, a little bird flew into the small opening
between two of these petrified flowers, behind
which was his nest, quite out of sight. After
some attempts to find the verger, we went back
to the hotel. . . .

In the morning my wife and Julian went
back to see the interior of the cathedral, while
I strayed at large about the town, again passing
round the castle site, and thence round the city,
where I found some inconsiderable portions
of the wall which once girt it about. It was
market-day in Carlisle, and the principal streets
were much thronged with human life and business on that account; and in as busy a street
as any stands a marble statue, in robes of antique state, fitter for a niche in Westminster
Abbey than for the thronged street of a town.
It is a statue of the Earl of Lonsdale, Lord

Lieutenant of Cumberland, who died about twenty years ago.

[Here follows the record of the visits to the Haunts of Burns, already published in Our Old Home. — S. H.]

GLASGOW, *July* 1. — Immediately after our arrival yesterday we went out and inquired our way to the cathedral, which we reached through a good deal of Scotch dirt, and a rabble of Scotch people of all sexes and ages. The women of Scotland have a faculty of looking exceedingly ugly as they grow old. The cathedral I have already noticed in the record of my former visit to Scotland. I did it no justice then, nor shall do it any better justice now; but it is a fine old church, although it makes a colder and severer impression than most of the Gothic architecture which I have elsewhere seen. I do not know why this should be so; for portions of it are wonderfully rich, and everywhere there are arches opening beyond arches, and clustered pillars and groined roofs, and vistas lengthening along the aisles. The person who shows it is an elderly man of jolly aspect and demeanor; he is enthusiastic about the edifice, and makes it the thought and object of his life; and being such a merry sort of man, always saying something mirthfully, and yet, in all his thoughts, words, and actions, having reference to this sol-

376

emn cathedral, he has the effect of one of the
corbels or gargoyles, — those ludicrous, strange
sculptures which the Gothic architects appended
to their arches.

The upper portion of the minster, though
very stately and beautiful, is not nearly so ex-
traordinary as the crypts. Here the intricacy of
the arches, and the profound system on which
they are arranged, is inconceivable, even when
you see them, — a whole company of arches
uniting in one keystone; arches uniting to form
a glorious canopy over the shrine or tomb of a
prelate; arches opening through and beyond
one another, whichever way you look, — all
amidst a shadowy gloom, yet not one detail
wrought out the less beautifully and delicately
because it could scarcely be seen. The wreaths
of flowers that festoon one of the arches are cut
in such relief that they do but just adhere to the
stone on which they grow. The pillars are massive and the arches very low, the effect being a
twilight, which at first leads the spectator to
imagine himself underground; but by and by I
saw that the sunshine came in through the narrow windows, though it scarcely looked like sunshine then. For many years these crypts were
used as burial ground, and earth was brought
in for the purpose of making graves; so that
the noble columns were half buried, and the
beauty of the architecture quite lost and for-

gotten. Now the dead men's bones and the earth that covered them have all been removed, leaving the original pavement of the crypt, or a new one in its stead, with only the old relics of saints, martyrs, and heroes underneath, where they have lain so long that they have become a part of the spot. . . . I was quite chilled through, and the old verger regretted that we had not come during the late hot weather, when the everlasting damp and chill of the spot would have made us entirely comfortable. These crypts originated in the necessity of keeping the floor of the upper cathedral on one level, the edifice being built on a declivity, and the height of the crypt being measured by the descent of the site.

After writing the above, we walked out and saw something of the newer portion of Glasgow; and really I am inclined to think it the stateliest of cities. The Exchange and other public buildings, and the shops in Buchanan Street are very magnificent; the latter especially, excelling those of London. There is, however, a pervading sternness and grimness resulting from the dark gray granite, which is the universal building-material both of the old and new edifices. Later in the forenoon we again walked out, and went along Argyle Street, and through the Trongate and the Salt-Market. The two latter were formerly the principal business streets,

and, together with High Street, the abode of
the rich merchants and other great people of
the town.   High Street, and, still more, the
Salt-Market, now swarm with the lower orders
to a degree which I never witnessed elsewhere;
so that it is difficult to make one's way among
the sullen and unclean crowd, and not at all
pleasant to breathe in the noisomeness of the
atmosphere.   The children seem to have been
unwashed from birth. Some of the gray houses
appear to have once been stately and handsome,
and have their high gable-ends notched at the
edges, like a flight of stairs. We saw the Tron
steeple, and the statue of King William III.,
and searched for the Old Tolbooth. . . . Wandering up the High Street, we turned once
more into the quadrangle of the University, and
mounted a broad stone staircase which ascends
square, and with right-angular turns on one corner, on the outside of the edifices. It is very
striking in appearance, being ornamented with a
balustrade, on which are large globes of stone,
and a great lion and unicorn curiously sculptured on the opposite side.   While we waited
here, staring about us, a man approached, and
offered to show us the interior. He seemed to
be in charge of the College buildings. We ac-
cepted his offer, and were led first up this stone
staircase, and into a large and stately hall, panelled high towards the ceiling with dark oak,

and adorned with elaborately carved cornices, and other wood-work. There was a long reading-table towards one end of the hall, on which were laid pamphlets and periodicals; and a venerable old gentleman, with white head and bowed shoulders, sat there reading a newspaper. This was the Principal of the University, and as he looked towards us graciously, yet as if expecting some explanation of our entrance, I approached and apologized for intruding on the plea of our being strangers and anxious to see the College. He made a courteous response, though in exceedingly decayed and broken accents, being now eighty-six years old, and gave us free leave to inspect everything that was to be seen. This hall was erected two years after the Restoration of Charles II., and has been the scene, doubtless, of many ceremonials and high banquetings since that period; and, among other illustrious personages, Queen Victoria has honored it with her presence. Thence we went into several recitation or lecture rooms in various parts of the buildings — but they were all of an extreme plainness, very unlike the rich old Gothic libraries and chapels and halls which we saw in Oxford. Indeed, the contrast between this Scotch severity and that noble luxuriance, and antique majesty, and rich and sweet repose of Oxford, is very remarkable, both within the edifices and without. But we saw one or two

curious things, — for instance, a chair of mahogany, elaborately carved with the arms of Scotland and other devices, and having a piece of
the kingly stone of Scone inlaid in its seat.
This chair is used by the Principal on certain
high occasions, and we ourselves, of course, sat
down in it.   Our guide assigned to it a date
preposterously earlier than could have been the
true one, judging either by the character of the
carving or by the fact that mahogany has not
been known or used much more than a century
and a half.

Afterwards he led us into the Divinity Hall,
where, he said, there were some old portraits of
historic people, and among them an original
picture of Mary Queen of Scots.   There was,
indeed, a row of old portraits at each end of the
apartment, — for instance, Zachariah Boyd, who
wrote the rhyming version of the Bible, which
is still kept, safe from any critical eye, in the
library of the University, to which he presented
this, besides other more valuable benefactions,
— for which they have placed his bust in a niche
in the principal quadrangle ; also, John Knox
makes one of the row of portraits ; and a dozen
or two more of Scotch worthies, all very dark
and dingy.   As to the picture of Mary of Scotland, it proved to be not hers at all, but a picture of Queen Mary, the consort of William
III., whose portrait, together with that of her

sister, Queen Anne, hangs in the same row. We told our guide this, but he seemed unwilling to accept it as a fact. There is a museum belonging to the University; but this, for some reason or other, could not be shown to us just at this time, and there was little else to show. We just looked at the gardens, but, though of large extent, they are so meagre and bare — so unlike that lovely shade of the Oxford gardens — that we did not care to make further acquaintance with them.

Then we went back to our hotel, and if there were not already more than enough of description, both past and to come, I should describe George's Square, on one side of which the hotel is situated. A tall column rises in the grassy centre of it, lifting far into the upper air a fine statue of Sir Walter Scott, which we saw to great advantage last night, relieved against the sunset sky; and there are statues of Sir John Moore — a native of Glasgow — and of James Watt, at corners of the square. Glasgow is certainly a noble city.

After lunch we embarked on board the steamer, and came up the Clyde. Ben Lomond, and other Highland hills, soon appeared on the horizon; we passed Douglas Castle on a point of land projecting into the river; and, passing under the precipitous height of Dumbarton Castle, which we had long before seen, came to our voyage's end at this village, where we have put up at the Elephant Hotel.

July 2. — After tea, not far from seven o'clock, it being a beautiful decline of day, we set out to walk to Dumbarton Castle, which stands apart from the town, and is said to have been once surrounded by the waters of the Clyde. The rocky height on which the castle stands is a very striking object, bulging up out of the Clyde, with abrupt decision, to the elevation of five hundred feet. The summit is cloven in twain, the cleft reaching nearly to the bottom on the side towards the river, but not coming down so deeply on the landward side. It is precipitous all around; and wherever the steepness admits, or does not make assault impossible, there are gray ramparts round the hill, with cannon threatening the lower world. Our path led us beneath one of these precipices several hundred feet sheer down, and with an ivied fragment of ruined wall at the top. A soldier who sat by the wayside told us that this was called the " Lover's Leap," because a young girl, in some love-exigency, had once jumped down from it, and came safely to the bottom. We reached the castle gate, which is near the shore of the Clyde, and there found another artillery soldier, who guided us through the fortress. He said that there were now but about

a dozen soldiers stationed in the castle, and no .
officer.

The lowest battery looks towards the river,
and consists of a few twelve-pound cannon; but
probably the chief danger of attack was from
the land, and the chief pains have been taken
to render the castle defensible in that quarter.
There are flights of stone stairs ascending up
through the natural avenue, in the cleft of the
double-summited rock; and about midway there
is an arched doorway, beneath which there used
to be a portcullis, — so that if an enemy had
won the lower part of the fortress, the upper
portion was still inaccessible. Where the cleft
of the rock widens into a gorge, there are several buildings, old, but not appertaining to the
ancient castle, which has almost entirely disappeared. We ascended both summits, and, reaching the loftiest point on the right, stood upon
the foundation of a tower that dates back to the
fifth century, whence we had a glorious prospect
of Highlands and Lowlands; the chief object
being Ben Lomond, with its great dome, among
a hundred other blue and misty hills, with the
sun going down over them; and, in another
direction, the Clyde, winding far downward
through the plain, with the headland of Dum-
beck close at hand, and Douglas Castle at no
great distance. On the ramparts beneath us
the soldier pointed out the spot where Wallace

scaled the wall, climbing an apparently inaccessible precipice, and taking the castle.   The
principal parts of the ancient castle appear to
have been on the other and lower summit of
the hill, and thither we now went, and traced
the outline of its wall, although none of it is
now remaining.   Here is the magazine, still containing some powder, and here is a battery of
eighteen-pound guns, with pyramids of balls,
all in readiness against an assault; which, however, hardly any turn of human affairs can hereafter bring about.   The appearance of a fortress
is kept up merely for ceremony's sake; and
these cannon have grown antiquated.   Moreover, as the soldier told us, they are seldom or
never fired, even for purposes of rejoicing or
salute, because their thunder produces the singular effect of depriving the garrison of water.
There is a large tank, and the concussion causes
the rifts of the stone to open, and thus lets the
water out.   Above this battery, and elsewhere
about the fortress, there are warders' turrets of
stone, resembling great pepper boxes.   When
Dr. Johnson visited the castle, he introduced
his bulky person into one of these narrow re-
ceptacles, and found it difficult to get out again.
A gentleman who accompanied him was just
stepping forward to offer his assistance, but Boswell whispered him to take no notice, lest Johnson should be offended; so they left him to get

out as he could.   He did finally extricate himself, else we might have seen his skeleton in the
turret.   Boswell does not tell this story, which
seems to have been handed down by local tradition.

The less abrupt declivities of the rock are
covered with grass, and afford food for a few
sheep, who scamper about the heights and seem
to have attained the dexterity of goats in clambering.   I never knew a purer air than this
seems to be, nor a lovelier golden sunset.

Descending into the gorge again, we went
into the armory, which is in one of the buildings occupying the space between the two hill-
tops.   It formerly contained a large collection
of arms ; but these have been removed to the
Tower of London, and there are now only
some tattered banners, of which I do not know
the history, and some festoons of pistols, and
grenades, shells, and grape and canister shot,
kept merely as curiosities ; and, far more interesting than the above, a few battle-axes, dag-
gers, and spearheads from the field of Bannockburn ; and, more interesting still, the sword
of William Wallace.   It is a formidable looking weapon, made for being swayed with both
hands, and, with its hilt on the floor, reached
about to my chin ; but the young girl who
showed us the armory said that about nine
inches had been broken off the point.   The

blade was not massive, but somewhat thin, compared with its great length; and I found that I
could brandish it, using both hands, with perfect ease.   It is two-edged, without any gaps,
and is quite brown and lustreless with old rust
from point to hilt.

These were all the memorables of our visit
to Dumbarton Castle, which is a most interesting spot, and connected with a long series of
historical events.   It was first besieged by the
Danes, and had a prominent share in all the
warfare of Scotland, so long as the old warlike
times and manners lasted.   Our soldier was
very intelligent and courteous, but, as usual
with these guides, was somewhat apocryphal in
his narrative; telling us that Mary Queen of
Scots was confined here before being taken to
England, and that the cells in which she then
lived are still extant, under one of the ramparts.
The fact is, she was brought here when a child
of six years old, before going to France, and
doubtless scrambled up and down these heights
as freely and merrily as the sheep we saw.

We now returned to our hotel, a very nice
one, and found the street of Dumbarton all
alive in the summer evening with the sports of
children and the gossip of grown people.   There
was almost no night, for at twelve o'clock there
was still a golden daylight, and Yesterday, before it died, must have met the Morrow.

In the lower part of the fortress there is a large sundial of stone, which was made by a French officer imprisoned here during the Peninsular War. It still numbers faithfully the hours that are sunny, and it is a lasting memorial of him, in the stronghold of his enemies.

INVERANNAN, *Evening*. — After breakfast at Dumbarton, I went out to look at the town, which is of considerable size, and possesses both commerce and manufactures. There was a screw-steamship at the pier, and many sailor-looking people were seen about the streets. There are very few old houses, though still the town retains an air of antiquity which one does not well see how to account for, when everywhere there is a modern front, and all the characteristics of a street built to-day. Turning from the main thoroughfare, I crossed a bridge over the Clyde, and gained from it the best view of the cloven crag of Dumbarton Castle that I had yet found. The two summits are wider apart, more fully relieved from each other, than when seen from other points ; and the highest ascends into a perfect pyramid, the lower one being obtusely rounded. There seem to be iron-works, or some kind of manufactory, on the farther side of the bridge, — and I noticed a quaint, château-like mansion, with hang-

388

ing turrets, standing apart from the street, probably built by some person enriched by business.

We left Dumbarton at noon, taking the rail
to Balloch, and the steamer to the head of Loch
Lomond.

Wild mountain scenery is not very good to
describe, nor do I think any distinct impressions
are ever conveyed by such attempts; so I mean
to be brief in what I say about this part of our
tour, especially as I suspect that I have said whatever I knew how to say in the record of my former
visit to the Highlands. As for Loch Lomond,
it lies amidst very striking scenery, being poured
in among the gorges of steep and lofty mountains, which nowhere stand aside to give it
room, but, on the contrary, do their best to
shut it in. It is everywhere narrow, compared
with its length of thirty miles; but it is the
beauty of a lake to be of no greater width than
to allow of the scenery of one of its shores being
perfectly enjoyed from the other. The scenery
of the Highlands, so far as I have seen it, cannot
properly be called rich, but stern and impressive, with very hard outlines, which are unsoft-
ened, mostly, by any foliage, though at this
season they are green to their summits. They
have hardly flesh enough to cover their bones,
— hardly earth enough to lie over their rocky
substance, — as may be seen by the minute va-

riety, — the notched and jagged appearance of the profile of their sides and tops; this being caused by the scarcely covered rocks wherewith these great hills are heaped together.

Our little steamer stopped at half a dozen places on its voyage up the lake, most of them being stations where hotels have been established. Morally, the Highlands must have been more completely sophisticated by the invention of railways and steamboats than almost any other part of the world; but physically it can have wrought no great change. These mountains, in their general aspect, must be very much the same as they were thousands of years ago; for their sides never were capable of cultivation, nor even with such a soil and so bleak an atmosphere could they have been much more richly wooded than we see them now. They seem to me to be among the unchangeable things of nature, like the sea and sky; but there is no saying what use human ingenuity may hereafter put them to. At all events, I have no doubt in the world that they will go out of fashion in due time; for the taste for mountains and wild scenery is, with most people, an acquired taste, and it was easy to see to-day that nine people in ten care nothing about them. One group of gentlemen and ladies — at least, men and women — spent the whole time in listening to a trial for murder, which

was read aloud by one of their number from a
newspaper. I rather imagine that a taste for
trim gardens is the most natural and universal
taste as regards landscape. But perhaps it is
necessary for the health of the human mind and
heart that there should be a possibility of taking refuge in what is wild and uncontaminated
by any meddling of man's hand, and so it has
been ordained that science shall never alter the
aspect of the sky, whether stern, angry, or beneficent, — nor of the awful sea, either in calm
or tempest, — nor of these rude Highlands.
But they will go out of general fashion, as I
have said, and perhaps the next fashionable
taste will be for cloud-land, — that is, looking
skyward, and observing the wonderful variety
of scenery, that now constantly passes unno-
ticed, among the clouds.

At the head of the lake, we found that there
was only a horse cart to convey our luggage to
the hotel at Inverannan, and that we ourselves
must walk, the distance being two miles. It had
sprinkled occasionally during our voyage, but
was now sunshiny, and not excessively warm ;
so we set forth contentedly enough, and had an
agreeable walk along an almost perfectly level
road ; for it is one of the beauties of these hills
that they descend abruptly down, instead of
undulating away forever. There were lofty
heights on each side of us, but not so lofty as

to have won a distinctive name; and adown their sides we could see the rocky pathways of cascades, which, at this season, are either quite dry or mere trickles of a rill. The hills and valleys abound in streams, sparkling through pebbly beds, and forming here and there a dark pool; and they would be populous with trout if all England, with one fell purpose, did not come hither to fish them. A fisherman must find it difficult to gratify his propensities in these days; for even the lakes and streams in Norway are now preserved. Julian, by the way, threatens ominously to be a fisherman. He rode the latter portion of the way to the hotel on the luggage cart; and when we arrived, we found that he had already gone off to catch fish, or to attempt it (for there is as much chance of his catching a whale as a trout), in a mountain stream near the house. I went in search of him, but without success, and was somewhat startled at the depth and blackness of some of the pools into which the stream settled itself and slept. Finally, he came in while we were at dinner. We afterwards walked out with him, to let him play at fishing again, and discovered on the bank of the stream a wonderful oak, with as many as a dozen boles springing either from close to the ground or within a foot or two of it, and looking like twelve separate trees, at least, instead of one.

INVERSNAID, *July* 3. — Last night seemed to close in clear, and even at midnight it was still light enough to read; but this morning rose on us misty and chill, with spattering showers of rain. Clouds momentarily settled and shifted on the hill-tops, shutting us in even more completely than these steep and rugged green walls would be sure to do, even in the clearest weather. Often these clouds came down and enveloped us in a drizzle, or rather a shower, of such minute drops that they had not weight enough to fall. This, I suppose, was a genuine Scotch mist; and as such it is well enough to have experienced it, though I would willingly never see it again. Such being the state of the weather, my wife did not go out at all, but I strolled about the premises, in the intervals of rain-drops, gazing up at the hillsides, and recognizing that there is a vast variety of shape, of light and shadow, and incidental circumstance, even in what looks so monotonous at first as the green slope of a hill. The little rills that come down from the summits were rather more distinguishable than yesterday, having been refreshed by the night's rain; but still they were very much out of proportion with the wide pathways of bare rock adown which they ran. These little rivulets, no doubt, often lead through the wildest scenery that is to be found in the Highlands, or anywhere else, and to the

formation and wildness of which they have
greatly contributed by sawing away for count-
less ages, and thus deepening the ravines.

I suspect the American clouds are more picturesque than those of Great Britain, whatever
our mountains may be ; at least, I remember
the Berkshire hills looking grander, under the
influence of mist and cloud, than the Highlands
did to-day. Our clouds seem to be denser and
heavier, and more decided, and form greater
contrasts of light and shade. I have remarked
in England that the cloudy firmament, even on
a day of settled rain, always appears thinner
than those I had been accustomed to at home,
so as to deceive me with constant expectations
of better weather. It has been the same to-day.
Whenever I looked upward, I thought it might
be going to clear up ; but, instead of that, it
began to rain more in earnest after midday, and
at half past two we left Inverannan in a smart
shower. At the head of the lake we took the
steamer, with the rain pouring more heavily
than ever, and landed at Inversnaid under the
same dismal auspices. We left a very good
hotel behind us, and have come to another that
seems also good. We are more picturesquely
situated at this spot than at Inverannan, our
hotel being within a short distance of the lake
shore, with a glen just across the water, which
will doubtless be worth looking at when the

mist permits us to see it.   A good many tour-
ists were standing about the door when we
arrived, and looked at us with the curiosity of
idle and weather-bound people.   The lake is
here narrow, but a hundred fathoms deep; so
that a great part of the height of the mountains
which beset it round is hidden beneath its surface.

July 4. — This morning opened still misty,
but with a more hopeful promise than yesterday,
and when I went out, after breakfast, there were
gleams of sunshine here and there on the hillsides, falling, one did not exactly see how,
through the volumes of cloud.   Close beside
the hotel of Inversnaid is the waterfall; all
night, my room being on that side of the house,
I had heard its voice, and now I ascended beside it to a point where it is crossed by a wooden
bridge.   There is thence a view, upward and
downward, of the most striking descents of the
river, as I believe they call it, though it is but a
mountain stream, which tumbles down an irregular and broken staircase in its headlong haste
to reach the lake.   It is very picturesque, however, with its ribbons of white foam over the
precipitous steps, and its deep black pools, overhung by black rocks, which reverberate the
rumble of the falling water.   Julian and I ascended a little distance along the cascade, and

then turned aside; he going up the hill, and I taking a path along its side which gave me a view across the lake. I rather think this particular stretch of Loch Lomond, in front of Inversnaid, is the most beautiful lake and mountain view that I have ever seen. It is so shut in that you can see nothing beyond, nor would suspect anything more to exist than this watery vale among the hills; except that, directly opposite, there is the beautiful glen of Inveruglass, which winds away among the feet of Ben Crook, Ben Ein, Ben Vain, and Ben Voirlich, standing mist-enwreathed together. The mists, this morning, had a very soft and beautiful effect, and made the mountains tenderer than I have hitherto felt them to be; and they lingered about their heads like morning dreams flitting and retiring, and letting the sunshine in, and snatching it away again. My wife came up, and we enjoyed it together, till the steamer came smoking its pipe along the loch, stopped to land some passengers, and steamed away again. While we stood there, a Highlander passed by us, with a very dark tartan, and bare shanks, most enormously calved. I presume he wears the dress for the sole purpose of displaying those stalwart legs; for he proves to be no genuine Gael, but a manufacturer, who has a shooting-box, or a share in one, on the hill above the hotel.

We now engaged a boat, and were rowed to Rob Roy's cave, which is perhaps half a mile distant up the lake. The shores look much more striking from a rowboat, creeping along near the margin, than from a steamer in the middle of the loch ; and the ridge, beneath which Rob's cave lies, is precipitous with gray rocks, and clothed, too, with thick foliage. Over the cave itself there is a huge ledge of rock, from which immense fragments have tumbled down, ages and ages ago, and fallen together in such a way as to leave a large irregular crevice in Rob Roy's cave. We scrambled up to its mouth by some natural stairs, and scrambled down into its depths by the aid of a ladder. I suppose I have already described this hole in the record of my former visit. Certainly Rob Roy, and Robert Bruce, who is said to have inhabited it before him, were not to be envied their accommodations ; yet these were not so very intolerable when compared with a Highland cabin, or with cottages such as Burns lived in.

Julian had chosen to remain to fish. On our return from the cave, we found that he had caught nothing ; but just as we stepped into the boat, a fish drew his float far under water, and Julian tugging at one end of the line, and the fish at the other, the latter escaped with the hook in his mouth. Julian avers that he saw the fish, and gives its measurement as about eighteen inches; but the fishes that escape us are always of tremendous size. The boatman thought, however, that it might have been a pike.

THE TROSACHS' HOTEL. — ARDCHEANO-CHROCHAN, *July 5.* — . . . Not being able to get a post-chaise, we took places in the omnibus for the head of Loch Katrine. Going up to pay a parting visit to the waterfall before starting, I met with Miss C——, as she lately was, who is now on her wedding tour as Mrs. B——. She was painting the falls in oil, with good prospect of a successful picture. She came down to the hotel to see my wife, and soon afterwards Julian and I set out to ascend the steep hill that comes down upon the lake of Inversnaid, leaving the omnibus to follow at leisure. The Highlander who took us to Rob Roy's cave had foreboded rain, from the way in which the white clouds hung about the mountain-tops; nor was his augury at fault, for just at three o'clock, the time he foretold, there were a few raindrops, and a more defined shower during the afternoon, while we were on Loch Katrine. The few drops, however, did not disturb us; and, reaching the top of the hill, Julian and I turned aside to examine the old stone fortress which was erected in this mountain pass to bridle the Highlanders after the rebellion of 1745. It stands in a very desolate and dismal situation, at the foot of long bare slopes, on mossy ground, in the midst of a disheartening loneliness, only picturesque because it is so exceedingly ungenial and unlovely. The chief interest of this spot is the fact that Wolfe, in his earlier military career, was stationed here. The fortress was a very plain structure, built of rough stones, in the form of a parallelogram, one side of which I paced, and found it between thirty and forty of my paces long. The two ends have fallen down; the two sides that remain are about twenty feet high, and have little portholes for defence, but no openings of the size of windows. The roof is gone, and the interior space overgrown with grass. Two little girls were at play in one corner, and, going round to the rear of the ruin, I saw that a small Highland cabin had been built against the wall. A dog sat in the doorway, and gave notice of my approach, and some hens kept up their peculiarly domestic converse about the door.

We kept on our way, often looking back towards Loch Lomond, and wondering at the grandeur which Ben Vain and Ben Voirlich, and the rest of the Ben fraternity, had suddenly put on. The mists which had hung about them all day had now descended lower, and lay among the depths and gorges of the hills, where also the sun shone softly down among them, and filled those deep mountain laps, as it were, with a dim-mer sunshine.   Ben Vain, too, and his brethren, had a veil of mist all about them, which seemed to render them really transparent ; and they had unaccountably grown higher, vastly higher, than when we viewed them from the shore of the lake. It was as if we were looking at them through the medium of a poet's imagination.   All along the road, since we left Inversnaid, there had been the stream which there formed the waterfall, and which here was brawling down little declivities, and sleeping in black pools, which we disturbed by flinging stones into them from the roadside. We passed a drunken old gentleman, who civilly bade me " Good-day ; " and a man and woman at work in a field, the former of whom shouted to inquire the hour ; and we had come in sight of little Loch Arklet before the omnibus came up with us.   It was about five o'clock when we reached the head of Loch Katrine, and went on board the steamer Rob Roy ; and, setting forth on our voyage, a Highland piper made music for us the better part of the way.

We did not see Loch Katrine, perhaps, under its best presentment ; for the surface was roughened with a little wind, and darkened even to inky blackness by the clouds that overhung it. The hilltops, too, wore a very dark frown.   A lake of this size cannot be terrific, and is therefore seen to best advantage when it is beautiful. The scenery of its shores is not altogether so

Loch Katrine

rich and lovely as I had preimagined ; not equal, indeed, to the best parts of Loch Lomond, — the hills being lower and of a more ridgy shape, and exceedingly bare, at least towards the lower end.   But they turn the lake aside with headland after headland, and shut it in closely, and open one vista after another, so that the eye is never weary, and, least of all, as we approach the end.   The length of the loch is ten miles, and at its termination it meets the pass of the Trosachs, between Ben An and Ben Venue, which are the rudest and shaggiest of hills.   The steamer passes Ellen's Isle, but to the right, which is the side opposite to that on which Fitz-James must be supposed to have approached it. It is a very small island, situated where the loch narrows, and is perhaps less than a quarter of a mile distant from either shore.   It looks like a lump of rock, with just soil enough to support a crowd of dwarf oaks, birches, and firs, which do not grow so high as to be shadowy trees.   Our voyage being over, we landed, and found two omnibuses, one of which took us through the famous pass of the Trosachs, a distance of a mile and a quarter, to a hotel, erected in castellated guise by Lord Willoughby d'Eresby.   We were put into a parlor within one of the round towers, panelled all round, and with four narrow windows, opening through deep embrasures.   No play-castle was ever more like the reality, and it is a very good hotel, like all that we have had experience of in the Highlands.   After tea we walked out, and visited a little kirk that stands near the shore of Loch Achray, at a good point of view for seeing the hills round about.

This morning opened cloudily ; but after breakfast I set out alone, and walked through the pass of the Trosachs, and thence by a path along the right shore of the lake.   It is a very picturesque and beautiful path, following the windings of the lake, — now along the beach, now over an impending bank, until it comes opposite to Ellen's Isle, which on this side looks more worthy to be the island of the poem than as we first saw it.   Its shore is craggy and precipitous, but there was a point where it seemed possible to land, nor was it too much to fancy that there might be a rustic habitation among the shrubbery of this rugged spot.   It is foolish to look into these matters too strictly. Scott evidently used as much freedom with his natural scenery as he did with his historic incidents ; and he could have made nothing of either one or the other if he had been more scrupulous in his arrangement and adornment of them.   In his description of the Trosachs, he has produced something very beautiful, and as true as possible, though certainly its beauty has a little of the scene painter's gloss on it. Nature is better, no doubt, but Nature cannot be exactly reproduced on canvas or in print ; and the artist's only resource is to substitute something that may stand instead of and suggest the truth.

The path still kept onward, after passing Ellen's Isle, and I followed it, finding it wilder, more shadowy with overhanging foliage of trees, old and young, — more like a mountain-path in Berkshire or New Hampshire, yet still with an Old World restraint and cultivation about it, — the farther I went.   At last I came upon some bars, and though the track was still seen beyond, I took this as a hint to stop, especially as I was now two or three miles from the hotel, and it just then began to rain.   My umbrella was a poor one at best, and had been tattered and turned inside out, a day or two ago, by a gust on Loch Lomond — but I spread it to the shower, and, furthermore, took shelter under the thickest umbrage I could find.   The rain came straight down, and bubbled in the loch ; the little rills gathered force, and plashed merrily over the stones ; the leaves of the trees condensed the shower into large drops, and shed them down upon me where I stood.   Still I was comfortable enough in a thick Skye Tweed, and waited patiently till the rain abated ; then took my way homeward, and admired the pass of the Trosachs more than when I first traversed it. If it has a fault, it is one that few scenes in

Great Britain share with it, — that is, the trees and shrubbery with which the precipices are shagged, conceal them a little too much. A crag, streaked with black and white, here and there shows its head aloft, or its whole height from base to summit, and suggests that more of such sublimity is hidden than revealed. I think, however, that it is this unusual shagginess which made the scene a favorite with Scott, and with the people on this side of the ocean generally. There are many scenes as good in America, needing only the poet.

July 6. — We dined yesterday at the *table d'hôte*, at the suggestion of the butler, in order to give less trouble to the servants of the hotel, and afford them an opportunity to go to kirk. The dining-room is in accordance with the rest of the architecture and fittings-up of the house, and is a very good reproduction of an old baronial hall, with high panellings and a roof of dark polished wood. There were about twenty guests at table ; and if they and the waiters had been dressed in mediæval costume, we might have imagined ourselves banqueting in the Middle Ages.

After dinner we all took a walk through the Trosachs' pass again, and by the right-hand path along the lake as far as Ellen's Isle. It was very pleasant, there being gleams of calm evening sunshine gilding the mountain-sides, and putting a golden crown occasionally on the head of Ben Venue. It is wonderful how many aspects a mountain has, — how many mountains there are in every single mountain ! — how they vary, too, in apparent attitude and bulk. When we reached the lake its surface was almost un- ruffled, except by now and then the narrow pathway of a breeze, as if the wing of an unseen spirit had just grazed it in flitting across. The scene was very beautiful, and, on the whole, I do not know that Walter Scott has overcharged his description, although he has symbolized the reality by types and images which it might not precisely suggest to other minds. We were re- luctant to quit the spot, and cherish still a hope of seeing it again, though the hope does not seem very likely to be gratified.

This was a lowering and sullen morning, but soon after breakfast I took a walk in the oppo- site direction to Loch Katrine, and reached the Brig of Turk, a little beyond which is the new Trosachs' Hotel, and the little rude village of Duncraggan, consisting of a few hovels of stone, at the foot of a bleak and dreary hill. To the left, stretching up between this and other hills, is the valley of Glenfinlas, — a very awful region in Scott's poetry and in Highland tradition, as the haunt of spirits and enchantments. It pre- sented a very desolate prospect. The walk back to the Trosachs showed me Ben Venue and Ben An under new aspects,— the bare summit of the latter rising in a perfect pyramid, whereas from other points of view it looks like quite a different mountain.   Sometimes a gleam of sunshine came out upon the rugged side of Ben Venue, but his prevailing mood, like that of the rest of the landscape, was stern and gloomy. I wish I could give an idea of the variety of surface upon one of these hillsides,— so bulging out and hollowed in, so bare where the rock breaks through, so shaggy in other places with heath, and then, perhaps, a thick umbrage of birch, oak, and ash, ascending from the base high upward.   When I think I have described them, I remember quite a different aspect, and find it equally true, and yet lacking something to make it the whole or an adequate truth.

Julian had gone with me part of the way, but stopped to fish with a pin-hook in Loch Achray, which bordered along our path.   When I returned, I found him much elated at having caught a fish, which, however, had got away, carrying his pin-hook along with it.   Then he had amused himself with taking some lizards by the tail, and had collected several in a small hollow of the rocks.   We now walked home together, and at half past three we took our seats in a genuine old-fashioned stage-coach, of which there are few specimens now to be met with.   The coachman was smartly dressed in the Queen's scarlet, and was a very pleasant and affable personage, conducting himself towards the passengers with courteous authority. Inside we were four, including Julian, but on the top there were at least a dozen, and I would willingly have been there too, but had taken an inside seat, under apprehension of rain, and was not allowed to change it. Our drive was not marked by much describable incident. On changing horses at Callander, we alighted, and saw Ben Ledi behind us, making a picturesque background to the little town, which seems to be the meeting-point of the Highlands and Lowlands. We again changed horses at Doune, an old town, which would doubtless have been well worth seeing, had time permitted. Thence we kept on till the coach drew up at a spacious hotel, where we alighted, fancying that we had reached Stirling, which was to have been our journey's end; but after fairly establishing ourselves, we found that it was the Brig of Allan. The place is three miles short of Stirling. Nevertheless, we did not much regret the mistake, finding that the Brig of Allan is the principal Spa of Scotland, and a very pleasant spot, to all outward appearance. After tea we walked out, both up and down the village street, and across the bridge, and up a gentle eminence beyond it, whence we had a fine view of a glorious plain, out of which rose several insulated headlands. One of these was the height on which stands Stirling Castle, and which reclines on the plain like a hound or a lion or a sphinx, holding the castle on the highest part, where its head should be. A mile or two distant from this picturesque hill rises another, still more striking, called the Abbey Craig, on which is a ruin, and where is to be built the monument to William Wallace. I cannot conceive a nobler or more fitting pedestal. The sullenness of the day had vanished, the air was cool but invigorating, and the cloud scenery was as fine as that below it. . . . Though it was nearly ten o'clock, the boys of the village were in full shout and play, for these long and late summer evenings keep the children out of bed interminably.

STIRLING, *July* 7. — We bestirred ourselves early this morning, . . . and took the rail for Stirling before eight. It is but a few minutes' ride, so that doubtless we were earlier on the field than if we had slept at Stirling. After our arrival our first call was at the post-office, where I found a large package containing letters from America, but none from Una. We then went to a bookseller's shop, and bought some views of Stirling and the neighborhood; and it is surprising what a quantity and variety of engravings there are of every noted place that we

have visited.   You seldom find two sets alike.
It is rather nauseating to find that what you
came to see has already been looked at in all its
lights, over and over again, with thousand-fold
repetition ; and, beyond question, its depictment
in words has been attempted still oftener than
with the pencil.   It will be worth while to go
back to America, were it only for the chance of
finding a still virgin scene.

We climbed the steep slope of the Castle
Hill, sometimes passing an antique-looking
house with a high, notched gable, perhaps with
an ornamented front, until we came to the sculptures, and battlemented wall, with an archway,
that stands just below the castle. . . . A shabby
looking man now accosted us, and could hardly
be shaken off.   I have met with several such
boors in my experience of sight-seeing.   He
kept along with us, in spite of all hints to the
contrary, and insisted on pointing out objects
of interest.   He showed us a house in Broad
Street, below the castle and cathedral, which he
said had once been inhabited by Henry Darnley,
Queen Mary's husband.   There was little or
nothing peculiar in its appearance ; a large, gray,
gabled house standing lengthwise to the street,
with three windows in the roof, and connected
with other houses on each side.   Almost directly
across the street, he pointed to an archway,
through the side of a house, and peeping through

it, we found a soldier on guard in a courtyard, the sides of which were occupied by an old mansion of the Argyle family, having towers at the corners, with conical tops, like those reproduced in the hotel at the Trosachs. It is now occupied as a military hospital. Shaking off our self-inflicted guide, we now made our way to the castle parade, and to the gateway, where a soldier with a tremendously red nose and two medals at once took charge of us.

Beyond all doubt, I have written quite as good a description of the castle and Cärse of Stirling in a former portion of my journal as I can now write. We passed through the outer rampart of Queen Anne; through the old round gate tower of an earlier day, and beneath the vacant arch where the portcullis used to fall, thus reaching the inner region, where stands the old palace on one side, and the old Parliament House on the other. The former looks aged, ragged, and rusty, but makes a good appearance enough pictorially, being adorned all round about with statues, which may have been white marble once, but are as gray as weather-beaten granite now, and look down from between the windows above the basement story. A photograph would give the idea of very rich antiquity, but as it really stands, looking on a gravelled courtyard, and with "CANTEEN" painted on one of its doors, the spectator does not find it

very impressive.   The great hall of this palace
is now partitioned off into two or three rooms,
and the whole edifice is arranged to serve as
barracks.   Of course, no trace of ancient magnificence, if anywise destructible, can be left in
the interior. We were not shown into this palace, nor into the Parliament House, nor into
the tower, where King James stabbed the Earl
of Douglas.   When I was here a year ago, I
went up the old staircase, and into the room
where the murder was committed, although it
had recently been the scene of a fire, which consumed as much of it as was inflammable.   The
window whence the Earl's body was thrown
then remained ; but now the whole tower seems
to have been renewed, leaving only the mullions
of the historic window.

   We merely looked up at the new, light-colored freestone of the restored tower in passing,
and ascended to the ramparts, where we found
one of the most splendid views, morally and
materially, that this world can show.   Indeed,
I think there cannot be such a landscape as the
Cärse of Stirling, set in such a frame as it is, —
the Highlands, comprehending our friends, Ben
Lomond, Ben Venue, Ben An, and the whole
Ben brotherhood, with the Grampians surrounding it to the westward and northward, and in
other directions some range of prominent objects
to shut it in ; and the plain itself, so worthy of

the richest setting, so fertile, so beautiful, so
written over and over again with histories. The
silver Links of Forth are as sweet and gently
picturesque an object as a man sees in a lifetime.
I do not wonder that Providence caused great
things to happen on this plain ; it was like
choosing a good piece of canvas to paint a great
picture upon.   The battle of Bannockburn
(which we saw beneath us, with the Gillie's Hill
on the right) could not have been fought upon
a meaner plain, nor Wallace's victory gained ;
and if any other great historic act still remains
to be done in this country, I should imagine the
Cärse of Stirling to be the future scene of it.
Scott seems to me hardly to have done justice
to this landscape, or to have bestowed pains
enough to put it in strong relief before the
world ; although it is from the lights shed on
it, and so much other Scottish scenery, by his
mind, that we chiefly see it, and take an interest in it. . . .

I do not remember seeing the hill of execution before, — a mound on the same level as
the castle's base, looking towards the Highlands.   A solitary cow was now feeding upon
it. I should imagine that no person could ever
have been unjustly executed there ; the spot is
too much in the sight of heaven and earth to
countenance injustice.

Descending from the ramparts, we went into

the Armory, which I did not see on my former
visit. The superintendent of this department
is an old soldier of very great intelligence and
vast communicativeness, and quite absorbed in
thinking of and handling weapons; for he is a
practical armorer. He had few things to show
us that were very interesting, — a helmet or two,
a bomb and grenade from the Crimea; also
some muskets from the same quarter, one of
which, with a sword at the end, he spoke of ad-
miringly, as the best weapon in the collection,
its only fault being its extreme weight. He
showed us, too, some Minie rifles, and whole
ranges of the old-fashioned Brown Bess, which
had helped to win Wellington's victories; also
the halberds of sergeants now laid aside, and
some swords that had been used at the battle
of Sheriffmuir. These latter were very short,
not reaching to the floor, when I held one of
them, point downward, in my hand. The short-
ness of the blade and consequent closeness of the
encounter must have given the weapon a most
dagger-like murderousness. Hanging in the
hall of arms, there were two tattered banners
that had gone through the Peninsular battles,
one of them belonging to the gallant 42d Regiment. The armorer gave my wife a rag from
each of these banners, consecrated by so much
battle-smoke; also a piece of old oak, half
burned to charcoal, which had been rescued

from the panelling of the Douglas Tower. We saw better things, moreover, than all these rusty weapons and ragged flags; namely, the pulpit and communion - table of John Knox. The frame of the former, if I remember aright, is complete; but one or two of the panels are knocked out and lost, and, on the whole, it looks as if it had been shaken to pieces by the thunder of his holdings forth, — much worm-eaten, too, is the old oak wood, as well it may be, for the letters MD (1500) are carved on its front. The communion-table is polished, and in much better preservation.

Then the armorer showed us a Damascus blade, of the kind that will cut a delicate silk handkerchief while floating in the air; and some inlaid matchlock guns. A child's little toy gun was lying on a workbench among all this array of weapons; and when I took it up and smiled, he said that it was his son's. So he called in a little fellow four years old, who was playing in the castle yard, and made him go through the musket exercise, which he did with great good will. This small Son of a Gun, the father assured us, cares for nothing but arms, and has attained all his skill with the musket merely by looking at the soldiers on parade. . . .

Our soldier, who had resigned the care of us to the armorer, met us again at the door, and

led us round the remainder of the ramparts,
dismissing us finally at the gate by which we
entered. All the time we were in the castle
there had been a great discordance of drums and
fifes, caused by the musicians who were prac-
tising just under the walls; likewise the sergeants were drilling their squads of men, and
putting them through strange gymnastic mo-
tions. Most, if not all, of the garrison belongs
to a Highland regiment, and those whom we
saw on duty, in full costume, looked very martial and gallant. Emerging from the castle, we
took the broad and pleasant footpath, which
circles it about midway on the grassy steep
which descends from the rocky precipice on
which the walls are built. This is a very beautiful walk, and affords a most striking view of
the castle, right above our heads, the height of
its wall forming one line with the precipice.
The grassy hillside is almost as precipitous as
the dark gray rock that rises out of it, to form
the foundations of the castle; but wild rose-
bushes, both of a white and red variety, are
abundant here, and all in bloom; nor are these
the only flowers. There is also shrubbery in
some spots, tossing up green waves against the
precipice; and broad sheets of ivy here and
there mantle the headlong rock, which also has
a growth of weeds in its crevices. The castle
walls above, however, are quite bare of any such

growth. Thus, looking up at the old storied fortress, and looking down over the wide, historic plain, we wandered halfway round the castle, and then, retracing our steps, entered the town close by an old hospital.

A hospital it was, or had been intended for; but the authorities of the town had made some convenient arrangement with those entitled to its charity, and had appropriated the ancient edifice to themselves. So said a boy who showed us into the Guildhall, — an apartment with a vaulted oaken roof, and otherwise of antique aspect and furniture; all of which, however, were modern restorations. We then went into an old church or cathedral, which was divided into two parts; one of them, in which I saw the royal arms, being probably for the Church of England service, and the other for the Kirk of Scotland. I remember little or nothing of this edifice, except that the Covenanters had uglified it with pews and a gallery, and whitewash; though I doubt not it was a stately Gothic church with innumerable enrichments and incrustations of beauty, when it passed from popish hands into theirs. Thence we wandered downward, through a back street, amid very shabby houses, some of which bore tokens of having once been the abodes of courtly and noble personages. We paused before one that displayed, I think, the sign of a spirit retailer, and looked as disreputable as a house could, yet was built of stalwart stone, and had two circular towers in front, once, doubtless, crowned with conical tops.   We asked an elderly man whether he knew anything of the history of this house ; and he said that he had been acquainted with it for almost fifty years, but never knew anything noteworthy about it.   Reaching the foot of the hill, along whose back the streets of Stirling run, and which blooms out into the Castle Craig, we returned to the railway, and at noon took leave of Stirling.

I forgot to tell of the things that awakened rather more sympathy in us than any other objects in the castle armory.   These were some rude weapons — pikes, very roughly made ; and old rusty muskets, broken and otherwise out of order ; and swords, by no means with Damascus blades — that had been taken from some poor weavers and other handicraft men who rose against the government in 1820.   I pitied the poor fellows much, seeing how wretched were their means of standing up against the cannon, bayonets, swords, shot, shell, and all manner of murderous facilities possessed by their oppressors.   Afterwards, our guide showed, in a gloomy quadrangle of the castle, the low windows of the dungeons where two of the leaders of the insurrectionists had been confined before their execution.   I have not the least shadow of doubt that these men had a good cause to fight for ; but what availed it with such weapons ! and so few even of those !

. . . I believe I cannot go on to recount any further this evening the experiences of to-day. It has been a very rich day ; only that I have seen more than my sluggish powers of reception can well take in at once. After quitting Stirling, we came in somewhat less than an hour to Linlithgow, and, alighting, took up our quarters at the Star and Garter Hotel, which, like almost all the Scottish caravansaries of which we have had experience, turns out a comfortable one. . . . We stayed within doors for an hour or two, and I busied myself with writing up my journal. At about three, however, the sky brightened a little, and we set forth through the ancient, rusty, and queer-looking town of Linlithgow, towards the palace and the ancient church, which latter was one of St. David's edifices, and both of which stand close together, a little removed from the long street of the village. But I can never describe them more worthily, and shall make nothing of the description if I attempt it now.

July 8. — At about three o'clock yesterday, as I said, we walked forth through the ancient street of Linlithgow, and, coming to the market-place, stopped to look at an elaborate and heavy stone fountain, which we found by an inscription to be a facsimile of an old one that used to stand on the same site. Turning to the right, the outer entrance to the palace fronts on this market-place, if such it be; and close to it, a little on one side, is the church. A young woman, with a key in her hand, offered to admit us into the latter; so we went in, and found it divided by a wall across the middle into two parts. The hither portion, being the nave, was whitewashed, and looked as bare and uninteresting as an old Gothic church of St. David's epoch possibly could do. The interior portion, being the former choir, is covered with pews over the whole floor, and further defaced by galleries, that unmercifully cut midway across the stately and beautiful arches. It is likewise whitewashed. There were, I believe, some mural monuments of Bailies and other such people stuck up about the walls, but nothing that much interested me, except an ancient oaken chair, which the girl said was the chair of St. Crispin, and it was fastened to the wall, in the holiest part of the church. I know not why it was there; but as it had been the chair of so distinguished a personage, we all sat down in it. It was in this church that the apparition of St. James appeared to King James IV., to warn him against engaging in that war which resulted in the battle of Flodden, where he and the flower of his nobility were slain.   The young woman showed us the spot where the apparition spake to him, — a side chapel, with a groined roof, at the end of the choir next the nave.   The Covenanters seem to have shown some respect to this one chapel, by refraining from drawing the gallery across its height; so that, except for the whitewash, and the loss of the painted glass in the window, and probably of a good deal of rich architectural detail, it looks as it did when the ghostly saint entered beneath its arch, while the king was kneeling there.

We stayed but a little while in the church, and then proceeded to the palace, which, as I said, is close at hand.   On entering the outer enclosure through an ancient gateway, we were surprised to find how entire the walls seemed to be ; but the reason is, I suppose, that the ruins have not been used as a stone quarry, as has almost always been the case with old abbeys and castles.   The palace took fire and was consumed, so far as consumable, in 1745, while occupied by the soldiers of General Hawley ; but even yet the walls appear so stalwart that I should imagine it quite possible to rebuild and restore the stately rooms on their original plan. It was a noble palace, one hundred and seventy-five feet in length by one hundred and sixty-five in breadth, and though destitute of much architectural beauty externally, yet its aspect from the

quadrangle which the four sides enclose is venerable and sadly beautiful.   At each of the interior angles there is a circular tower, up the whole
height of the edifice and overtopping it, and
another in the centre of one of the sides, all
containing winding staircases.   The walls facing
upon the enclosed quadrangle are pierced with
many windows, and have been ornamented with
sculpture, rich traces of which still remain over
the arched entrance-ways ; and in the grassy
centre of the court there is the ruin and broken
fragments of a fountain which once used to play
for the delight of the king and queen, and lords
and ladies, who looked down upon it from hall
and chamber.   Many old carvings that belonged
to it are heaped together there; but the water
has disappeared, though, had it been a natural
spring, it would have outlasted all the heavy
stone work.

As far as we were able, and could find our
way, we went through every room of the palace, all round the four sides.   From the first
floor upwards it is entirely roofless. In some of
the chambers there is an accumulation of soil,
and a goodly crop of grass ; in others there is
still a flooring of flags or brick tiles, though
damp and moss-grown, and with weeds sprouting between the crevices. Grass and weeds, indeed, have found soil enough to flourish in, even
on the highest ranges of the walls, though at a

dizzy height above the ground ; and it was like
an old and trite touch of romance, to see how
the weeds sprouted on the many hearthstones
and aspired under the chimney flues, as if in
emulation of the long-extinguished flame.   It
was very mournful, very beautiful, very delightful, too, to see how Nature takes back the palace, now that kings have done with it, and adopts
it as a part of her great garden.

On one side of the quadrangle we found the
roofless chamber where Mary Queen of Scots
was born, and in the same range the bedchamber that was occupied by several of the Scottish
Jameses ; and in one corner of the latter apartment there is a narrow, winding staircase, down
which I groped, expecting to find a door, either
into the enclosed quadrangle or to the outside
of the palace.   But it ends in nothing, unless it
be a dungeon ; and one does not well see why
the bedchamber of the king should be so convenient to a dungeon.   It is said that King
James III. once escaped down this secret stair,
and lay concealed from some conspirators who
had entered his chamber to murder him.   This
range of apartments is terminated, like the other
sides of the palace, by a circular tower enclosing
a staircase, up which we mounted, winding round
and round, and emerging at various heights,
until at last we found ourselves at the very topmost point of the edifice ; and here there is a

small pepper box of a turret, almost as entire as when the stones were first laid. It is called Queen Margaret's bower, and looks forth on a lovely prospect of mountain and plain, and on the old red roofs of Linlithgow town, and on the little loch that lies within the palace grounds. The cold north wind blew chill upon us through the empty window frames, which very likely were never glazed; but it must be a delightful nook in a calmer and warmer summer evening.

Descending from this high perch, we walked along ledges and through arched corridors, and stood, contemplative, in the dampness of the banqueting-hall, and sat down on the seats that still occupy the embrasures of the deep windows. In one of the rooms, the sculpture of a huge fireplace has recently been imitated and restored, so as to give an idea of what the richness of the adornments must have been when the building was perfect. We burrowed down, too, a little way in the direction of the cells, where prisoners used to be confined; but these were too ugly and too impenetrably dark to tempt us far. One vault, exactly beneath a queen's very bedchamber, was designated as a prison. I should think bad dreams would have winged up, and made her pillow an uncomfortable one.

There seems to be no certain record as respects the date of this palace, except that the most recent part was built by James I. of England, and bears the figures 1620 on its central tower. In this part were the kitchens and other domestic offices. In Robert Bruce's time there was a castle here, instead of a palace, and an ancestor of our friend Bennoch was the means of taking it from the English by a stratagem in which valor went halves. Four centuries afterwards, it was a royal residence, and might still have been nominally so, had not Hawley's dragoons lighted their fires on the floors of the magnificent rooms ; but, on the whole, I think it more valuable as a ruin than if it were still perfect. Scotland, and the world, needs only one Holyrood ; and Linlithgow, were it still a perfect palace, must have been second in interest to that, from its lack of association with historic events so grand and striking.

After tea we took another walk, and this time went along the High Street, in quest of the house whence Bothwellhaugh fired the shot that killed the Regent Murray. It has been taken down, however; or, if any part of it remain, it has been built into and incorporated with a small house of dark stone which forms one range with two others that stand a few feet back from the general line of the street. It is as mean-looking and commonplace an edifice as is anywhere to be seen, and is now occupied by one Steele, a tailor. We went under a square arch (if an arch can be square), that goes quite through the

424

house, and found ourselves in a little court; but it was not easy to identify anything as connected with the historic event, so we did but glance about us, and returned into the street. It is here narrow, and as Bothwellhaugh stood in a projecting gallery, the Regent must have been within a few yards of the muzzle of his carbine. The street looks as old as any that I have seen, except, perhaps, a vista here and there in Chester, — the houses all of stone, many of them tall, with notched gables, and with stone staircases going up outside, the steps much worn by feet now dust; a pervading ugliness, which yet does not fail to be picturesque; a general filth and evil odor of gutters and people, suggesting sorrowful ideas of what the inner houses must be when the outside looks and smells so badly; and finally, a great rabble of the inhabitants, talking, idling, sporting, staring about their own thresholds and those of dram-shops, the town being most alive in the long twilight of the summer evening. There was nothing uncivil in the deportment of these dirty people, old or young; but they did stare at us most unmercifully.

We walked very late, entering, after all that we had seen, into the palace grounds, and skirting along Linlithgow Loch, which would be very beautiful if its banks were made shadowy with trees, instead of being almost bare. We viewed the palace on the outside, too, and saw what had once been the principal entrance, but now looked like an arched window, pretty high in the wall; for it had not been accessible except by a draw-bridge. I might write pages in telling how venerable the ruin looked, as the twilight fell deeper and deeper around it; but we have had enough of Linlithgow, especially as there have been so many old palaces and old towns to write about, and there will still be more. We left Linlithgow early this morning, and reached Edinburgh in half an hour. To-morrow I suppose I shall try to set down what I see; at least some points of it.

July 9. — Arriving at Edinburgh, and acting under advice of the cabman, we drove to Addison's Alma Hotel, which we find to be in Prince's Street, having Scott's monument a few hundred yards below, and the Castle Hill about as much above.

The Edinburgh people seem to be accustomed to climb mountains within their own houses; so we had to mount several staircases before we reached our parlor, which is a very good one, and commands a beautiful view of Prince's Street, and of the picturesque old town, and the valley between, and of the castle on its hill.

Our first visit was to the castle, which we reached by going across the causeway that bridges the valley, and has some edifices of

Grecian architecture on it, contrasting strangely
with the nondescript ugliness of the old town,
into which we immediately pass. As this is my
second visit to Edinburgh, I surely need not
dwell upon describing it at such length as if I
had never been here before.   After climbing up
through various wards of the castle to the topmost battery, where Mons Meg holds her station, looking like an uncouth dragon, — with a
pile of huge stone balls beside her for eggs, —
we found that we could not be admitted to
Queen Mary's apartments, nor to the crown-
room, till twelve o'clock; moreover, that there
was no admittance to the crown-room without
tickets from the crown-office, in Parliament
Square.   There being no help for it, I left my
wife and Julian to wander through the fortress,
and came down through High Street in quest of
Parliament Square, which I found after many
inquiries of policemen, and after first going to
the Justiciary Court, where there was a great
throng endeavoring to get in; for the trial of
Miss Smith for the murder of her lover is caus-
ing great excitement just now.   There was no
difficulty made about the tickets, and, returning, found Sophia and Julian; but Julian grew
tired of waiting, and set out to return to our
hotel, through the great strange city, all by himself. Through means of an attendant, we were
admitted into Queen Margaret's little chapel,

427

on the top of the rock ; and then we sat down, in such shelter as there was, to avoid the keen wind, blowing through the embrasures of the ramparts, and waited as patiently as we could.

Twelve o'clock came, and we went into the crown-room, with a throng of other visitors, — so many that they could only be admitted in separate groups. The Regalia of Scotland lie on a circular table within an iron railing, round and round which the visitors pass, gazing with all their eyes. The room was dark, however, except for the dim twinkle of a candle or gas-light ; and the regalia did not show to any advantage, though there are some rich jewels, set in their ancient gold. The articles consist of a two handed sword, with a hilt and scabbard of gold, ornamented with gems, and a mace, with a silver handle, all very beautifully made ; besides the golden collar and jewelled badge of the Garter, and something else which I forget. Why they keep this room so dark I cannot tell ; but it is a poor show, and gives the spectator an idea of the poverty of Scotland, and the minuteness of her sovereignty, which I had not gathered from her royal palaces.

Thence we went into Queen Mary's room, and saw that beautiful portrait — that very queen and very woman — with which I was so much impressed at my last visit. It is wonderful that this picture does not drive all the other portraits of Mary out of the field, whatever may be the comparative proofs of their authenticity. I do not know the history of this one, except that it is a copy by Sir William Gordon of a picture by an Italian, preserved at Dunrobin Castle.

After seeing what the castle had to show, which is but little except itself, its rocks, and its old dwellings of princes and prisoners, we came down through the High Street, inquiring for John Knox's house. It is a strange-looking edifice, with gables on high, projecting far, and some sculpture, and inscriptions referring to Knox. There is a tobacconist's shop in the basement story, where I learned that the house used to be shown to visitors till within three months, but it is now closed, for some reason or other. Thence we crossed a bridge into the new town, and came back through Prince's Street to the hotel, and had a good dinner, as preparatory to fresh wearinesses; for there is no other weariness at all compared to that of sight-seeing.

In mid-afternoon we took a cab and drove to Holyrood Palace, which I have already described, as well as the chapel, and do not mean to meddle with either of them again. We looked at our faces in the old mirrors that Queen Mary brought from France with her, and which had often reflected her own lovely

face and figure ; and I went up the winding
stair through which the conspirators ascended.
This, I think, was not accessible at my former
visit.   Before leaving the palace, one of the attendants advised us to see some pictures in the
apartments occupied by the Marquis of Bread-
albane during the queen's residence here.   We
found some fine old portraits and other paintings, by Vandyke, Sir Peter Lely, Sir Godfrey
Kneller, and a strange head by Rubens, amid
all which I walked wearily, wishing that there
were nothing worth looking at in the whole
world.   My wife differs altogether from me in
this matter ; . . . but we agreed, on this occasion, in being tired to death.   Just as we got
through with the pictures, I became convinced
of what I had been dimly suspecting all the
while, namely, that at my last visit to the palace
I had seen these selfsame pictures, and listened
to the selfsame woman's civil answers, in just
the selfsame miserable weariness of mood.

We left the palace, and toiled up through the
dirty Canongate, looking vainly for a fly, and
employing our time, as well as we could, in
looking at the squalid mob of Edinburgh, and
peeping down the horrible vistas of the closes,
which were swarming with dirty life, as some
mouldy and half-decayed substance might swarm
with insects, — vistas down alleys where sin,
sorrow, poverty, drunkenness, all manner of

sombre and sordid earthly circumstances, had imbued the stone, brick, and wood of the habitations for hundreds of years. And such a multitude of children too ; that was a most striking feature.

After tea I went down into the valley between the old town and the new, which is now laid out as an ornamental garden, with grass, shrubbery, flowers, gravelled walks, and frequent seats. Here the sun was setting, and gilded the old town with its parting rays, making it absolutely the most picturesque scene possible to be seen. The mass of tall, ancient houses, heaped densely together, looked like a Gothic dream ; for there seemed to be towers and all sorts of stately architecture, and spires ascended out of the mass ; and above the whole was the castle, with a diadem of gold on its topmost turret. It wanted less than a quarter of nine when the last gleam faded from the windows of the old town, and left the crowd of buildings dim and indistinguishable, to reappear on the morrow in squalor, lifting their meanness skyward, the home of layer upon layer of unfortunate humanity. The change symbolized the difference between a poet's imagination of life in the past — or in a state which he looks at through a colored and illuminated medium — and the sad reality.

This morning we took a cab, and set forth

between ten and eleven to see Edinburgh and its environs; driving past the University, and other noticeable objects in the old town, and thence out to Arthur's Seat. Salisbury Crags are a very singular feature of the outskirts. From the heights, beneath Arthur's Seat, we had a fine prospect of the sea, with Leith and Portobello in the distance, and of a fertile plain at the foot of the hill. In the course of our drive our cabman pointed out Dumbiedikes' house; also the cottage of Jeanie Deans,— at least, the spot where it formerly stood; and Muschat's Cairn, of which a small heap of stones is yet remaining. Near this latter object are the ruins of St. Anthony's Chapel, a roofless gable, and other remains, standing on the abrupt hillside. We drove homeward past a parade ground on which a body of cavalry was exercising, and we met a company of infantry on their route thither. Then we drove near Calton Hill, which seems to be not a burial ground, although the site of stately monuments. In fine, we passed through the Grass-Market, where we saw the cross in the pavement in the street, marking the spot, as I recorded before, where Porteous was executed. Thence we passed through the Cowgate, all the latter part of our drive being amongst the tall, quaint edifices of the old town, alike venerable and squalid. From the Grass-Market the rock of the castle looks more pre-

cipitous than as we had hitherto seen it, and its
prisons, palaces, and barracks approach close to
its headlong verge, and form one steep line with
its descent. We drove quite round the Castle
Hill, and returned down Prince's Street to our
hotel. There can be no other city in the world
that affords more splendid scenery, both natural and architectural, than Edinburgh.

Then we went to St. Giles's Cathedral, which
I shall not describe, it having been kirkified
into three interior divisions by the Covenanters; and I left my wife to take drawings, while
Julian and I went to Short's Observatory, near
the entrance of the castle. Here we saw a
camera obscura, which brought before us, without our stirring a step, almost all the striking
objects which we had been wandering to and
fro to see. We also saw the mites in cheese,
gigantically magnified by a solar microscope;
likewise some dioramic views, with all which
Julian was mightily pleased, and for myself, being tired to death of sights, I would as lief see
them as anything else. We found, on calling
for mamma at St. Giles's, that she had gone
away; but she rejoined us between four and
five o'clock at our hotel, where the next thing
we did was to dine. Again after dinner we
walked out, looking at the shop windows of
jewellers, where ornaments made of cairngorm
pebbles are the most peculiar attraction. As it

433

was our wedding-day, . . . I gave Sophia a golden and amethyst-bodied cairngorm beetle with a ruby head; and after sitting awhile in Prince's Street Gardens, we came home.

July 10. — Last evening I walked round the castle rock, and through the Grass-Market, where I stood on the inlaid cross in the pavement, thence down the High Street beyond John Knox's house. The throng in that part of the town was very great. There is a strange fascination in these old streets, and in the peeps down the closes; but it doubtless would be a great blessing were a fire to sweep through the whole of ancient Edinburgh. This system of living on flats, up to I know not what story, must be most unfavorable to cleanliness, since they have to fetch their water all that distance towards heaven, and how they get rid of their rubbish is best known to themselves.

My wife has gone to Roslin this morning, and since her departure it has been drizzly, so that Julian and I, after a walk through the new part of the town, are imprisoned in our parlor with little resource except to look across the valley to the castle, where Mons Meg is plainly visible on the upper platform, and the lower ramparts, zigzagging about the edge of the precipice, which nearly in front of us is concealed or softened by a great deal of shrubbery, but

434

farther off descends steeply down to the grass
below.   Somewhere on this side of the rock
was the point where Claverhouse, on quitting
Edinburgh before the battle of Killiecrankie,
clambered up to hold an interview with the
Duke of Gordon.   What an excellent thing it
is to have such striking and indestructible land-
marks and time-marks that they serve to affix
historical incidents too, and thus, as it were, nail
down the Past for the benefit of all future ages !

The old town of Edinburgh appears to be
situated, in its densest part, on the broad back
of a ridge, which rises gradually to its termination in the precipitous rock, on which stands
the castle.   Between the old town and the new
is the valley, which runs along at the base of
this ridge, and which, in its natural state, was
probably rough and broken, like any mountain
gorge.   The lower part of the valley, adjacent
to the Canongate, is now a broad hollow space,
fitted up with dwellings, shops, or manufactories ; the next portion, between two bridges, is
converted into an ornamental garden free to the
public, and contains Scott's beautiful monument,
— a canopy of Gothic arches and a fantastic
spire, beneath which he sits, thoughtful and ob-
servant of what passes in the contiguous street ;
the third portion of the valley, above the last
bridge, is another ornamental garden, open only
to those who have pass-keys.   It is an admira-

ble garden, with a great variety of surface, and extends far round the castle rock, with paths that lead up to its very base, among leafy depths of shrubbery, and winds beneath the sheer, black precipice.   Julian and I walked there this forenoon, and took refuge from a shower beneath an overhanging jut of the rock, where a bench had been placed, and where a curtain of hanging ivy helped to shelter us.   On our return to the hotel, we found mamma just alighting from a cab.   She had had very bad fortune in her excursion to Roslin, having had to walk a long distance to the chapel, and being caught in the rain ; and, after all, she could only spend seven minutes in viewing the beautiful Roslin architecture.

436

𝕮𝖍𝖊 𝕽𝖎𝖛𝖊𝖗𝖘𝖎𝖉𝖊 𝕻𝖗𝖊𝖘𝖘

Electrotyped and printed by H. O. Houghton & Co.
Cambridge, Mass., U. S. A.

DATE DUE
